MW00803663

Warm and Welcoming

Warm and Welcoming

How the Jewish Community Can Become Truly Diverse and Inclusive in the 21st Century

Edited by Warren Hoffman and Miriam Steinberg-Egeth

ROWMAN & LITTLEFIELD
Lanham • Boulder • New York • London

Published by Rowman & Littlefield
An imprint of The Rowman & Littlefield Publishing Group, Inc.
4501 Forbes Boulevard, Suite 200, Lanham, Maryland 20706
www.rowman.com

86-90 Paul Street, London EC2A 4NE, United Kingdom

Copyright © 2022 by The Rowman & Littlefield Publishing Group, Inc.

All rights reserved. No part of this book may be reproduced in any form or by
any electronic or mechanical means, including information storage and retrieval
systems, without written permission from the publisher, except by a reviewer who
may quote passages in a review.

British Library Cataloguing in Publication Information Available

Library of Congress Cataloging-in-Publication Data
Names: Hoffman, Warren, 1976– editor. | Steinberg-Egeth, Miriam, 1981–
   editor.
Title: Warm and welcoming : how the Jewish community can become truly
   diverse and inclusive in the 21st century / edited by Warren Hoffman and
   Miriam Steinberg-Egeth.
Description: Lanham : Rowman & Littlefield Publishing Group, [2022] |
   Includes bibliographical references and index. | Summary: "This book
   tackles institutionalized biases and barriers to inclusion within Jewish
   communities, offering stories and context about the issues facing Jews
   of all backgrounds, as well as practical, concrete advice to change how
   Jewish institutions of all sizes, capacities, and histories engage with
   diverse populations"— Provided by publisher.
Identifiers: LCCN 2021032033 (print) | LCCN 2021032034 (ebook) | ISBN
   9781538149690 (cloth) | ISBN 9781538149706 (paperback) | ISBN
   9781538149713 (epub)
Subjects: LCSH: Jews—United States—Social life and customs—21st century.
   | Social integration—Religious aspects—Judaism. | Marginality,
   Social—Religious aspects—Judaism. | Multiculturalism—Religious
   aspects—Judaism. | United States—Ethnic relations.
Classification: LCC E184.36.S65 W37 2022 (print) | LCC E184.36.S65
   (ebook) | DDC 305.892/4073—dc23
LC record available at https://lccn.loc.gov/2021032033
LC ebook record available at https://lccn.loc.gov/2021032034

♾™ The paper used in this publication meets the minimum requirements of
American National Standard for Information Sciences—Permanence of Paper for
Printed Library Materials, ANSI/NISO Z39.48-1992.

Contents

Foreword

Rabbi Sid Schwarz

The stated goal of this volume is, in the words of its editors, "to help Jewish communal organizations, whether long-standing legacy institutions or recent start-ups . . . understand the various challenges facing a new generation of Jews and, more than that, learn about specific steps and actions that they can take to transform their organizations into the inclusive and diverse spaces that they aspire to be." It is a noble goal, and the volume contains outstanding chapters by Jewish leaders who provide important insights and guidance about how Jewish institutions can do a better job at this very important task. Not surprisingly, I find many of the sentiments and recommendations in the book well aligned with my own work in the Jewish community as a congregational rabbi, the CEO of several Jewish organizations, and the director of national initiatives focused on rethinking the modus operandi of American Jewish institutions.

THE EVOLUTION OF THE AMERICAN SYNAGOGUE

As with any attempt to change a social system that has been in place for multiple generations, suggestions that seem patently obvious to one constituency are, nevertheless, not so easily achieved. Understanding why requires a bit of historical context. Religious and ethnic groups coming to the United States during the 19th and early 20th centuries (before draconian immigration restrictions were put in place by Congress) were fleeing persecution in Europe and hoping to improve economic opportunities for themselves and their children. The United States turned out to make both aspirations possible. America's principles of religious liberty and cultural pluralism made it possible for religious minorities to establish faith communities and cultural institutions that allowed each group to perpetuate their ethnic identities. And America's abundant natural resources and free market system created a robust economy that would allow immigrants to see their children enter the middle class in one generation.

By the 1950s, faith communities became enshrined as part of "the American Way," a phenomenon well described (and endorsed) in Will Herberg's classic book, *Protestant, Catholic, Jew: An Essay in American Religious Sociology* (1955). Somewhat counterintuitively, one joined a church or a synagogue in order to be a better American. Religious authorities, recognizing the benefits of this odd cultural phenomenon to the growth of their institutions, harmonized the teachings of scriptures with the blessings of the American way of life, thus giving acculturation an explicit endorsement. In turn, American political leaders gave preferential tax status to religious institutions, and every speech included the obligatory, "God bless America." The marriage of "God and Country" worked well for both sides of the equation.

As Jews prospered in the period after World War II, they moved from the cities to the suburbs, built and joined synagogues, and created Jewish communal organizations like Jewish Community Centers (JCCs) and Federations. Grand edifices were built, comparing favorably to the neighboring Catholic, Methodist, and Presbyterian churches. Rabbis gave sermons about how Judaism and American values were aligned, and the Jews who earned the most money rose into leadership positions, first in the Jewish community and, soon, in American public life as well. If you were white, male, middle class (or better), heterosexual, and married with children, with politics that were not too extreme, it was darn near perfect.

Fast forward 70 years: Virtually all of the sociological factors that allowed the American Jewish community to grow and flourish in the post–World War II era have changed. Jews no longer need synagogues to acculturate into America. The American project is, itself, badly sullied: misguided foreign wars, racism, xenophobia, the growing gap between the wealthy and the poor, ecological devastation driven by monied interests, a dysfunctional political system, and more. Long marginalized groups—women, those identifying as LGBTQI, communities of color, the differently abled—have found their voices and are demanding a seat at the tables of American society. And interest in religion by Americans has declined dramatically for a host of reasons too numerous to detail here.[1] A March 2021 Gallup poll now shows that only 47 percent of Americans affiliate with a faith community. From 1937 until 1999, that number held steady at about 70 percent.[2] The lowest affiliation rates are among millennials and Generation X, an ominous indicator for the future, based on traditional metrics developed by past generations.

Beginning in the 1990s, a series of national efforts was launched that sought to help synagogues adapt to the changing American social landscape. These synagogue transformation initiatives included Synagogue 2000 (later renamed 3000); STAR: Synagogues, Transformation and Renewal; the Legacy Heritage

Innovation Project; and the Experiment in Congregational Education. Books were published that both analyzed the current state of the American synagogue and proposed a series of ideas that could help make synagogues more responsive to the times.

My own contribution to the field was *Finding a Spiritual Home: How a New Generation of Jews Can Transform the American Synagogue* (2000), in which I traced the evolution of the American synagogue through three stages, the last being the synagogue-center that was created in the go-go growth days of post–World War II suburbanization. I argued that while the synagogue-center model met the needs of first-generation Jews, it was poorly aligned with the needs and values of that generation's children as they grew into adulthood. I profiled four synagogues that were attracting the very Jews who, for the most part, were disinclined to join the large and affluent synagogue-centers in their neighborhoods. The specific operating principles common to all four pathbreaking institutions were the following: (1) they were mission driven; (2) they focused on "serious Judaism" including Jewish learning, spirituality, social justice, and personal acts of *hesed* (lovingkindness); (3) they effectively empowered laypeople and encouraged their widespread, active participation in leadership; and (4) they presented Judaism as a toolkit to advance human flourishing. What made these principles compelling is that the four congregations from which I derived the principles represented four different denominational affiliations, including Adat Shalom, a Reconstructionist congregation in Bethesda, Maryland, where I was the founding rabbi.[3]

If one were to survey the dozen or so books written about synagogue transformation from 1990 to 2010, many rooted in significant field research around North America, there was widespread agreement about why the synagogue-center was no longer a model that could work for American Jews and a strong sense as to what needed to change to make synagogues relevant and vibrant again. But there was no consensus around nomenclature. Some used the term "visionary synagogues"; some used the term "emergent synagogues." I used the term "synagogue-communities" in *Finding a Spiritual Home*, but, more recently, I prefer the term "covenantal communities." More important, spiritual communities that embodied many of the principles articulated by the synagogue transformation field were founded and began to flourish, even as synagogue-centers around the country were experiencing dramatic declines in membership. Dozens of synagogues closed or pursued mergers to survive.

Seven new paradigm spiritual communities that operationalized many of the principles mentioned above created a consortium called the Jewish Emergent Network (JEN). It is no coincidence that none of the seven used the term "synagogue" or "congregation" in their names, signaling that these sacred communities were not your mom's or dad's suburban synagogue-centers. They include IKAR (Los Angeles), The Kitchen (San Francisco), Mishkan Chicago (Chicago), Kavana Cooperative (Seattle), 6th and I (Washington, DC),

Romemu (New York), and Lab Shul (New York). These communities, by dint of their creative and charismatic rabbis and their ability to attract large and enthusiastic followings (both in person and online), have attracted outsized attention from both the media and researchers. But there are easily another two to three dozen communities around North America following in the organizational footsteps of the JEN affiliates. This is over and above the thriving network of independent *minyanim*, most without rabbis, attracting next-generation Jews who might once have joined more conventional synagogues.

What comes through loud and clear in the chapters in *Warm and Welcoming* is the way that Jews who relate strongly to certain issues, identities, life choices, origins, and cultural preferences have found their voice and, rightfully, are demanding that they get a seat (or more) at the communal table. Synagogue-centers were (and many still are) conformist to a fault. They privileged heterosexual, Ashkenazi, white men who were married with children. Everyone else was made to feel unwelcome or invisible. This included not only LGBTQI Jews or Jews of color but also the intermarried, singles, widows and widowers, the differently abled, those who were too politically left on Israel/Palestine, and those who weren't sufficiently well positioned as middle-class professionals. These Jews were rarely made to feel welcome in Jewish communal institutions, and they certainly were not part of the leadership elite. And here—I will admit—even in new paradigm spiritual communities that pride themselves as having rejected the organizational cultures of suburban synagogue-centers, there is a ton of work that still needs to be done to raise consciousness about all of the Jews who still feel that they have been left out in the cold.

It is worth celebrating the fact that, today, the Jewish community is paying more and more attention to issues of diversity, equity, and inclusion (or DEI, for short). Large Jewish foundations are funding these efforts. Even legacy Jewish organizations have task forces looking into hiring practices and how to create more eclectic program offerings that might appeal to long-ignored constituencies of Jews. Change will come, even if slowly. Think of how hard it is to erase generations of systemic racism in the United States. But there are many blind spots. Today there is a hyper-focus on Next Gen Jews, but it has been pointed out that the Jewish community is also failing to engage tens of thousands of baby boomers who have drifted away from Jewish life as empty nesters and who have both wisdom and resources that could benefit the Jewish world.[4] What has been called the "ashkenormativity" of the Jewish community—centering the white, European/Ashkenazi experience over all other manifestations of the Jewish experience—is similarly deeply rooted in the way that Jewish institutions function. Part of the good news that the publication of *Warm and Welcoming* represents is that, for almost every essay in the book, one can point to one or more recently formed organizations committed to championing the particular issue that has, for too long, been ignored.

JEWISH LIFE BEYOND SYNAGOGUES

While on the issue of "normativity" and inclusion, it is important to mention one other major shift that is taking place in the Jewish community that relates to the themes of *Warm and Welcoming*. In the 20th century, the synagogue was the primary retail outlet where Jews went to learn about and express their Jewish identity. In the 21st century, the synagogue is one of many retail platforms where Jews can learn about and express their Jewish identity. Even in the 20th century, Jewish identity manifested itself differently than was the case for American Christians. For a highly identified American Christian, church was the primary locus where religious identity was shaped and expressed. But many Jews who would describe themselves as "strongly identified" with being Jewish might not even be members of a synagogue. Arguably, Jews have created the most sophisticated communal infrastructure of any ethnic group in America. Jews who are averse to religion might be deeply involved with a JCC, Jewish social service agencies, the philanthropic work of a Jewish Federation, Israel advocacy, the universe of Jewish public affairs agencies, and/or Jewish theater, music, or arts organizations. The list of settings in which Jews could express their Jewish identity is a long one. Studies that show that American Jews compare unfavorably with Christians in terms of church/synagogue attendance or belief in God do not take into account that, for Jews, religion is just one facet of Jewish identity.

In *Jewish Megatrends: Charting the Course of the American Jewish Future* (2013), I argued that synagogues will continue to lose market share among Jews, but that may not represent a decline in the strength of the Jewish identity of American Jews. Even though only about 30 percent of Jews are affiliated with a synagogue—far fewer than almost any other religious group in the United States—the 2013 Pew Research Center study of American Jewish life reported that a whopping 94 percent of surveyed Jews are "proud to be Jewish."[5] That represents a vast pool of Jews available for the right kind of engagement. But if standard demographic surveys of the Jewish community continue to measure Jewish identity by asking people whether they (a) belong to a synagogue, (b) contribute to the Jewish Federation, and (c) take trips to Israel, we will continue to get narratives of a Jewish community in decline. The motivation for writing *Jewish Megatrends* was that it was clear to me that there was tremendous energy among Next Gen Jews to reinvent Jewish life, even as they turned their backs on the Jewish institutions built by the previous generation.

As a way to test the thesis that I offered in *Jewish Megatrends* about the changing nature of Jewish identity in the Jewish community, in 2015, I, along with a staff team, launched a national initiative called Kenissa: Communities of Meaning Network. *Kenissa* is the Hebrew word for entranceway or portal, and we used the term because we saw that thousands of younger Jews were finding their way into Jewish life through pathways other than legacy Jewish institutions. Kenissa was designed to identify, convene, and mobilize those "creatives" who were creating new models of Jewish life and community in North America. We identified specific sectors that were attracting an enthusiastic following of younger Jews, which included social justice; spiritual practice; independent *minyanim*; Jewish learning groups; new paradigm congregations, most of which were founded since the year 2000; eco-sustainability; and arts and culture. In each of these sectors, new organizations were being created, many operating under the radar screen of the organized Jewish community. Ironically, these "communities of meaning" were more successful at attracting Next Gen Jews than were many legacy Jewish organizations with exponentially larger budgets.

Over the course of five years, we mapped the "communities of meaning" phenomenon in North America, building a database of more than 400 organizations. During that same period of time, we convened some 300 of the founders of these organizations at nine different national consultations, and we used that opportunity to have them help define the very phenomenon that they were a part of. Kenissa Network members wrote essays on their understanding of the Jewish community and how it must function. They offered "How We Built This" narratives about how they grew their organizations and built a following. They even created graphical representations of their aspirational models of American Jewish life. All of these can be found on the Kenissa website, and they underscore that Next Gen Jews see Jewish life very differently than do the current custodians of the organized Jewish community.[6]

In a study of Kenissa participants by Dr. Tobin Belzer, we learned a lot more about what is driving the communities of meaning phenomenon. When asked to identify themselves among a long list of possible Jewish descriptors, 85 percent of the sample listed "just Jewish" or "post-denominational."[7] Very few checked boxes like "Conservative Jew" or "Reform Jew." Contrary to the findings of the 2013 Pew study and other heavily cited studies of Jewish attitudes, less than 20 percent said that they would respond well to appeals to Jewish loyalty based on memories of the Holocaust. An even smaller number said they would respond well to appeals to Jewish loyalty based on the existence of the State of Israel. Close to 70 percent said that their loyalties were primarily global and universal rather than particularistic, but more than 90 percent said they felt an affinity to the ethics and values of Judaism. Elsewhere, I have argued that the organized Jewish community was built by tribal Jews for tribal Jews.[8] If the Jewish community wants to capture the interests and passions of Generations X, Y, and Z, it will have to pivot to a community that better understands a post-tribal Jewish generation.[9]

We asked Kenissa Network members to describe the kind of atmosphere and ethos that they wanted their organizations to manifest. The words they used most frequently included "transformative," "welcoming," "nonjudgmental," "pluralistic," "risk-taking," "playful," and "unconventional." As we spent more time in Kenissa gatherings, we heard more and more stories about experiences that Network members had growing up in legacy Jewish organizations in which they felt judged and marginalized if they did not reflect "mainstream" attitudes, life choices, and mores. No one knows how many thousands of Jews were totally alienated by such experiences and have been lost to the Jewish community for this very reason. But Kenissa members made a different choice. They wanted Judaism to be a piece of their personal identity constructs, but they needed to create organizations and platforms in their own image to make it work for them and those like them.

WHAT MIGHT THE AMERICAN JEWISH FUTURE LOOK LIKE?

It is fair to ask whether the two worldviews that I have outlined above are too far apart to ever come together in some organic way that can serve the needs of the entire Jewish community. I believe it is possible. If I am wrong, we have two, unsatisfactory, zero-sum scenarios. In one, the legacy community continues to hold sway by ignoring or marginalizing all new manifestations of Jewish life. In the second, less likely scenario, the emerging communities of meaning simply seek to displace the legacy Jewish community, squandering the significant resources, expertise, and credibility that it has amassed for more than a century.

I have had the privilege of working professionally in both the legacy Jewish community and several new paradigm organizations that were part of the cultural milieu that has given birth to so many new Jewish communities of meaning. Each of the sectors has significant assets and some significant liabilities. I do believe that bridge building between the two sectors can generate a huge win-win for the Jewish future, and I am already seeing that collaborative future starting to take shape.

For the past several years, I have made presentations about the Kenissa project to dozens of Jewish audiences, almost exclusively sponsored by legacy Jewish organizations like Federations, synagogues, and JCCs. The average age of most of these audiences was considerably older than the audiences of our Kenissa national convenings. At my speaking engagements, the audiences were made up of the people who have built and who are currently stewards of the organized Jewish community. And without exception, at the Q&A following my presentations, one (or more) participant says something like "You just described my kids." This is not offered as a critique. It is offered more as a revelation. To paraphrase and telescope dozens of such comments: "I thought my kids were rejecting all of the Jewish things to which I have devoted my time and philanthropy. I thought I had lost them. But their interests and values sound similar to the Jewish creatives that you talked about. And the kinds of organizations you have described sound like the kinds of places my kids might actually be willing to try." I believe that many individuals and institutions of the generation that has funded and led the organized Jewish community to date stand ready and willing to help fund and support the emergence of new models of Jewish life.

Getting even more granular, for the last two years, we have invited small delegations of senior professionals from 20 of the largest Jewish Federations in the country to attend a National Kenissa Consultation. Because we work hard to create a "safe space" for our Kenissa creatives, we asked that the Federation professionals attend in "listen and learn" mode. We knew that they would hear some things that they might not agree with, but the conversation was designed to be exclusively for Kenissa Network members. On the final day of the three-day Consultation, we held a think tank attended by only the Federation professionals while the rest of the Kenissa staff facilitated the last day for participants. In our think tank, we asked these questions: What did you observe? What did you learn? What might this mean for your work back home? Sure enough, the Federation professionals heard a lot that challenged and even upset them. The working assumptions of our Network members do not reflect the kinds of opinions that Federation pros usually hear. But, more important, the Federation pros were deeply impressed by the commitment of Kenissa members to Jewish life, and they were blown away by the creativity of their various endeavors. It was immediately obvious to them how compelling such offerings might be to Next Gen Jews. The Federation pros left the gathering with their heads spinning about how the communities of meaning phenomenon could enhance Jewish life in their respective communities if they could come up with a formula for how to make such collaborations happen.

To my mind, such collaborations represent a winning formula not only for Federations but also for American synagogues and other legacy institutions. If, in the 20th century, Jews looked to their synagogues to help them acculturate into American society, in the 21st century, the Jewish communal experiences that will have the most appeal to Next Gen Jews are those that offer a cultural alternative to the prevailing lifestyles and mores of America. Even as interest in traditional religion has declined in the United States, the interest in spirituality and alternative lifestyles has grown. The Facebook generation might be able to boast thousands of "friends" or followers on Twitter, but people report that they can't find a single person with whom to have an intimate conversation or, for that matter, a community that will allow them to feel seen and heard.[10] This is an environment ripe for spiritual communities that are mission driven, that build a deep relational culture among members, and that bring the collective power of the community to bear on the social and political issues that are tearing our nation apart.

During the days of the Temple in Jerusalem, there was a tension between the priests, who were the custodians of the Temple rites and worked in close collaboration with the ruling elite, and the prophets, who, speaking in the name of God, critiqued the moral failings of the society. It is a tension inherent in the way the institution of religion positions itself vis-à-vis the society in which it functions. Shall we be "insiders" or "outsiders"? Reverend Michael-Ray Mathews, a contemporary Black Baptist minister who works for Faith in Action in the Bay Area, has said of clergy, "you can choose to be chaplains of the empire or prophets of the resistance."[11] While that quote has a clear progressive bent, I believe there is a deep truth embedded in his charge that transcends political partisanship. The appeal of Orthodox Judaism, even to those who were raised with little to no religion, is precisely because Orthodoxy promotes a lifestyle that puts limits on American culture. There are things you can't eat. There are times when you need to shut down all of your technological devices. There are days when you can't engage in commerce. This is not the "counterculture" of the 1960s, but it is distinctively "countercultural," and, to adherents of Orthodoxy, it offers a glimpse of how one can carve out a life of sacred purpose in a society that is so spiritually shallow.

Next Gen Jews are attracted to organizations and communities that stand for something, another way of being "countercultural" or "prophets for the resistance." It might be racial justice. It might be combatting food insecurity or mass incarceration. It might be gender equality. It might be a commitment to ecological sustainability. It might be working for human rights. For each of these issues, one could name one or more Jewish organizations that have done outstanding work in the realm of education, advocacy, and/or service. And there are now emerging a few dozen synagogues that have put such social issues at the very center of their institutional missions. These are examples of the "communities of meaning" that will have particular appeal to Next Gen Jews in the foreseeable future.

One additional organizational strategy that needs to be explored is for Jewish institutions to engage in partnerships with organizations and communities of meaning that have expertise and passion for specific civic issues. What if synagogues stopped seeing themselves as private clubs exclusively serving their dues-paying members and, instead, positioned themselves as "wisdom/action centers"? They could help Jews deepen their knowledge of and commitment to Judaism and, at the same time, bring the considerable talent and resources of the Jewish people to bear on the issues affecting our communities, our nation, and the world. I could think of dozens of communities of meaning led by young, creative individuals that would welcome the chance to establish mutually beneficial partnerships that would bring a dynamic new programmatic dimension into synagogues. In turn, synagogues and other more established organizations can provide these fledging organizations with a platform and administrative support that is often desperately needed but not always affordable to them.

I am aware that not all rabbis and Jewish communal leaders feel equal to the task of balancing the inward-focused agenda with the more outward-facing agenda, and many lay leaders of congregations and other Jewish institutions will resist such a shift. Synagogues, in particular, can be notoriously conservative (small *c*) when it comes to changing the way things are done, be it in the realm of worship, congregational programming, or governance and finances. Here it is worth noting that the COVID-19 pandemic precipitated some truly bold innovations in synagogues of all denominations all across North America. Rabbis and staff of Jewish organizations were challenged to meet the needs of their respective communities under very difficult constraints, and there are numerous examples of innovations that were introduced that might never have otherwise been tried.[12] Many leaders took note that the range of possibilities for their institutions might be a lot greater than they previously assumed.

My early Jewish education took place in an Orthodox yeshiva where it was clear that the rabbi in the front of the room would proclaim some "truth," and we, his students, would provide a modern replay of the children of Israel at Mt. Sinai by responding, "we will do and we will listen" (*naaseh v'nishma*). The Jewish community still has both religious and communal leaders who expect that top-down model of leadership to work. It doesn't. One of the positive consequences of the internet age that we live in is that the voices that once were silent can now be heard. It is a new and challenging terrain for would-be leaders because, with so many voices in the mix, building consensus can be very hard. But with open minds and open hearts, I believe that when leaders both encourage and pay attention to all of those disparate voices, something better can be created. *Warm and Welcoming* provides a platform for much wisdom from a wide array of innovative voices. If the stewards of the Jewish community take in that wisdom with open minds and open hearts, we can build a more vibrant Jewish future together.

NOTES

1. See Kevin McCaffree, *The Secular Landscape: The Decline of Religion in America* (Cham, Switzerland: Palgrave Macmillan, 2017).

2. Jeffrey Jones, "U.S. Church Membership Falls Below Majority for the First Time," Gallup, March 29, 2021, https://news.gallup.com/poll/341963/church-membership -falls-below-majority-first-time.aspx.

3. The other synagogues profiled were Beth El of Sudbury, Massachusetts (Reform); B'nai Jeshurun in New York City (chartered as a Conservative synagogue before they dropped their affiliation in the mid-1990s); and the Hebrew Institute of Riverdale in Bronx, New York (Orthodox).

4. See the work of B3, the Jewish Boomer Platform: https://www.b3platform.org/.

5. Pew Research Center, *A Portrait of Jewish Americans* (Washington, DC: Pew Research Center, October 1, 2013), 13, https://www.pewresearch.org/wp-content/ uploads/sites/7/2013/10/jewish-american-full-report-for-web.pdf.

6. Kenissa Network members' essays on Jewish life can be found at https://kenissa.org/blog/; "How We Built This" narratives can be found at https://kenissa.org/national-gatherings/national-consultations/2020-national-consultation/how-we-built-this-2020/; the graphic representations of an ideal Jewish community can be found at https://kenissa.org/about-kenissa/conceptual-frameworks/.

7. Tobin Belzer, *Jewish Communal Transformation: A Look at What's Happening and Who's Making It Happen*, November 2016, https://kenissa.org/wp-content/uploads/2016/12/NPSCI-report-Nov-16-final.pdf.

8. See Rabbi Sidney Schwarz, *Judaism and Justice: The Jewish Passion to Repair the World* (Woodstock, VT: Jewish Lights, 2006), chapters 2 and 16.

9. My preferred term for "post-tribal" Jews is "covenantal Jews," and I explain the term and why I use it in *Jewish Megatrends: Charting the Course of the American Jewish Future* (Woodstock, VT: Jewish Lights, 2013), 10ff.

10. There is a growing literature on the negative impact that technology has had on American culture and on the spiritual well-being of Americans. One seminal analysis is Sherry Turkle's *Alone Together: Why We Expect More from Technology and Less from Each Other* (New York: Basic Books, 2011).

11. Michael-Ray Mathews, "Will You Be Chaplain to the Empire or Prophet of the Resistance?" *Sojourners Magazine*, February 16, 2017, https://sojo.net/articles/faith-action/will-you-be-chaplain-empire-or-prophet-resistance.

12. Sidney Schwarz, "Synagogue Innovation in the Age of Corona," *eJewish Philanthropy*, May 11, 2020, https://ejewishphilanthropy.com/synagogue-innovation-in-the-age-of-corona/.

Acknowledgments

The opportunity to work on this project with a close friend has been one of the most rewarding aspects of writing this book. The two of us met in Philadelphia's Jewish community, where, from 2008 to 2017, we planned Purim parties, Shavuot programs, Shabbat dinners, and a host of other events to serve as many Jews in the region as we could. Throughout the years, we talked about various projects we could do together. (Our favorite was an initiative in which the two of us would set up a table in Philadelphia's Rittenhouse Square doling out advice to passersby à la Lucy in *Peanuts:* Miriam on love and relationships and Warren on fashion. Suffice it to say that this initiative never came to fruition.) The book you hold in your hands is a reflection of our love of building Jewish community in all sorts of forms and locations. Thank you to all of you who attended those events with us and taught us so much in the process.

We are grateful to so many people for making this book happen. First off, we are most grateful to each of the contributors to this book. The chapters in this book were written throughout the course of the COVID-19 pandemic, and amid the stresses of dealing with the pandemic and juggling family and work issues, each contributor made time in their lives to write for this project. We thank them for sharing their knowledge, wisdom, and experience and for sharing their own commitment to creating inclusive communities with us and with all of you.

Thank you as well to Rowman & Littlefield for publishing this book and believing in our vision. We are particularly grateful to Michael Gibson, Sylvia Landis, and our editor Natalie Mandziuk. Natalie was there every step of the way, helping us navigate challenges and bumps and making sure we made it to the finish line.

I would like to thank the board of the Association for Jewish Studies, especially executive committee members Noam Pianko, Christine Hayes, Laura

Leibman, Kenneth Koltun-Fromm, Jeffrey Shoulson, Robin Judd, and Sarah Benor, for giving me the time to write and work on this project. I would also like to thank Pam Nadell, Lila Corwin-Berman, Laura Levitt, and Jeffrey Veidlinger, all of whom gave advice and publishing guidance along the way.

I am grateful to everyone who taught me new things about inclusion and how to build Jewish community, many of whom have contributed to this volume. While Jewish community goes far beyond synagogues, over the years I have been privileged to experience welcoming community through a variety of rabbis and religious institutions, including Rabbi Mayer Seligman at Temple Sholom in Broomall, Pennsylvania; Rabbi Linda Potemken at Congregation Beth Israel of Media, Pennsylvania; and Rabbi Lauren Grabelle Herrmann at Kol Tzedek in West Philadelphia. I would also like to thank the Schusterman Foundation, not only for providing funding for this project but also, and more important, for including me in the ROI community, where for nearly 10 years I have gotten to meet, collaborate, and work with the next generation of Jewish communal innovators. Thank you as well to all the organizers of the annual Collaboratory gathering, which has been one of the most inspiring and energizing places to engage with the current and next wave of Jewish communal practitioners.

Thank you to Seth Pamperin, who taught me how to see Judaism through non-Jewish eyes, showing me all the places where even the most well-intentioned Jewish spaces unintentionally became less than welcoming. Friends and chosen family are so important in my life, and having their support through this last year was so needed; thank you to Mitch Ginsburgh, Evan Noch, Sam Longair, Janette Amadio, Matt Durso, Sarah Schonberg, and Tessa Andermann. I am grateful to the participants in the Heymish *minyan* for providing consistent, loving, friendly, and warm Jewish space (as well as delicious food) throughout my many years in Philadelphia. Finally, thank you to Miriam Steinberg-Egeth, who has been the most amazing partner on this project. She made the challenging process of co-editing a collection of essays fun and manageable, and the book itself is so much better because of her.

                                                        Warren Hoffman

I would like to thank the Philadelphia Jewish community for its willingness to collaborate, its openness to change, and its role in shaping me into the Jewish professional I am today. In particular, I want to acknowledge the organizations and representatives that make up the Center City Kehillah, as well as the rabbis of the Board of Rabbis of Greater Philadelphia. These incredible networks exemplify partnerships and model how to explore the limits of what our communities can do together.

I want to express my deepest gratitude to my family, who were literally physically present for every step of this project as we spent the pandemic at home together. Thank you to Marc for your endless love and patience, and for believing in me and the value of my work. To my children, Aliza and Solomon, thank you for your insights, creativity, thoughtfulness, tech support, and growing independence. This world, and the Jewish community, will be yours next, and I am inspired every day by seeing how you are poised to be leaders.

Thank you to Jenny Berggren, Elizabeth Drellich, Joan Fanwick, Tamar Fox, Rabbanit Dasi Fruchter, Rabbi Annie Lewis, Beverly and Naomi Socher-Lerner, and Adrienne Westwood for being my constant texting companions throughout this past year and for supporting me, my family, and my work, each in your own way. No personal or professional question has ever been too insignificant or too problematic for the lot of you, and I am lucky to call you my friends.

I simply wouldn't be who I am today without my parents, Phyllis and Ted, who modeled for me, from my very earliest memories, what it means to nurture and sustain Jewish communities. For so long, being Jewish was entirely wrapped up in being your daughter, and I am grateful for the unique and completely non-replicable Jewish education I received from you and from the Temple Beth El community in Dunkirk/Fredonia, New York. Thank you also to my siblings, Gillian and Dan, for showing me what it means to be a writer and for demonstrating what it looks like to be true to your own Jewish paths.

Thank you so very much to Warren for being a colleague, collaborator, and friend, and for bringing me into this project. While in some ways this book is a far cry from planning Purim drag shows and serving salmon on Shavuot, in the ways that matter, it is an extension of every important conversation we've ever had. I am grateful for your vision of this project, your dedication to Jewish communities, and, most of all, your friendship.

Miriam Steinberg-Egeth

* * *

Thank you to everyone who sees themselves in these pages and feels seen as a result. Thank you to the clergy and Jewish professionals who work relentlessly to improve and widen what our Jewish experiences and institutions look like. And finally, thank you to those of you who don't see yourself in these pages and who want to yell and scream at us that we missed an issue that is at the core of your identity. Thank you for being who you are, and thank you for your patience as the Jewish community gets closer to welcoming you as your full self.

Introduction

Warren Hoffman

It was Friday night, *erev* Shabbat, and I was walking into a synagogue I had never visited before for services. Entering the rear of the sanctuary, I watched the fading light from the stained-glass windows begin to cast gentle shadows on the pews and walls, and I saw five individuals sitting in a circle having a conversation. One of the individuals I quickly recognized as the rabbi from the synagogue's website. Excited to have the opportunity to meet the rabbi before services, I still distinctly remember how all five people looked up at me, turned in my direction, and then, as if I were a ghost, quickly turned away again. Not a hello. Not a welcome. Not a "Shabbat Shalom." Perhaps they were deep in the middle of a story and couldn't be bothered. Perhaps they thought I was a long-time member. By the time their discussion finished, the sanctuary had filled up with people who settled in for services. The sanctuary buzzed, and yet no one greeted me, asked where I was from, or even said hello. Services ended and I left, never to return. Like a spirit who had passed through the aisles, unseen, it was as if I had never been there at all. I could have been a member in the making, a donor, or (who knows?), maybe somewhere down the line, even the next synagogue president, but one will never know, as no one there had taken the time to say hello. I was "low-hanging fruit," a young person under 30 who had walked in the doors of a synagogue at a time when the average age of synagogue members seemed to be 50 and up.[1]

On the surface, this story might sound like nothing more than an unfortunate missed opportunity in capturing a new member, but the whole experience left me feeling hurt. Years later, when I recounted this experience to a friend and named the synagogue, her eyes got big, and she exclaimed, "Oh, the same thing happened to me at that place!" So maybe it wasn't just me, or maybe it was just me and her. But in some ways, the number of people who were turned off by their experience at this synagogue doesn't matter, because if even just one person was ignored or not welcomed by an institution, it's an organizational failure, an indication of the inability of an organization to fulfill its mission of building community. And while it's true that making connections can go both ways—there's no reason why I can't introduce myself to others—one would like to think that upon entering a new space, the regulars would do their utmost to welcome a stranger into their midst.

My story is not unique or even the most traumatic, but it's happened to me and others more than once at Jewish Federations, Jewish Community Centers (JCCs), synagogues, and other Jewish organizations around the country, many of which claim to be "warm and welcoming," yet repeatedly fall short at the very basic action of welcoming newcomers. Sometimes this absence of welcoming behavior is nothing more than the failure to greet someone, but usually, on a much more profound level, it's a failure to welcome in and make space for people who are different from the majority of attendees or those who have needs that are not currently being met by the organization. I've spent my life and much of my career volunteering at and working in Jewish communal organizations, witnessing firsthand both the challenges and missteps that organizations, whether legacy institutions or start-ups, have faced in attempting to engage the next generation of participants, both Jewish and not.

While we can sometimes chock up the inability to be truly welcoming to unfortunate obliviousness, in other cases, the actions of a Jewish organization can feel like unwarranted acts of aggression, callousness, and outright insensitivity. Jews of color are regularly interrogated and questioned in Jewish spaces by individuals who are suspicious of their presence. Are they really Jews? Maybe they're just visiting with a Jewish friend. Did they convert? There's the interfaith couple who is welcomed into the synagogue only to experience rhetoric from the *bimah* (raised prayer platform) that describes the "problem" of interfaith relationships. How can one feel welcomed if they are defined and seen as a "problem"? Or there's the nonbinary Jew who wants to join their local JCC but is confronted by an application form that only has options for male or female. Or there's the single gay Jew in his 20s or 30s who is told about all the programming at his local Federation for young singles, but it's really programming geared toward matchmaking straight couples so that they procreate and have children. How about the Hebrew-illiterate partner who can't follow along at services because the organization doesn't use transliterations? What about the Jew who would be happy to support the local Federation with a donation, but because the individual also supports IfNotNow, a group that advocates for Palestinian rights, a group that the Federation refuses to recognize, the person does not feel like they are part of the larger organized Jewish community? What happens to the young Jew who has much energy and knowledge to offer the local synagogue but can't afford to pay dues because of student loan debt and feels uncomfortable having to plead poverty to the synagogue administrator? The list goes on and on.

The truth is, every time one of these incidents occurs, Jewish institutions potentially lose another member, another donor, another supporter, all while their core number of supporters continues to dwindle. The loss also goes beyond the monetary. These organizations lose new perspectives, diversity, energy, and excitement that individuals who want to be a part of something meaningful have to offer. These organizations do lasting damage not only to the unwelcomed individuals but also to themselves and to Judaism itself. How many "unfortunate" situations or off-putting remarks can one person reasonably tolerate before they decide that they're done with Judaism altogether?

At New York's Central Synagogue, one of the largest Reform congregations in the city and in all of North America with 2,600 member households, there is actually a waiting list to become a synagogue member that lasts about 18–24 months.[2] Central Synagogue, though, is an anomaly, as many Federations, JCCs, and synagogues in the 21st century are hurting for members and donors. Gone are the decades following World War II when Jews built large synagogue complexes with swimming pools in the suburbs and elsewhere where Jews could celebrate their Jewishness in bolder ways than ever before.[3] The 1950s and 1960s were the golden years of such institutions, and, unfortunately, many such institutions, despite now having a Twitter channel and Facebook page, are still very much operating with programs, marketing, and beliefs as if the 1950s never left, scratching their heads over where everyone went.

If you were to ask the leaders of such communal organizations for the reasons behind these trends of attrition, they would have a ready answer, one that was handed to them on October 1, 2013, complete with facts and figures in the form of a 214-page document titled *A Portrait of Jewish Americans*, researched and compiled by the Pew Research Center. The "Pew study" or "Pew survey," as it was often called in shorthand, was the first major demographic study of the American Jewish community since the 2000–2001 National Jewish Population Survey. The 2013 study tried to determine how people identified Jewishly, how they practiced their Judaism (if at all), how certain political issues resonated with Jews, and more. Distilled to a 20-page summary, the 2013 Pew study revealed a number of big takeaways:

- 62 percent of American Jews said that being Jewish was tied more to ancestry or culture than religion.
- Approximately 44 percent of American Jews were in interfaith relationships, with that number increasing as the age of the respondent decreased.
- Only 43 percent of surveyed Jews expressed a connection with Israel, with that number dropping to 23 percent for so-called Jews of no religion.[4]

When the study was first released, it was all that Jewish communal professionals could talk about for weeks and months afterward, as Jewish publications and pundits spilled a great deal of ink trying to unpack what the study meant for the future of Judaism in the United States.[5] The response among Jewish professionals (and Jews themselves) was unsurprisingly mixed. For many, it was a "sky is falling" moment, amplifying the woes and anxieties that many legacy organizations had long been experiencing. Many of these organizations quickly moved into panic or triage mode (if they weren't already there), asking how even more dollars could be spent on outreach to millennials and other underengaged individuals in the Jewish community. Innovation grants sprang up, and committees were formed to try to diagnose and treat the situation. Many of these efforts were well intentioned but often misguided in their approach, attempting to provide Band-Aids to Jewish institutions that in many cases needed a major overhaul. For other individuals, the results of the Pew study were nothing more than a shrug of the shoulders. "Tell us something we don't know," they seemed to say. Not letting the results of the study distract them from their missions or core activities, such agencies decided that ultimately it was, for better or worse, business as usual. While a new Pew study on American Jewry was released more recently in 2021, many of the statistics from 2013 had not changed that much.

The 2013 Pew study confirmed the fears of many legacy Jewish institutions that could now point with dismay to numbers showing how their woes of attrition were not unimagined or insignificant. Jews, especially those in their 20s and 30s, were identifying as less religious than before (a trend that was not unique to Jews, although that point was somewhat buried in the Pew study), and it was the job of legacy organizations to win them back.[6] In reality, though, this was only half the story. While it's true that factors beyond the control of Jewish legacy organizations had accounted for shifts in Jewish affiliation, what was unexamined by the Pew study were the ways in which Jewish communal institutions, many of which describe themselves as "warm and welcoming," had unwittingly alienated, turned away, and even offended the exact individuals whom they were trying to engage.

For those of you from Jewish communal institutions who are reading these words at this very moment, I'm sure this assertion may be hard to process or accept. "That's not us!" you'll exclaim. "We're a wonderful organization. How could anyone not like us?" After all, you view yourselves as positive spaces in the Jewish community. But in many cases, Jewish communal institutions are unwilling and sometimes even incapable of effecting the change necessary to be truly inclusive organizations in the 21st century. *Saying that you are "warm and welcoming" is very different from actually being "warm and welcoming."* Rather, being "warm and welcoming" is a continuous, evolving, and never-ending process that requires a great deal of concerted effort, energy, and work; it's not a simple statement of fact.

The goal of this book is to help Jewish communal organizations, whether long-standing legacy institutions or recent start-ups, as well as everything in between, understand the various challenges facing a new generation of Jews and, more than that, learn about specific steps and actions that they can take to transform their organizations into the inclusive and diverse spaces that they aspire to be. While there have been a number of books over the years, such as Rabbi Ron Wolfson's *Relational Judaism* (2013) and Rabbi Sid Schwarz's *Jewish Megatrends* (2013), that have worked to chart new strategies for how Jewish institutions can continue to evolve and remain relevant, *Warm and Welcoming* appears at a very particular moment not only in Jewish history but also in American history. This book was written during the COVID-19 pandemic when the United States and the world at large experienced unprecedented barriers toward connecting with people as well as huge advancements in technologically assisted accessibility for people isolated at home. Perhaps most significantly during the pandemic, the United States also witnessed mass protests and a new movement for racial justice and equity for African Americans. The movement was a reckoning and wake-up call for many organizations, including Jewish organizations, to take a hard and honest look at the need to be more open and inclusive not just to people of color but also to individuals from a variety of backgrounds that have typically not seen themselves represented or truly welcomed by the Jewish American community.

This book features chapters, insights, and resources by some of the top practitioners and up-and-coming thinkers in the Jewish world who are leading the way and modeling how true inclusivity works. In fact, the idea to make this book a collection of essays rather than instructions from a single person was a conscious decision to show how there is a real need to hear and learn from a variety of people, especially the populations that one is trying to serve, to make them feel not only included but also part of the conversation itself.

Such thinking derives in part from work known as "design theory" that has developed out of Stanford's d.school. Design theory, while originally conceived as a way to address problems and challenges between customers and businesses in the for-profit world, has been adapted and utilized by nonprofit practitioners in recent years. There are a number of elements that define design theory, and this book is not meant to be a guide in how design theory works, but there is one essential component that is worth considering—namely, giving a voice to the stakeholders who will be served by an institution to enable them to give feedback to the product under investigation. Consider for a moment this question: Does your Jewish institution have individuals under the age of 30 on your board or in key leadership positions? Have individuals who aren't white, Ashkenazi, male, straight, or even (heaven forbid) Jewish serving in major leadership positions? I once sat on a funding panel where suburban Jewish women between the ages of 40 and 70 had to determine how to serve and fund the needs of Jewish millennials who lived in the city. The targets of such funding were never brought into the process or asked what they thought, creating a further disconnect between the institution and the individuals served. In a moment when boards are still predominantly run by

Jews of a certain age who have the means to pay board dues and make significant contributions (not unworthy actions in and of themselves), what might it
mean to radically shake up the leadership and boards of legacy organizations
with a younger and more diverse demographic that can actually speak to the
issues and challenges facing their communities and offer insight into funding
decisions to serve interests that are relevant to them? What might be gained in
buy-in and renewed support that would compensate, at least at the outset, by
a potential partial decrease in revenue by young individuals who don't (yet)
have the capacity to give? Might short-term financial losses be a hedging strategy against long-term stakeholder cultivation?

For many communal professionals and probably for even more board
members, there will be parts of this book that will be hard to digest and may
even make you uncomfortable. Like the call of the shofar that is meant to wake
us up during Rosh Hashanah, to get us to perform *heshbon ha-nefesh* (taking
account of one's soul), so, too, is this book a type of wake-up call, encouraging institutions to take stock of how they function and operate. The changes
may be outside the scope of your personal or organizational Jewish identity
or even your identity at large. I've seen these reactions firsthand in staff and
board meetings. Unfortunate reactions to new ideas have ranged from outright
dismissal to public ridicule of new strategies for engagement. Design thinking, though, encourages us to embrace ambiguity and uncertainty and to try
new things. Simply doubling down on failing strategies because it's what you
know—a strategy that far too many organizations utilize—is unacceptable.

Embracing new ideas, though, can be a challenge. Take, for example, asking
people to conceive of gender as something that isn't binary. Asking this of
some people and, more important, trying to get them to change their institution's forms or policies to reflect those new understandings can be unsettling,
"silly," or incomprehensible to someone who has grown up in the world
where everything seemed clearly "male" and "female." But what does your
organization lose by making this change? Will older donors really abandon
the institution if they are no longer presented with binary options? Asking
someone to be more inclusive of gender difference doesn't require that they
rethink their own personal sense of gender (although that may happen and
that's not a bad thing), but what might be gained by expanding gender definitions? Making space for others need not be a threat to one's own position,
status, or identity.

Depending on your organization's structure, religious viewpoints, or financial capacity, some of the strategies in this book may be difficult to enact. An
Orthodox synagogue, for example, may feel ideologically restricted in how it
addresses issues of gender and sexuality, and a small-town JCC may not have
the resources to make their physical space fully inclusive for individuals with
wheelchairs. Even the most energetic, forward-thinking organization with the
best intentions will probably, due to funding limitations, staffing limitations,

and finite bandwidth, not be able to do everything suggested in this book. And that's OK. Becoming an inclusive organization is a process, not a checklist. Not every adjustment is right for every community, although ideally, discussions around change and inclusion should be *communal* activities with as much buy-in as possible, not decisions made by an exclusive group. More than that, change is hard and scary, and the older and more established an organization is, the harder it is to change. What an organization may possess in size and resources, it often lacks in nimbleness and flexibility.

Enacting change also requires a team effort. For many years, I served in a number of legacy organizations as what's been known colloquially as an "intrapreneur," someone who works in an established organization to bring about and foster change. While my passion for change is legion, one person alone cannot right a ship. If you are an executive director or a board chairperson reading this book, and you are inspired to implement some of the ideas contained in these pages, good for you! But it won't be enough. You'll have to cultivate allies so that they understand why such changes are needed and necessary. It will take time and, in some cases, may even require a reconsideration of personnel in terms of both staff and lay leaders to construct a team that is ready, willing, and able to bring about the modifications necessary to transform your organization into a 21st-century operation. And lest you think that change is nothing more than needing a new logo or rebrand for your organization, let me simply say this: it's not. One Jewish legacy organization I am familiar with, which was struggling to engage new audiences, went through a multi-month, very expensive rebranding process, only to tell its audience at the brand relaunch that its logo was new, but it was the same organization it had always been—a most unfortunate of announcements, in my assessment. Rather than ask difficult questions and really grapple with who it was and the audiences it was serving or, more important, not serving, the organization settled for a new look (and a new font) without altering its outdated substance.

And for those organizations that are unable to pivot in a new direction or are adamantly opposed to change, it's my strong belief that such organizations are committing themselves to a trajectory where they will effectively put themselves out of business or, at the very least, reconciling themselves to serving only a limited subset of the Jewish population. This self-inflicted damage might not be felt today or even next year, but, like the slow, seemingly imperceptible changes that climate change is wreaking on our world, the devastating effects of not changing course will develop into catastrophic consequences in the next 10–20 years. A crisis of this magnitude cannot be solved overnight or when things have gotten so bad that we have already passed the point of no return. How many members can a synagogue or JCC afford to lose before it's too late? How many lapsed or deceased donors, who are not replaced, can you manage to lose before you have to start curtailing the amount of money you allocate? And what if that organization does go out of business? Sometimes that isn't the worst thing. Not everything in this world is meant to last forever, and Jewish organizations are no exception. If they are no longer effectively serving the populations that they intend to serve, or have lost touch with the changing needs of the community, perhaps it's not terrible if they fade away. As we will see from some of the contributors in this collection, there are a number of smaller, energetic, and relevant Jewish organizations ready to fill the gaps and serve the needs of contemporary Jews that legacy organizations are unable to meet. Despite what the 2013 and 2020 Pew studies might say, younger generations of Jewish Americans are actively "doing Jewish" and feeding their Jewish identities—but in ways and in places that may look very different from Judaism of the past.

Jewish tradition itself teaches us how to be welcoming; it's the principle of *ahavat ger* (loving the stranger). It's true that for many years, and even today to some extent, Jews felt so marginalized by mainstream American society that there was a real need and even joy in creating environments where they could be among other Jews. There was safety, both literal and figurative, in these spaces: a way to feel at home with others who were like them. But in achieving and establishing such places of cultural and religious refuge, Jews have sometimes failed to remember *ahavat ger*, even forgetting the ways that they themselves were once marginalized and now may be inadvertently reproducing the behaviors of mainstream society within their own walls. Until everyone is fully welcomed and embraced into the Jewish community and made to feel truly at home, every individual, Jewish or not, who walks through your doors is a stranger.

Parshat vayera (Exodus 18:1–22:24) drives home this need to welcome the stranger. The Jewish forefather, Abraham, greets three strangers at his door; more than simply saying "hello" or asking what they may need, he and his wife Sarah go out of their way to provide them with food, water, and hospitality. Abraham and Sarah don't wait to learn who these people are or what they might get out of being hospitable. All they know is that these three strangers must be properly welcomed. This in and of itself is a good principle to live by, but to be practical about it as well, gracious hospitality is a potential investment in a future member, donor, or volunteer. The person we are meeting might have the capacity to give or to play a major role in our institution. Even more basic than this, the inclusion of other voices and perspectives in our communities will make Judaism a more vibrant, flexible, and inclusive community for the future. In the case of Abraham and Sarah, one of the strangers tells the elderly couple that they will have a son in the coming year, despite their advanced age, a proclamation that causes Sarah to laugh. There's no indication that the hospitality offered by Abraham and Sarah brought about this prognostication, but, clearly, it didn't hurt. Again, we shouldn't welcome people because of what we think we may get out of it, but for those individuals wondering what's in it for their institution, it's about cultivating people, as we don't know where our greatest supporters may come from. And even if a particular individual isn't going to join your organization for whatever reason, if that person has a bad experience, they may end up saying negative things about your organization (regardless of the prohibition against *l'shon ha'ra*, or gossip) that can quickly poison the well of a small, tight-knit community.

This work of welcoming takes conscious effort. It's more than just saying hello at the entrance like you're a door greeter at Walmart. While it might not seem practical or possible to engage with every individual yourself, creating a corps of volunteers who can be tasked with this role is equally important. A friend of mine, who is part of the Vivace group (donors aged 21–45) of Opera Philadelphia, told me how on his second attendance at one of the Opera's performances, he found a handwritten note on his seat from another Vivace member expressing how excited they were that my friend had come to this event and had joined the group. Not a difficult or costly action, to say the least, but one that required some forethought, planning, and a little bit of time. In our digital age when so much feels particularly fleeting and ephemeral, receiving this handwritten note, this personal touch, made my friend feel special, included, and eager to play a continuing role in Vivace, stewarding him toward both board leadership and donor potential.

Warm and Welcoming begins with several chapters that focus on the myriad of Jewish American Identities, including LGBTQ Jews, Jews of color, individuals with disabilities, interfaith families, and those who belong to the generations labeled millennials and Gen Z. All of these groups have been marginalized, denied access in some way, or been misunderstood or underserved by mainstream institutions. While the Jewish American community is often discussed as a sort of monolith with the "average" Jew depicted as white, Ashkenazi, male, straight, and non-disabled, a strategy developed to counter Jewish minority status in mainstream America, the fact is that the community is and always has been more diverse than it seems at a quick pass. While the contributors in these chapters discuss the issues facing a number of specific populations within the Jewish community, this list is not meant to be, by any means, comprehensive. In talking about difference, one could talk about the diversity of Jewish cultural backgrounds (Sephardic, Mizrahi, Persian, African, etc.) or the diversity of Jewish religious movements themselves (Reform, Reconstructionist, Conservative, and Orthodox). How do we acknowledge difference in our communities? This is more than "tolerance"; this is learning about what makes people different and understanding and celebrating their presence. These are lessons that can be applied to any subgroup within the Jewish American community, but it should be said that such inclusion goes for everyone. Even Jews who do not fall into any of these subareas and might identify as your "average" mainstream Jew need to be welcomed, greeted, and cultivated. In fact, one could go even further and say that the real goal here is not merely to welcome someone in and carve out space for them but also to change the Jewish landscape substantially so that people from all backgrounds and with all different needs are seamlessly woven into the fabric of the Jewish community, thereby making a whole new cloth in the process.

The chapters that follow offer a range of strategies for creating programming and inclusive engagement opportunities that remove barriers of entry into the Jewish community while fostering spaces that are more open to a variety of experiences and points of view. These strategies include arts and culture and music that will engage new audiences, navigating fraught topics like Israel/Palestine and social justice, and learning how to communicate and market your institution's story in an inclusive way. The experts who have contributed these chapters impart actionable ideas for how the content you offer can itself model inclusivity. In fairness, not all of these models can be repurposed by every institution, but legacy institutions in particular need to know what's working elsewhere in the Jewish community, and leaders of such organizations might be inspired by the grassroots, start-up nature of Jewish engagement outside their own doors. Young people want authenticity and have strong "BS" meters, often able to judge whether a program is really about engagement and serving their needs or just a ploy to capture their dollars.

A common theme that runs through many of these chapters is that, in order to make the Jewish community more diverse and inclusive, welcoming isn't enough. Rather, true inclusiveness means enabling individuals and populations who have been previously disempowered to articulate their own needs and chart their own Jewish journeys within the larger Jewish communal structure. The definition of Jewish community needs to expand, and the previous generation's gatekeepers must share the reins of decision making, program creation, and community building with a new set of individuals who want and deserve to see themselves at the forefront of Jewish life. Being "warm and welcoming" is more than making room at the table; it's about rethinking what the table looks like.

This work of becoming "warm and welcoming" is a process not an endpoint. Like any personal relationship, making people feel welcome and at home in your organization takes constant work and effort. The moment we think we can coast on our successes is when we risk losing people again. In a world in which all we want are quick results at the tap of a button, sent by text, making such an investment can seem difficult, overwhelming, and even scary. This work requires that we be vulnerable, admitting what we don't know and what our weaknesses may be, but recognizing that if we start asking questions and talking to people, we may learn new things about others and ourselves.

In fact, Miriam and I, as the co-editors of this book, learned new things about inclusion and made our own mistakes along the way. We learned new perspectives on the value of building authentic relationships with people whose backgrounds may be different from our own, as well as learning that sometimes even the best intentions do not make for perfect solutions.

Learning from our mistakes, though, was part of the process, and we encourage readers not to be scared by the possibility of doing or saying the wrong thing; the opposite—doing nothing—we believe, is even worse than making a mistake. This work will force most of us out of our comfort zones, engaging with people whose backgrounds, ideas, values, identities, experiences, and politics might be greatly different from our own. Yet, at the same time, these same individuals share a common connection through Judaism that binds us together. Knowing that community is not monolithic is a powerful realization that can make an organization stronger. As much as tradition can be comforting and nourishing, it can, without adapting, also be enervating and stultifying, preventing us from moving forward and embracing change. Whether we like it or not, the world is moving forward, and both Jews and Judaism are changing. That's the one thing we can agree on from the recent Pew studies. The question is, will you and your organization be there to meet and grapple with those challenges? Hopefully, this book will help you along the way as you navigate the many paths, options, identities, and manifestations available on the path to becoming an inclusive organization in the 21st century.

NOTES

1. According to the 2020 Pew Research Center study, among respondents to the survey, 27 percent of synagogue members are between the ages of 18 and 29, while the largest group at 35 percent are individuals between the ages of 50 and 64. Pew Research Center, *Jewish Americans in 2020* (Washington, DC: Pew Research Center, May 11, 2021), 82, https://www.pewforum.org/2021/05/11/jewish-americans-in-2020/.

2. "Becoming a Member," Central Synagogue, accessed February 15, 2021, https://www.centralsynagogue.org/community/becoming_a_member.

3. See, for example, David Kaufman, *Pool with a Shul: The "Synagogue-Center" in American Jewish History* (Waltham, MA: Brandeis University Press, 1999).

4. Pew Research Center, *A Portrait of Jewish Americans* (Washington, DC: Pew Research Center, October 1, 2013), 8, 35, 55, https://www.pewresearch.org/wp-content/uploads/sites/7/2013/10/jewish-american-full-report-for-web.pdf.

5. Gary Rosenblatt, "What Pew Does and Doesn't Tell Us," *Times of Israel*, October 9, 2013, https://jewishweek.timesofisrael.com/what-pew-does-and-doesnt-tell-us-2/; Jack Wortheimer and Steven M. Cohen, "The Pew Survey Reanalyzed: More Bad News, but a Glimmer of Hope," *Mosaic*, November 2, 2014, https://mosaicmagazine.com/essay/uncategorized/2014/11/the-pew-survey-reanalyzed/; "'Jews of No Religion': Haaretz Contributors Unpack the Pew Survey," *Haaretz*, October 15, 2013, https://www.haaretz.com/jewish/.premium-jews-of-no-religion-analyzed-1.5273974; J. J. Goldberg, "Pew Survey about Jewish America Got It All Wrong," *Forward*, October 13, 2013, https://forward.com/opinion/185461/pew-survey-about-jewish-america-got-it-all-wrong/; Laurence Kotler-Berkowitz, "2015 after Pew: Thinking about American Jewish Cohesion, Assimilation and Division," Berman Jewish Databank, October 1, 2015, https://www.jewishdatabank.org/databank/search-results/study/793.

6. Pew Research Center, *A Portrait of Jewish Americans,* 7–8. The 2020 Pew study revealed that the majority of American Jews in all age groups identified more culturally as Jews than religiously. See Pew Research Center, *Jewish Americans in 2020,* chapter 3.

CHAPTER 1

LGBTQ Jews

Idit Klein

A 15-year-old lesbian tentatively knocks just below the bronze plate marked "Head of School" on the thick oak door. She has an appointment and has rehearsed what she wants to say, but she is nervous.

"Come in, Shula."

She enters and sits and takes a deep breath.

"Rabbi, I think you know that I came out at school recently. I'm the only out gay person here. I want to tell you what that feels like. I want to tell you my story." She exhales. She reminds herself: *I'll share, he'll listen, and then he'll understand why the school needs a Gay-Straight Alliance.* She starts to speak.

The rabbi holds up his hand to stop her from continuing. "Shula, I don't want to hear about your sex life."

Conversation over.

This exchange transpired more than 20 years ago and is described in the 2005 documentary film, produced by Keshet, *Hineini: Coming Out in a Jewish High School.* The film portrays how that 15-year-old channeled her isolation and despair into a vision of community and hope and organized to establish the first ever Gay-Straight Alliance at a Jewish high school.

At the time, I had just become the founding executive director of Keshet, a then-local organization in Boston with a mission of attaining lesbian, gay, bisexual, transgender, and queer (LGBTQ) equality and inclusion in Jewish life.[1] We helped support Shula in her campaign. As I started to build Keshet, I had many of my own disheartening exchanges with Jewish community leaders. When I would introduce myself and describe Keshet, people commonly replied, "How is that a Jewish issue? How is what you're doing relevant to the Jewish community?" Others responded with barely concealed disgust. I recall standing behind a Keshet information table at a Boston Jewish community fair and watching the shift in expression on people's faces—from neutral curiosity to perception and aversion—as they approached me and quickly turned away.

Twenty years later, it is rare for someone to question the relevance of Keshet's work, and about one-fourth of Jewish high schools have Gender and Sexuality Alliances.[2] Yet Keshet staff continue to hear from many LGBTQ Jewish teens that they feel alone. We also continue to hear from many LGBTQ Jewish adults that they feel alienated at synagogues, Jewish community centers, Federations, and other Jewish institutions. While LGBTQ people in Jewish life and the broader world have made undeniable strides toward legal and social equality since Shula first knocked on the rabbi's office door, we still have far to go. What must we do to build on our progress and chart a path forward?

DATA AND DISCRIMINATION

We must begin with a clear grasp of how inequality and discrimination impact the lives of lesbian, gay, bisexual, transgender, and queer people. Ultimately, a Jewish community that truly embraces its LGBTQ members must understand how the broader political and social context affects people's lives. No matter how warmly embraced LGBTQ people may be within a particular Jewish community, we continue to suffer legal inequality and social bias in American society. Queer Jews need our cisgender,[3] heterosexual allies to understand the ongoing impact of living without consistent legal protection from discrimination in housing, employment, health care, government services, and other spheres of life.

According to the 2020 Pew Research Center's survey of Jewish Americans, 9 percent of American Jews identify as lesbian, gay, or bisexual. Whereas approximately 88 percent of American Jews of all ages identify as straight, that figure plunges to 75 percent among Jews under age 30.[4] It is notable, and regrettable, that the Pew study did not ask about gender identity in addition to sexual orientation, so the survey does not yield data on the percentage of Jews who identify as transgender. A 2016 Williams Institute survey estimates that 0.6 percent of Americans identify as transgender, a percentage that also skews higher with younger ages.[5]

Despite significant progress in legal rights in the United States in the past 20 years, LGBTQ people still lack federal protections against discrimination based on sexual orientation and gender identity. The need for these protections is clear: nearly two-thirds of LGBTQ Americans report having experienced discrimination in employment, housing, public accommodations, health care, or another realm in their lives. The risks are even higher for LGBTQ people of color, particularly trans and nonbinary Black and Brown people.

Numerous studies show a dramatic link between experiences of anti-LGBTQ prejudice and harm to the health of LGBTQ people.[6] Acts of bias and discrimination substantially raise the risks of depression, anxiety, suicidality, and other signs of psychological concern. The data is particularly troubling among

LGBTQ youth. According to a CDC study, lesbian, gay, and bisexual (LGB) students were more than three times as likely to seriously consider attempting suicide as heterosexual youth (48 percent versus 13 percent). LGB students were nearly five times as likely to attempt suicide as their heterosexual peers (23 percent versus 5 percent).[7] The data is even more alarming in studies that look specifically at trans and nonbinary youth: according to an American Academy of Pediatrics study, more than half of transgender boys and nearly one-third of transgender girls reported attempting suicide.[8] Although studies focused on LGB(TQ) Jewish youth do not exist, it is reasonable to assume that the data would be the same. Indeed, our experience at Keshet working closely with hundreds of LGBTQ Jewish youth each year reflects the national data.

Moreover, a study published in the *American Journal of Preventive Medicine* shows that increased religious affiliation among LGBTQ youth increases the likelihood of suicidality.[9] Although the vast majority of research subjects in this study belong to Christian denominations, our experience with LGBTQ Jewish youth at Keshet shows similar vulnerabilities. Numerous queer youth have told us how they internalized the messages of shame and stigma from their Jewish communities. Just a few months ago, a trans teen said, "I felt like G-d was telling me there is something wrong with me," which led them to think about self-harm and suicide.[10]

The good news is that youth professionals know how to interrupt this cycle of despair and, instead, catalyze hope. The Trevor Project's 2020 survey on LGBTQ youth mental health shows that connection with an LGBTQ-affirming person significantly decreases a queer youth's likelihood of attempting suicide.[11] The same trans teen who was suicidal connected with queer Jewish peers and adult mentors through Keshet who made them feel "holy, seen, and loved."[12] Today, they are supporting other LGBTQ Jewish teens in online forums and advocating for a more inclusive Jewish community in their home Jewish community. Together with another queer Jewish teen, they lead Zoom gatherings for LGBTQ Jewish youth. This teen who once struggled with the ultimate despair now provides a lifeline for teens who live in hostile family situations.

I am heartened that this teen was able to connect with their own strength and resilience through Keshet, but I am also dismayed that they absorbed such damaging messages about being transgender from their Jewish community and our broader society. Jewish tradition teaches that we must honor the divine spark in each and every person. Clearly, this teen did not feel seen and validated in their Jewish community. Only by finding their way to Keshet did they start to write a new, more positive story of self.

CHARTING PATHWAYS TO CHANGE

Not every teen who comes to Keshet is suicidal, but nearly every teen talks about feeling alone in their home Jewish community. Many of their families belong to synagogues that would describe themselves as "warm," "welcoming," and "inclusive," and yet teens often tell us they feel isolated and unseen in these communities. In 2012, Keshet started to bring LGBTQ and ally Jewish teens together at weekend retreats in order to give them a space where they would feel seen and affirmed, a space where they could breathe and be themselves as unselfconsciously as possible. Indeed, we hear from queer teens who come to Keshet Shabbaton weekend retreats, "I can't believe how amazing it feels to be in a space where I can be fully myself as a queer Jew. I've never felt this way before." What can we do to reach the day when LGBTQ Jewish youth can find that ease and sense of wholeness in their home Jewish communities? What can we do to reach the day when LGBTQ Jews of all ages feel that sense of belonging?

Every Jewish community needs to engage in a process that starts with looking inward. Keshet has identified five typologies, or stages in progress, toward a community where LGBTQ people feel a full sense of belonging: Hostile | Indifferent | Tolerant | Inclusive | Belonging.

In a hostile community, LGBTQ people experience antagonism and rejection. Several years ago, Keshet staff heard from a newly out young gay man and longtime summer camp counselor that he was told by his camp director that he couldn't be placed in a boys' bunk again "because it might make parents uncomfortable." Other examples of a hostile community include the following:

- A rabbi's contract is not renewed after she comes out as transgender.
- A camp counselor does nothing while kids bully a nonbinary child.
- A day school teacher says it is "unnatural" or "against the Torah" to be lesbian, gay, bisexual, or transgender.

In an indifferent community, LGBTQ people don't experience blatant, aggressive homo/bi/transphobia, but they do experience erasure and isolation. I recall attending a major Jewish community event in Boston on May 17, 2004, the day same-sex marriage became legal in Massachusetts, and waiting in vain for this watershed moment to be mentioned. It never was. No one intended to be hurtful; I'm sure no one thought of it. And that is exactly what was so painful and alienating about that evening. Other examples of an indifferent community include the following:

- No one, or very few people, are openly LGBTQ, and this absence is never discussed.

- Efforts to engage in LGBTQ-focused initiatives are rebuffed.
- Leadership ignores concerns about lack of inclusion.

In a tolerant community, LGBTQ people are accepted as long as they abide by certain norms, and generally community leaders don't advocate for LGBTQ rights. For years, a Chicago synagogue proudly proclaimed its commitment to being "welcoming and tolerant" of LGBTQ people, but its leaders consistently refused to speak out in support of LGBTQ civil rights. Other examples of a tolerant community include the following:

- A cisgender gay couple is embraced, while a transgender woman is shunned.
- LGBTQ people are accepted after they come out, but community leaders don't otherwise communicate positive messages about people of all sexual orientations and gender identities.
- The community doesn't engage in LGBTQ rights advocacy work in the broader world. The focus is on the status quo, not on change.

In an inclusive community, LGBTQ people may feel welcomed but not fully a part of the community. Recently, a Jewish Federation in the Midwest took key steps toward LGBTQ inclusion by doing an LGBTQ audit of its policies and programs. These are critical first steps in a much longer process. Other examples of an inclusive community include the following:

- Leaders take concrete steps to ensure that organizational policy, program, leadership, and culture include LGBTQ people.
- LGBTQ members are asked for their input into matters of LGBTQ concern.
- LGBTQ-focused educational programs are offered, such as a text study class looking at transgender and nonbinary experiences in traditional Jewish texts.

In a community of belonging, LGBTQ people feel a sense of ownership; they feel at home. A Manhattan synagogue with which Keshet frequently partners gives queer people a sense of belonging by including LGBTQ voices in programming year round, not just during Pride Month. Other examples of a community of belonging include the following:

- LGBTQ people are represented at all levels of leadership and are asked for input on all topics, not only LGBTQ issues.
- The community engages in LGBTQ rights work in the broader world.
- Program offerings include both LGBTQ-focused programs (e.g., a reading by a trans Jewish author of a memoir) and LGBTQ-inclusive programs

(e.g., a series on issues in contemporary Jewish life includes a session on LGBTQ issues).

Critically, in a community of belonging, people understand that the work is never done: LGBTQ equality work is seen as an ongoing process of reflection, learning, and action.

In my experience, many American Jewish institutions perceive themselves as "warm and welcoming" or "inclusive," but these institutions are often experienced by LGBTQ people as tolerant and accepting. Tolerance doesn't feel good. I love my life in Boston, so I tolerate the long, cold winters. It's hard to imagine that I will ever love or embrace the months of dreary chill. So, too, in many American Jewish communities, LGBTQ people feel grudgingly accepted, tolerated despite our queerness. That's very different from feeling a sense of belonging and celebration as our full selves. I believe that a sense of ownership in a community should be what LGBTQ people seek and demand for ourselves, not simply a place at a table set by someone else. When we are included or welcomed, that dynamic presumes that LGBTQ people are not a part of the "we" who gets to extend the welcome. We stand outside and wait to be invited in. What all of us deserve to feel in our Jewish community is a sense of home; we don't need to feel included or welcomed by others because we are already home.

So how can a Jewish institution become a community of belonging for LGBTQ people? The work needs to encompass every level of institutional life: policy, program, leadership, and culture.

Jewish institutions often turn to policy as a starting point for LGBTQ equality work. Policies are concrete, and best practices can easily be applied to improve them. And yet policy changes are only meaningful if they are thoughtfully applied to realities on the ground. For example, a Bay Area Jewish day school added sexual orientation and gender identity to the school's antibullying policy, but teachers were never trained in how to respond when a student was bullied because of what others assumed to be their LGBTQ identity. It took the parent whose child was being harassed to point out to the head of school that teachers were violating the school's newly adopted policy. That intervention led the school to develop mandatory trainings that gave educators the tools they needed to respond to harassment and cultivate a culture of respect.

Similarly, a Hillel at a college in the Northeast added sexual orientation and gender identity to its employment nondiscrimination policy but never trained its staff or board in implementing that policy. Consequently, when an out lesbian applied for a position, she wasn't hired because a handful of board members weren't comfortable with her. In both of these examples, the policy *change* was the easy part. Effective and comprehensive *implementation* is what required attention, resources, and hard work. In other contexts, changing policies can be an arduous and controversial process that necessitates deep cultural change.

A Conservative synagogue in the Midwest engaged in a nearly year-long series of conversations before voting to amend its membership policy to develop a more expansive definition of "household." Previously, there were two household options: "single member" or "family," with places for the names of husband, wife, and children (if any). There was no option, however, for couples in same-sex marriages or people in committed relationships who were not legally married. Community forums on the proposed change were emotional and painful. Those who opposed the policy change spoke of their fears of how the community would shift and become unfamiliar. Those who supported the more inclusive membership policy talked about how they or their children struggled to feel a part of the community. A longtime older member talked about how her son and his husband wouldn't join the synagogue because they weren't treated as a family. Ultimately, the synagogue board voted to change the policy. Despite their fears, the synagogue didn't lose a single member; in fact, it gained several new members.

Program content communicates who and what matters in a community. LGBTQ Jews often look to an institution's programming to understand the degree to which queer people are integrated into communal life. It's become more common for synagogues and other Jewish institutions to mark LGBTQ Pride Month with a program: a speaker, a film, participating in a Pride March. While this is wonderful to see, Jewish community leaders should bring an LGBTQ lens to their programming year round, not just one month of the year. Jewish institutions can infuse LGBTQ content into programming in numerous ways:

- Educators can speak about Jewish family life in an LGBTQ-inclusive way. This can be done in simple ways, such as showing a photo of two men standing under a *chuppah* (wedding canopy) or mentioning a wedding of two women. With teens or adults, educators can look at how Jewish customs and laws around marriage have evolved to honor LGBTQ relationships.
- A series of LGBTQ Israeli films can be shown as part of a larger program about LGBTQ life in Israel or as a stand-alone set of programs.
- A queer perspective can be brought to Jewish holidays, such as Passover: What stands in the way of freedom for LGBTQ people? Or Sukkot: Who are the LGBTQ *ushpizin* (honored ancestral visitors) we would want to invite in to our sukkah?

Purim offers particularly rich opportunities for how LGBTQ perspectives can enrich Jewish life. A youth movement advisor in Boston led a discussion with high school students in which they looked at "Esther moments" in LGBTQ history—instances when coming out changed the course of history, just as Esther forever altered Jewish history when she came out as a Jew. A teacher at a Jewish high school in New York City asked his students to write a report about a historical figure who, like Esther, changed the dynamics of power by taking a risk and publicly claiming their own identity. A San Diego synagogue held a Purim carnival for families with young children that included a reading corner where an educator read *The Purim Superhero*, a Purim story about a boy with a daddy and an *abba* (father).

In addition to LGBTQ-inclusive programming within the community, Jewish institutions can dedicate social justice programs to advancing LGBTQ rights in the broader world. In 2018, when anti-trans groups sought to legalize discrimination against transgender people in Massachusetts, Jewish communities made history by coming together in the largest-ever Jewish campaign for trans civil rights. Seventy percent of all Massachusetts synagogues and other Jewish institutions joined Keshet's "Yes on 3" campaign to safeguard transgender rights. Our numbers made a difference in the public sphere and helped trans rights prevail at the ballot box. Jewish community mobilization also made a difference internally. For many Jewish institutions, this campaign marked the first time they engaged in LGBTQ rights advocacy. LGBTQ Jews and our family members took notice. A 21-year-old trans man said, "I never imagined that I would see synagogue members take action to protect my rights as a trans person. Often, queer and trans communities feel like we're isolated. To see that the Jewish community will show up and put in effort is not something I'm going to forget."[13]

All aspects of LGBTQ equality work require ongoing attention and effort, but creating a culture of belonging is the hardest part. LGBTQ inclusive policies and programs can feel like technical fixes; an LGBTQ-inclusive culture reflects fundamental shifts in how people act and feel. In thinking about culture change, we also must understand the distinction between sexual orientation and gender identity. A community in which people of all sexual orientations feel at home isn't necessarily a community where people of all gender identities feel a sense of belonging.

I often ask staff or leaders of Jewish community institutions to imagine a queer person walking into their building: "Think of a 12-year-old gay teen walking into a classroom at your synagogue. What does he see that tells him, 'I'm a part of this place'?" "Think of a six-year-old nonbinary child entering first grade in a Jewish day school. What do they hear that tells them, 'I can be myself here'?" "Think of a trans 42-year-old woman walking into the JCC. What does she notice that tells her, 'I am seen here'?" I encourage them to think about LGBTQ people who are Black, Latinx, Mizrahi, and/or Sephardi. What do they see that tells them, "You are a part of the 'we' of this community"?

Invariably, this exercise alerts Jewish community leaders to the absence of representation in the physical and digital spaces of their institutions. Often, when Jewish institutions make efforts to integrate visual representation that reflects the diversity of Jewish life, they are criticized for taking a tokenizing approach. Changes in any realm—organizational materials, leadership, programming—need to be accompanied by shifts in other spheres in order for the changes to feel authentic. Here are a few ways to incorporate LGBTQ representation into an organization's visual identity:

- Photos on websites and in marketing materials that include LGBTQ people in the institution's visual identity convey that LGBTQ people are a part of the community. Examples include photos of a gay couple and their kids celebrating Hanukkah, a nonbinary teen speaking from the *bimah* (raised prayer platform), and a group of people at a rally holding signs such as "Another Jew for LGBTQ Equality." It's important for photos not to be the only ways that LGBTQ people are visible in a community. The answer to inclusion is not tokenization through a photo or two; it is full representation and integration into the life of a community.
- LGBTQ Safe Zone stickers are an easy way to send a message of support. Many LGBTQ Jewish kids have told us that when they see a Safe Zone sticker on a teacher's desk or a youth group advisor's office door, they know that they can confide in that adult if and when they feel ready. They know that adult will look out for them.
- Posters of prominent LGBTQ Jews such as Harvey Milk, Kate Bornstein, Rabbi Sandra Lawson, and Michael Twitty, to name a few. Displaying such posters sends the message that this Jewish community celebrates and honors queer Jews.

In implementing any of these steps, the key is not simply to make room for difference; the key is to be open to how difference must fundamentally change the look and feel of a community for good. Consider how a poster of Rabbi Sandra Lawson, a Black lesbian, may change students' assumptions about what a rabbi looks like. Consider how a poster of Kate Bornstein, a transgender activist and writer, may change a congregation's conceptions of gender. And consider how providing an equally accessible All Gender bathroom option, or making all bathrooms All Gender, sends a powerful message to trans and nonbinary people: you matter; you belong here.

Jewish communities that engage in this work of culture change are communities where LGBTQ people thrive. In these communities, young people aren't supported only after they come out; they grow up hearing the message that people of every sexual orientation and gender identity are honored and loved. So many LGBTQ Jews experience a period of alienation from the Jewish community after coming out. Imagine a Jewish world in which queer Jews never for a single moment doubt that their Jewish community will embrace them. Think of the depth of connection and commitment to Jewish life that would be possible.

Two days after the November 2016 presidential election, I received an e-mail from Erin Schreiber, a Hillel director at a small college outside of St. Louis,

Missouri. She described how early in the morning on November 9, a trans student who was active in Hillel reached out to her in crisis. He said that he felt terrified about what the next four years held for him. Erin offered to meet him at the Hillel office to talk in person. As she drove there, she tried to think of what she could offer to reassure him. She walked into her office and nearly stepped on an envelope that had been tucked under her door. She opened it and saw that inside were the LGBTQ Safe Zone stickers she had ordered from Keshet. She pulled out a sticker just as her student walked in and held it up saying, "Look! There is hope in the world. We have a whole community that is standing with us."

It is no accident that this student reached out to Erin for support. She had worked hard to create a culture of belonging for LGBTQ students within Hillel. And so, without hesitation, on that despairing day, he reached out for the hand he knew would be there.

My hope is that we will reach a day when LGBTQ Jews know that in times of despair, celebration, and everything in between, we can turn to our Jewish community. No one will ever ask these questions: How will people respond when I come out? Will I be treated kindly? Will I still be loved?

We're not there yet, but I know that through policies, programs, and culture change, Jewish leaders can increasingly demonstrate that LGBTQ Jews are not simply tolerated or accepted but, instead, are fully integrated into the fabric of Jewish life. Then, and only then, we will be able to say *"Hineini"* without ever questioning whether we belong.

RESOURCES

Websites

Eshel (eshelonline.org) offers support and resources for Orthodox LGBT people and their families.

JQ International (jqinternational.org) offers education, support, and community building for LGBTQ Jews in Los Angeles.

JQY (jqyouth.org) is an organization for Orthodox, Chasidic, and Sephardic teens and young adults in the Metro New York area.

Keshet (keshetonline.org) is a national organization that provides resources and training for Jewish community institutions; offers support and leadership development for LGBTQ Jewish teens; and mobilizes Jewish communities to advocate for LGBTQ civil rights.

SOJOURN: The Southern Jewish Resource Center for Gender and Sexual Diversity (sojourngsd.org) provides Jewish and LGBTQ+ programming, education, support, and advocacy in the American South.

Books

Dzmura, Noach, ed. *Balancing on the Mechitza: Transgender in Jewish Community.* Berkeley, CA: North Atlantic Books, 2010.

Greenberg, Steven. *Wrestling with God and Men: Homosexuality in the Jewish Tradition.* Madison: University of Wisconsin Press, 2004.

Kabakov, Miriam, ed. *Keep Your Wives Away from Them: Orthodox Women, Unorthodox Desires.* Berkeley, CA: North Atlantic Books, 2010.

Ladin, Joy. *Through the Door of Life: A Jewish Journey between Genders.* Madison: University of Wisconsin Press, 2012.

Shneer, David, and Caryn Aviv, eds. *Queer Jews.* New York: Routledge, 2002.

Sienna, Noam, ed. *A Rainbow Thread: An Anthology of Queer Jewish Texts from the First Century to 1969.* Philadelphia: Print-O-Craft Press, 2019.

NOTES

1. "Queer" is used by some as an umbrella term that encompasses lesbian, gay, bisexual, and transgender people. Although the term was used historically as a slur targeting those perceived to transgress conventional norms of sexual orientation and/or gender expression—and still is used pejoratively by some—many people have reclaimed "queer" as a positive, affirming, and empowering identity term. Some people prefer "queer" because it transcends the gender binary and can expansively include attraction to people of a range of genders.

2. Today, the term "Gay-Straight Alliance" has largely been replaced by the more inclusive "Gender and Sexuality Alliance," which encompasses both sexual orientation and gender identity.

3. A term for anyone who understands their gender to be the same as what was announced at their birth (often also described as "assigned at birth"). "Cisgender" is used to contrast with "transgender" on the gender spectrum. Cisgender has its origin in the Latin-derived prefix *cis*, meaning "on the same side."

4. Pew Research Center, *Jewish Americans in 2020* (Washington, DC: Pew Research Center, May 11, 2021), 194, https://www.pewforum.org/2021/05/11/jewish-americans-in-2020/.

5. Andrew R. Flores, Jody L. Herman, Gary J. Gates, and Taylor N. T. Brown, *How Many Adults Identify as Transgender in the United States?* (Los Angeles, CA: Williams Institute, June 2016), 2, https://williamsinstitute.law.ucla.edu/wp-content/uploads/Trans-Adults-US-Aug-2016.pdf.

6. Nathaniel Frank and Kellan Baker, "Anti-LGBT Discrimination Has a Huge Human Toll: Research Proves It," *Washington Post,* December 19, 2019, https://www.washingtonpost.com/outlook/2019/12/19/anti-lgbt-discrimination-has-huge-human-toll-research-proves-it/.

7. "Infographic about LGB Suicidal Thoughts & Experiences Data," Centers for Disease Control and Prevention, https://www.cdc.gov/violenceprevention/communicationresources/infographics/yrbs-lgb-suicide.html.

8. Russell B. Toomey, Amy K. Syvertsen, and Maura Shramko, "Transgender Adolescent Suicide Behavior," *Pediatrics* 142, no. 4 (October 2018): 3, https://doi.org/10.1542/peds.2017-4218.

9. Carol Kuruvilla, "Chilling Study Sums Up Link between Religion and Suicide for Queer Youth," *Huff Post*, April 4, 2018, https://www.huffpost.com/entry/queer-youth-religion-suicide-study_n_5ad4f7b3e4b077c89ceb9774.

10. Private conversation with the author, October 28, 2020.

11. "National Survey on LGBTQ Youth Mental Health 2020," Trevor Project, https://www.thetrevorproject.org/survey-2020/.

12. Private conversation with the author, October 28, 2020.

13. Private conversation with the author, November 15, 2018.

CHAPTER 2

Interfaith Families

Jodi Bromberg

In 2021, when Kamala Harris became the vice president of the United States, she was the first woman and first person of color to hold this important position, and with her husband, Jewish American Douglas Emhoff, she became the first vice president who was part of a Jewish interfaith couple. They're not the first administration to be part of an interfaith family, but they are the first interfaith *couple*. Former president Donald Trump has Jewish grandchildren, and President Joe Biden does, too. Emhoff's kids call Harris by the Yiddish-inflected term of endearment "Mamaleh" (little Momma) to rhyme with Kamala. Cute, right? It makes sense that the first Jewish couple to make it to the White House is an interfaith couple. After all, 72 percent of progressive (non-Orthodox) Jews who have gotten married since 2000 have married someone who is not Jewish.[1] Interfaith families in Jewish life aren't a drop in the ocean; they *are* the ocean.

Early indications show that the Second Family won't be spared the mixed bag of reactions that many interfaith couples often receive from the broader Jewish community. At the same time, it's too early to know how the Jewish community is going to react to the first Second Family being a Jewish interfaith couple. The day after the election was called for President Biden and Vice President Harris, Twitter was aflame with conversation about Harris and Emhoff. "I am beyond delighted that the first Jewish 2nd family is interfaith and multiracial. Maybe now the Jewish community will be able to see such families as normal, sacred, and essential. We are the Jewish present and the Jewish future. That future is so damn bright," wrote Rabbi Emily Cohen, who grew up in a family with a Jewish parent and a Quaker parent.[2]

Cohen is the rabbi at West End Synagogue in New York City, and she is also a Rukin Rabbinic Fellow at 18Doors (formerly InterfaithFamily), the national organization focused on supporting interfaith families in Jewish life. The response to her tweet was swift and damning, as one reply told her that we should have "sat *shiva*" (the Jewish ritual of mourning) for Emhoff, while another wrote, "Multiracial Jewish families are undoubtedly essential to our people. Interfaith remains, at best, an open question."[3]

Later in the day, Rabbi Cohen noted, "So based on the responses to this tweet, along with a bunch of other rhetoric I've seen today, stuff for interfaith fams [*sic*] is about to get ugly." She was at least partially right: the replies to her tweet included a variety of disparaging comments, including that intermarriage was against Talmudic law and, horrifyingly, that interfaith couples must be relieved by the death of the six million Jews during the Holocaust so that we're no longer embarrassed by their "Jewishness."

Others responded with open arms, like Rabbi Ruth Abusch-Magder, who tweeted, "Interfaith families are part of the Jewish community. Multiracial families are part of the Jewish community. We see you. We are glad you are here. We welcome the possibilities and priorities you bring with you."[4] Interfaith families themselves responded to Rabbi Cohen with statements like "Thank you for standing for us. My husband is Jewish, I profess no faith, and our son is Jewish. So much for shrinking the faith." And also, "I'm the child of an interfaith marriage and I was raised Jewish. I'm waking up to the fact that this is controversial but so glad to hear voices like yours fighting for inclusion."[5]

The contradictory responses to the vice president's family are representative of the broader response to interfaith families in Jewish life, though perhaps more hospitable overall. Jewish press, leaders, and organizations often embrace celebrity interfaith couples while degrading their everyday counterparts. Though when former First Daughter Chelsea Clinton, who is Christian, married Mark Mezvinsky, who is Jewish, rabbis weren't kind. They offered their disapproval of the couple's decision to have their wedding co-officiated by a rabbi and a Methodist minister and of the couple's decision to get married shortly before the end of Shabbat.[6] Despite being the fastest growing population among progressive Jews, interfaith families continue to be treated as a demographic to be tolerated, but not accepted or embraced, in much of Jewish life. It's clear that we're at a crossroads in American Jewish life, and also that we've been heading toward this moment for a while. Because, as 18Doors director of professional development Tema Smith tweeted, "you don't get to 'claim' @DouglasEmhoff in one breath and disparage interfaith families in another."[7] How did we get here?

THE "PROBLEM" OF INTERMARRIAGE

Two weeks before the 2020 presidential election, the *Jewish Telegraphic Agency* tweeted this about a story it had published about European Jewry: "Rising rates of intermarriage, a low reproductive rate and high levels of antisemitism are chipping away at the continent's Jewish population, a study has found."[8]

Blaming the decline in the population of Jews on interfaith couples, or fearing they are responsible, is a tired trope that's been going on for years in the U.S. Jewish community, creating the falsehood that Jewish engagement or connection requires a Jewish spouse. But this idea is not borne out in the research.

While Jewish community studies overall find lower levels of Jewish engagement among interfaith couples than their Jewish-Jewish counterparts, in a further analysis of both the 2013 and the more recent 2020 Pew studies on Jewish Americans, the percentage of adult children who have a Jewish identity has increased with each generation. As Alan Cooperman and Gregory Smith write, "When we look at all adults who have just one Jewish parent—including both those who identify as Jewish and those who do not—we see that the Jewish retention rate of people raised in intermarried families appears to be rising. That is, among all adults (both Jewish and non-Jewish) who say they had one Jewish parent and one non-Jewish parent, younger generations are more likely than older generations to be Jewish today."[9]

This increase in interfaith families identifying Jewishly is likely due to early efforts to cultivate the belonging of interfaith families by pioneers such as Egon Mayer, as well as the Reconstructionist movement's resolution in 1968 adopting patrilineal descent and later the Reform movement's similar action in 1983. If no Jewish communities accepted interfaith couples, how could they raise Jewish children? It's a problem that continues to exist today, though significant progress has been made. In 18Doors' recent survey of interfaith couples with Benenson Strategy Group, more than half of the couples who reported they were not engaged Jewishly said they were interested in participating in Jewish life. But they reported that they had not found a Jewish community that felt comfortable for them or inclusive of interfaith families.[10] For those interfaith couples who have a rabbi officiate at their wedding, research shows that they subsequently engage in Jewish life at similar levels to Jewish-Jewish couples.[11] Although there is more work to be done to increase the number of Jewish institutions where interfaith couples and families feel like they belong, the rise in the population of progressive Jews in the United States is still directly attributable to the rise in interfaith families.[12]

Nonetheless, the ongoing idea that intermarriage is responsible for the downfall of Jewish life continues to be perpetuated in many circles and, with it, an adherence and commitment to endogamy, the continued stated importance of encouraging Jews to marry Jews. This barometer of "success" is so prevalent that at least one prominent Jewish organization that engages young adults continues to evaluate itself by how many of its participants marry someone who is Jewish, deeming it one of its key metrics of "success." Until 2015, another youth organization barred its student leaders from dating people who weren't Jewish; now, it has lifted the ban, though the switch was reportedly made out of respect for youth leaders who have a parent who is not Jewish—"not to make it more acceptable" for the youth leaders to date other students who aren't Jewish.

CLAIMING INTERFAITH IDENTITY (OR BOTH/AND)

I run 18Doors, the only national nonprofit that is laser focused on supporting interfaith couples, couples like Kamala and Doug, Chelsea and Mark, and the millions of interfaith family members living in the United States. In addition to supporting couples and families with programs, Jewish content, and access to more than 700 rabbis and cantors on its Jewish clergy referral service, 18Doors works to build a more inclusive Jewish community, where interfaith families can meet others like them and find a sense of belonging. We provide training and consulting services to Jewish organizations, their clergy, professionals, and lay leaders to help cultivate inclusive communities.

My family is similar to the couples and families we meet at 18Doors programs. Every branch of my family tree is an interfaith one: I'm a second-generation interfaith family—my wife is Catholic and I'm Jewish, and we're raising three synagogue-going, religious-school-educated Jewish kids. We also have a Christmas tree in our home, and our kids believe in Santa—something that my spouse said was important to her as we negotiated our religious differences. She agreed to raise our children Jewish and to have a Jewish home—something she has fully committed to—and I agreed to Christmas.

My mom converted to Judaism before marrying my Jewish-born dad and then raising my two brothers and me as Jews. My brothers married Christian and Catholic women. My wife's stepsister is Catholic, and her late husband, z"l (of blessed memory), was Jewish.

My life is full of experiences from both religious and cultural traditions that stay with me today, like Jewish overnight camp and Easter ham at my grandma's. Living in both worlds has provided me with the ability to understand the language of fasting on Yom Kippur, kosher dietary laws, and ritual garb, as well as the cultural Ashkenazi touchstones of gefilte fish and chopped liver, alongside the language and culture of Jesus, church, Christmas trees, and Easter egg hunts. As a Jew, while I don't identify with the beliefs of Christianity, I'm comfortable in Christian spaces. I have warm memories of sitting in Russian Orthodox church with my beloved grandma, z"l (of blessed memory), staring up at a larger-than-life portrait of Jesus on the crucifix. Those memories aren't about the church or Jesus for me. They are about the warm memories of my grandmother's love—the same grandmother who crocheted yarmulkes for my bat mitzvah and happily celebrated Jewish holidays with us.

And, while my spouse and I are raising our children exclusively religiously Jewish, other families make different choices. In the course of seeking to understand families who raise their children in both Christian and Jewish religious traditions, I've learned that while some Christians believe in Jesus as their messiah, others have more nuanced understandings of Jesus. Some families actively practice both Christianity and Judaism and don't see the two as contradictory.[13] At the same time, there is a large diversity of practice and experience of families who say they are raising their children in two religious traditions, including (1) those who practice two traditions culturally, not religiously, (2) those who practice one culturally and one religiously, or (3) those who practice two religions.

The benefit to being raised as part of an interfaith family is that I am comfortable in more than one cultural or religious tradition. The drawback, though, is a feeling of never quite fitting in, never quite cracking the code. Through my work, I've talked to many people who have converted to Judaism, and all reported that the thing that is most challenging to pick up and acculturate to is Jewish culture. I think that's true for children of interfaith families, and children of families where a parent has converted—and it's a reason that the most popular pages on 18Doors' website continue to be around Jewish culture, holidays, traditions, and food. The nuances of Jewish culture create a sometimes inadvertent barrier to participating in Jewish life, and members of interfaith families often pick up on these distinctions more than people who have been raised in monolithic Jewish communities for their whole lives.

I was in my mid-30s before I knew what *tzimmes* was. (And in case you don't know, it's an Ashkenazi Jewish dish made of stewed vegetables, often mixed with stewed fruits.) I didn't understand the Yiddish words and phrases my friends and colleagues sprinkled into their English conversations, and I remember being embarrassed when I used a Yiddish phrase incorrectly in college and a Jewish friend pointed it out. I remember being embarrassed at Hebrew school that I was celebrating Christmas with my grandma, rather than doing the stereotypical Ashkenazi Jewish American tradition of going to the movies and eating Chinese food. I didn't grow up knowing what a Federation or "day school" was. There are serious gaps in my Jewish literacy despite having attended 10 years of Hebrew school, eight summers of Jewish overnight camping and programming, and more youth group conclaves than I remember. It's a feeling that isn't exclusive to people in interfaith families— plenty of people who grew up in Jewish-Jewish families report a lack of Jewish knowledge as well, and the concurrent embarrassment that comes with it. In fact, Archie Gottesman and Stacy Stuart at the Jewish organization JewBelong created a term for it: "Jewbarassment."

I think the key difference between how children from Jewish-Jewish families experience those episodes and how children from interfaith families do is that those from Jewish-Jewish families don't ascribe their gaps in Jewish knowledge to a deficiency in their identity, that anything is wrong with them.

I, however, saw the holes in my Jewish literacy as evidence that I didn't belong; I connected my lack of cultural fluency with my mom's Russian Orthodox upbringing. This wasn't just some internalized self-projection; the Jewish community often helped. While the rabbi of the Reform synagogue I grew up in was warm, gentle, kind, inclusive, and thoughtful of the families in his midst, other members of the congregation weren't always so. On more than one occasion throughout my childhood, Jewish friends from Hebrew school would remark nonchalantly that I wasn't "really" Jewish or that I was only "half Jewish." These experiences have continued for me into adulthood. At my Reconstructionist synagogue—230 miles from my childhood synagogue—on more than one occasion, I've been told by friendly congregants that I have "one Irish son" and "one Jewish son," because my twin boys are named Jacob and Liam. It's said without malice, and I know that my family doesn't face the same challenges that people of color in Jewish spaces face, looks that are indicative of the racism within the Jewish community and our broader society. "No," I say politely with a smile, "I have two Jewish sons and two Irish sons." *Both/and*, not *either/or*.

It is the *both/and* that is in front of us that most people miss when it comes to interfaith families. The binary nature of language does not help us: you are either Jewish or not Jewish. Language fails us here. The word "interfaith" or any of the words in its wake—"multifaith," "intercultural," "multicultural," "modern"—are challenging because the words all connote a sameness that isn't there, as if we are monolithic. One of the predominant reasons that InterfaithFamily changed its name to 18Doors in February 2020 was a growing understanding that the old name didn't articulate the identities of the people we aimed to serve. "Interfaith" itself as a term does not capture the diversity of couples and families from different religious, cultural, ethnic, and spiritual backgrounds and the diversity of journeys they take, or doors that they open, in their exploration of Jewish life.[14]

There are myriad terms interfaith couples and families might use instead: mixed heritage, dual faith, intercultural, dual heritage, Blewish (Black and Jewish), Jew-theran (Jewish and Lutheran), Cashews (Catholic and Jewish), Hin-Jews (Hindu and Jewish), Bu-Jew (Buddhist Jews), Jewpanese (Jewish and Japanese), Jew-ish, half Jewish, Jewish-adjacent, a modern family, just Jewish, just a couple, or just a family. None is more right than the others—the main goal is to ensure that you're using terminology that resonates with the audience you are trying to reach. To that end, the best words and identities to use still remain the ones that the couple or family standing in front of you uses to describe themselves or that they tell you most resonate with them. At the same time, just because someone uses a term like "half Jew" or "Cashew" doesn't mean that you should use the term without permission. Otherwise, it might seem like you're disparaging or making fun of them. So, proceed with caution.

Identity is flexible, permeable, and nuanced. Yes, we are Catholic and Jewish and Baptist and Quaker and Muslim and Hindu and straight and gay and transgender and black and white and Latinx and differently abled—*and* the reality transcends even beyond those labels and identities. In the same way that gender is not binary, neither is religious identity. There are many Christian and Catholic people—including my wife—who have Jewish spouses, who belong to a synagogue, are raising their children Jewish, and are active lay leaders in the Jewish community with no other religious life outside of Judaism. They are not Jews, but they have an identity in the Jewish community.

The binary way in which most Jewish institutions and the people inside them think of who their membership encompasses leaves those of us with family members who dance in the middle of the binary, who are both/and, out in the cold. Alternatively, Jewish institutions that only think of those family members in the context of the Jews to whom they are connected also leads to feelings of exclusion. What happens if their spouse passes away or leaves, or if the kids grow up and move out? There are Christian, Catholic, Hindu, Buddhist, Quaker, and Muslim people who are part of Jewish life and community. While that identity may have started out as tied to someone Jewish—typically, a spouse or child—for some, as the person who is not Jewish becomes ingrained in that community, the original source of connection matters less. It is the ongoing, sustaining nature of the relationships forged in that community that matter going forward. They don't want to convert to Judaism, though some may later. But they are part of our community because they show up, they are there and want to be there, and they contribute to the Jewish community's enduring strength through their participation.[15]

The people inside our institutions are our people, regardless of their chosen identity. In order to embrace interfaith families, it is important for us to grapple with the complexity around identity, and then move beyond it. In an era where much of the marketing we see, and its related demand, is around customization, personalization, and an ability to "do it yourself" in the way that works for you, the growing perception is that identity is also malleable. As we think about the future of Jewish life, I think that might become part of its enduring strength—the ability to personalize Jewish life in the way that works for each of us.

Many people who hear and read about flexible Jewish identities may be fearful of what that means, thinking of a "dumbed-down" or "lesser-than" Judaism. But with the personalization comes meaning—the desire for an enduring connection to Jewish life and community—though that likely looks very different than it did in prior generations. The Jewish institutions and the people in them who are open to the possibility of permeable identities will find themselves transformed and changed in new, interesting, and beautiful ways.

My Catholic wife, Courtney, is an active member of our synagogue, Kerem Shalom in Concord, Massachusetts. Rabbi Darby Leigh, who leads the congregation, is profoundly deaf, and about three years ago, he founded what may be the only American Sign Language (ASL) synagogue choir in the country. They perform Hebrew songs and prayers at High Holiday services and at other times throughout the year.[16] The ASL choir meets with Rabbi Darby to pick songs and prayers, and then he translates them as a group from Hebrew into ASL. So while Courtney doesn't speak or read Hebrew, she is fluent in ASL, and it's through the ASL choir that she learns the meanings of the Hebrew prayers and songs the choir performs in a deep and transformative way.

In thinking about identities, we also know that "interfaithedness"—the identity that people from interfaith couples or families have—waxes and wanes as a salient identity—and that the prominence of this identity depends, in part, on the other identities each of us hold at any given time, and which of those identities might be most pronounced depending on the space we're in. From the work at 18Doors, it appears that "interfaithedness" is most prominent at life cycle events when topics of spirituality and religion are at the fore. The other time when these identities come to the surface is around potential holiday conflicts, most notably for Jewish-Christian couples, around Passover and Easter, and Hanukkah and Christmas. As a result, 18Doors provides discussion guides for interfaith families around holiday decision making, resources for connecting to rabbis for life cycle events, and local events to connect couples with others like them who have similar experiences and identities.

We have only begun to scratch the surface of the complexity of identities of interfaith couples. Little research has been done in Jewish life, particularly around the intersectionality of identities. For example, how does race, ethnicity, and culture influence identity when it intersects with interfaith families? How does the religion of the spouse who is not Jewish influence the family's connection to Jewish life or community through their conception of religion, religious tradition, and community? How does sexual orientation or gender identity impact their involvement in Jewish life? We know much less about interfaith couples and families than we think we do, and it is critically important that we remember that—and center those voices in the conversation moving forward.

WHY DO INTERFAITH COUPLES AND FAMILIES NEED A SAFE SPACE?

When I was younger, I would have appreciated meeting and knowing other families like mine, and I used 18Doors' resources long before I joined the organization. Consequently, do not be surprised, concerned, or hurt if the interfaith couples and families in your midst are primarily interested in meeting and engaging with others whose direct lived experiences mirror their own. When you are part of a historically marginalized group—and Jewish interfaith couples have been historically marginalized, and continue to be treated as sub-optimal—it is sometimes helpful to have peers and mentors with whom to connect, share ideas and stories, and, most important, to have a comfortable, safe space just to be. As long as interfaith couples and families continue to be treated as second best within Jewish institutional life, we will continue to need spaces to which we can retreat.

There are myriad institutional policies that have been in place for decades that prevent the Jewish community at large from being a place of inclusion and belonging for interfaith families. Four issues in particular stick out: (1) a pronounced emphasis on and overvaluation of endogamy, (2) the prohibition or inability for some rabbis to officiate or co-officiate at the weddings of interfaith couples, (3) the exclusion of candidates who are married to a non-Jewish partner from being admitted or ordained at most progressive Jewish seminaries, and (4) a proliferation of rabbis who will only agree to marry a couple "if they commit to raising their children Jewish" according to the rabbi's specifications. These policies and behaviors discriminate against Jews in interfaith relationships.

I expect that many would argue with my use of the word "discriminate"—after all, I imagine the response might be "It's not discrimination, it's boundary-keeping, it's *halacha* (Jewish law)." That, of course, is true for many Jews and their understanding of Jewish identity and Jewish law. But for many (if not most) interfaith couples, these policies feel like, and are received as, discrimination and rejection. Regardless of the intent, that is the impact, and the result is that interfaith couples and families encountering such boundaries may stop connecting to Jewish life entirely. As I tell my sons, building relationships is like putting marbles in a jar. Each time you have a positive connection, a marble goes in the jar. For each negative interaction, you take a marble out of the jar. How many marbles have to be taken from the jar before interfaith families say, "Enough!"? I once met a woman who called 65 rabbis before she found one who would marry her and her husband. (She wasn't Jewish; he was.) Most couples won't make that many calls.

The continued existence of these practices has no positive effect on the Jewish community. Perhaps such behaviors are meant to discourage Jews from getting into interfaith relationships in the first place, but there is no evidence that they have been effective in that regard. People who are discriminated against have no motivation to forge ongoing Jewish connections, identity, or practice. Rather, by institutionalizing discrimination, these policies open the door to Jews thinking it's sanctioned to make offhand remarks to people in interfaith families that range from casually insensitive to outright mean.

Consider the following: A member of a Reform congregation on the West Coast who was not Jewish but was raising Jewish kids with her Jewish husband once told me how a group of her supposed friends said, in front of her, that interfaith families were "dumbing down the gene pool." (She was a graduate of Harvard Business School.) Or this: A member of a Reform congregation in Massachusetts said that at her son's bar mitzvah, when she arrived on the *bimah* (raised prayer platform), there was a prayer sheet for her husband, who isn't Jewish, which said in large letters, "Prayer for the Non-Jew." I once spoke to a group of students getting their master's degrees in Jewish studies when a young Jewish woman told me that she was afraid that if people who aren't Jewish held the Torah, they "might rip it." And a Christian mom who is an active member of her synagogue and raising Jewish kids told me that the worst experiences she had had in Jewish life were the insensitive things her husband's Jewish family members said.

At 18Doors, we once held a breakfast at a large Jewish organization's conference, only to learn that many of the organization's staff were not "out" to their employer about the fact that they were either from an interfaith family or in an interfaith relationship. They feared that their supervisors would penalize them and that their careers would suffer if this information about their families were made public. More than one Jewish person has told me that they no longer bring their spouse of a different religion to Jewish events because the spouse has been treated poorly too many times.

Given a choice, Jewish people in interfaith couples will choose to honor and privilege their relationship and protect their partner if they think that the partner is at risk of being hurt in a Jewish space. Until we can change the attitudes and policies that continue to discriminate against interfaith families—and see the related shift and increase in the number of people from interfaith couples and families who are leaders in Jewish communal organizations—interfaith couples will participate in Jewish life at levels lower than their Jewish-Jewish counterparts.

WELCOMING VERSUS INCLUSION VERSUS BELONGING

Often 18Doors is approached by Jewish institutions who want to be "welcoming" to interfaith couples, and for many years, the conversation focused around how to involve those individuals who had been historically excluded from such institutions. Welcoming people is of course good and needed—the idea that when a stranger arrives at your home, they will receive a warm smile, a kind hello, and friendly banter makes sense. But that passive reception is nowhere near enough. If I'm *welcomed* into someone's home for a meal, I sit politely at the dinner table, waiting for someone to serve me and to take my dishes, but I'm not comfortable venturing into the kitchen on my own. It is the beginning of a relationship, the beginning of a journey together, but it's not yet my lived-in experience.

If I am *included* or *belong* in someone's home, well, they're closer to family. I'm walking into the kitchen with my dishes and helping to clean up. I'm initiating conversations that are interesting to me, sharing my favorite foods, or bringing a playlist to listen to during dinner. But those behaviors don't materialize overnight. The act of inclusion is a layered process that happens over days, weeks, months, and even years. Getting to that point of belonging is about building trust, a day-in, day-out process of ensuring the interfaith folks in your community feel and know that your organization is a place for them, and that the community is open to being transformed by the participation of interfaith families in their midst.

GETTING STARTED

Happily, there are many avenues of entry for cultivating a sense of inclusion and belonging. One great place to start is encouraging rabbis in your life to apply to become an 18Doors Rukin Rabbinic Fellow. This two-year, stipended program creates communities of practice of 11 to 15 rabbis each year to develop their skills and thinking on working with interfaith couples and families. It begins with an immersive retreat for each cohort, followed by ongoing professional development, coaching, and learning. Fellows also run programs for interfaith couples and families in their communities. At the time of this writing, there are 26 active Rukin Rabbinic Fellows in the United States and Canada.

Another way to foster inclusion is by checking out the professional development and community learning resources 18Doors has on interfaith inclusion. 18Doors offers community learning opportunities to help communities develop and grow their thinking on connecting with interfaith families, ranging from workshops on reviewing the language and optics of their organization to primers on engaging interfaith families and unpacking bias. In addition, there are e-learning modules that allow people to learn asynchronously when it's convenient for them, as well as an e-mail newsletter for Jewish communal leaders and professionals with helpful resources and information. And, for individuals looking to understand the lives of Jewish interfaith families and couples, reading stories of their lived experiences on the 18Doors website is a great way to do that. Or simply talk to the interfaith couples in your life about their experiences.

In addition, know that there is often a disconnect between how leaders and professionals at Jewish organizations perceive their organization's commitment to the inclusion of interfaith families, and how the families themselves experience those efforts. To counteract that phenomena, consider a listening campaign of interfaith couples or families in your organization so that you are getting useful feedback—and be open to what you may hear. Finally, here are some best practices for communicating with interfaith families:

- DO treat all members of your community with dignity, respect, and courtesy.
- DON'T use terms like "marrying out," or talk negatively about intermarriage.
- DO relax, smile, and say hello—even to those you don't know or who look different from you. Work through unfamiliar situations in a calm, courteous manner.
- DON'T assume that someone is not Jewish, or not part of your Jewish community, based on physical characteristics, like the color of their skin, hair, or eyes.

- DO let interfaith families choose the words to describe them: Do they call themselves an interfaith family? A Jewish family? A mixed culture family? A modern family? Follow their lead on language.
- DON'T use derogatory terms, whether in Yiddish or English, to refer to people who aren't Jewish, such as "non-Jew," "shiksa," or "goy."
- DO look and speak directly to people who aren't Jewish, and if the conversation turns to "Jewish geography" or childhood experiences like Jewish summer camp, be sure to include them by asking questions about their childhood summers and upbringing.
- DON'T comment on whether you think a person's name is a "Jewish name."
- DO congratulate members in your community on their wedding, regardless of whether they marry someone Jewish.
- DO talk openly to board members and organization members about how to welcome, include, and foster the belonging of interfaith families; do consider making it a communal priority.
- DON'T assume that someone who is not Jewish is not invested in being part of your Jewish community or is not raising their children with Judaism.
- DO create policies that provide as much access as possible to your organization and its gatherings and rituals as possible.

By following these guidelines, you'll be paving the way for the millions of members of interfaith families to feel and be included in your organizations, fostering a culture of belonging, and affirming that mixed faith couples are indeed a critically important part of Jewish life. Doing so will create opportunities for interfaith couples and families to connect to Jewish life, be more confident that Judaism holds a place for them, and be more comfortable in Jewish settings. Through that inclusion, the vibrancy and diversity of the entire Jewish community will be affirmed and strengthened, contributing to our enduring strength.

RESOURCES

Center for Radically Inclusive Judaism (cfrij.com) advocates for attitudes, policies, and programs that engage interfaith families in Jewish life and community.

18Doors (18doors.org) is the only national Jewish organization devoted to supporting interfaith families in their exploration of Jewish life, as well as Jewish leaders and organizations who want to welcome them.

jHUB (jHUBcle.org) is a local 18Doors affiliate in Cleveland, Ohio, that provides a new way for interfaith couples and families to comfortably explore, discover, and personalize the meaning of Jewish culture and values in the modern world.

Sherry and Alan Leventhal Center for Interfaith Families (jewishnola.com/interfaith) is an in-house initiative of the Jewish Federation of Greater New Orleans working to create a broader and more inclusive Jewish community through programs and community partnerships for families and households who identify as interfaith.

NOTES

1. Alan Cooperman and Gregory A. Smith, "What Happens When Jews Intermarry?" Pew Research Center Fact Tank, November 12, 2013, https://www.pewresearch.org/fact-tank/2013/11/12/what-happens-when-jews-intermarry.

2. Emily Cohen (@ThatRabbiCohen), "I am beyond delighted that the first Jewish 2nd family is interfaith and multiracial," Twitter, November 8, 2020, https://twitter.com/ThatRabbiCohen/status/1325448786697707525.

3. Yehuda Krohn (@YehudaKrohn), "Multiracial Jewish families are undoubtedly essential to our people. Interfaith remains, at best, an open question," Twitter, November 8, 2020, https://twitter.com/YehudaKrohn/status/1325510642057539590.

4. Rabbi Ruth Abusch-Magder (@RabbiRuth), "Interfaith families are part of the Jewish community," Twitter, November 8, 2020, https://twitter.com/RabbiRuth/status/1325549472340992001.

5. @kriegkm, "Thank you for standing for us. My husband is Jewish, I profess no faith, and our son is Jewish. So much for shrinking the faith," Twitter, November 8, 2020, https://twitter.com/kriegkm/status/1325590224634777602; @emmavan47, "I'm the child of an interfaith marriage and I was raised Jewish. I'm waking up to the fact that this is controversial but so glad to hear voices like yours fighting for inclusion," Twitter, November 8, 2020, https://twitter.com/emmavan47/status/1325551080453804032.

6. The retired founder of InterfaithFamily, Ed Case, and founder of the Center for Radically Inclusive Judaism, summed up the response to the Mezvinsky-Clinton wedding in "The Missing Mazel Tov," *Forward*, August 11, 2010, https://forward.com/opinion/129999/the-missing-mazel-tov/.

7. Tema Smith (@temasmith), "Just a friendly little reminder that you don't get to 'claim' @DouglasEmhoff in one breath and disparage interfaith families in another," Twitter, November 8, 2020, https://twitter.com/temasmith/status/1325471022510989313.

8. *Jewish Telegraphic Agency* (@JTANews), "Rising rates of intermarriage, a low reproductive rate and high levels of anti-Semitism are chipping away at the continent's Jewish population, a study has found," Twitter, October 22, 2020, https://twitter.com/JTAnews/status/1319278819543404551. For the full article, see Cnann Liphshiz, "The Global Proportion of Jews Living in Europe Is as Low as It Was 1,000 Years Ago: And the Future There Doesn't Look Bright," *Jewish Telegraphic Agency*, August 21, 2020, https://www.jta.org/2020/10/21/global/the-results-are-in-for-post-holocaust-european-jewry-it-doesnt-look-good.

9. Cooperman and Smith, "What Happens When Jews Intermarry?"

10. 18Doors / Benenson Strategy Group, *The Impact of COVID-19 on Interfaith Relationships: Research Findings and Implications*, unpublished report, October 2020.

11. Leonard Saxe, Fern Chertok, Graham Wright, and Shahar Hecht, *Under the Chuppah: Rabbinic Officiation and Intermarriage* (Waltham, MA: Cohen Center for Modern

Jewish Studies at Brandeis University, October 2016), https://bir.brandeis.edu/bit stream/handle/10192/33110/RabbinicOfficiation102616.pdf.

12. Leonard Saxe, "Is Intermarriage Really the Demise of Jews in America?" *Jerusalem Post*, August 7, 2019, https://www.jpost.com/opinion/intermarriage-in-america -597951.

13. Susan Katz Miller's work in this area has been helpful to my understanding, particularly her book *Being Both: Embracing Two Religions in One Interfaith Family* (Boston, MA: Beacon Press, 2013). See also https://susankatzmiller.com/ and Susan Katz Miller's blog at https://onbeingboth.wordpress.com/.

14. Jodi Bromberg and Bruce Taylor, "InterfaithFamily Becomes 18Doors," *eJewish Philanthropy*, February 13, 2020, https://ejewishphilanthropy.com/interfaithfamily -becomes-18doors/.

15. InterfaithFamily's now-retired founder, Ed Case, has written a book, *Radical Inclusion: Engaging Interfaith Families for a Thriving Jewish Future* (Newtonville, MA: Center for Radically Inclusive Judaism, 2019), that cogently articulates a series of ideas around how we might think about this in a meaningful and inclusive way.

16. Kerem Shalom, "Kerem Shalom's Rabbi: Author to ASL Chorus Conductor," *JewishBoston*, February 12, 2020, https://www.jewishboston.com/kerem-shaloms-rabbi -author-to-asl-chorus-conductor.

CHAPTER 3

Jews of Color

Gamal Palmer

When I was 13, having just become a bar mitzvah, I was in synagogue for Shabbat services, singing "L'dor v'dor"—"from generation to generation"—at the top of my lungs. I had my *tallis* (prayer shawl) and *kippah* (ritual head covering) on, I was totally decked out, and then this man tapped me on my shoulder, interrupting my *davening* (praying), and asked, "Are you Jewish?" (an absurd question given where I was and what I was doing and wearing). This line of questioning has happened to me many times in my life, but I had learned to smile and nod, to be accepting, letting people think it was OK to ask me these things, even though it wasn't OK then, and this line of questioning is not OK today. It's true, people are usually well intentioned and are "just asking" or "just being curious." But I have had to create a protective shield against the implications of questions like this.

This experience is not unique to me. When I became an adult, someone once said to me, "I totally get JOC slapped almost every time I go to synagogue." "What's that?" I asked. He said, "It's that experience a Jew of Color (JOC) has when they walk into a synagogue or a Jewish space and they're being questioned for being Jewish, being questioned for being there. It feels like a slap in the heart. A JOC slap." That's not a term that's widely used, but for me, hearing those words was really cathartic, because I finally had language for this experience that I'd had my whole life, whether it was inside or outside of Jewish community, where people questioned my Judaism.

There are many assumptions people have of you if you're a Jew of Color: that you're not really Jewish, that you've never been to Israel, that you don't believe in Israel's right to exist. A lot of this culminates in the assumption that you are also most likely antisemitic to some degree. For so many years, I don't think I even processed half of the things people said and were projecting onto me. Rather, I've felt like somebody was throwing a sharp dart at me, never quite hitting the bull's-eye, but they keep trying over and over and over again. After a while, the hurt just felt normal to receive.

That moment of being interrupted in synagogue has stayed with me, but that type of intrusion isn't the only way that Jews of Color experience their Jewish identities. Many years after that specific moment in synagogue, I moved to Los Angeles, well past my teenage years, after grad school, and after having lived abroad in South Africa. In Los Angeles, I met another JOC, Eric Green, who at the time was a part of Bend the Arc, a Jewish nonprofit committed to progressive social change. He said, "Hey, you got to come to this Hanukkah party." So I went, and I'll never forget my experience. I walked in the room, and there were 50–60 people there, most of whom were of color, and most of whom were Jewish. I had never had that experience before, and it was both overwhelming and beautiful. To be honest, I almost didn't believe what I was experiencing. I thought to myself, "Wait, is everybody here really Jewish?" It was my own moment of disbelief and even internalized racism after years of also being taught that people of color are not Jewish. My first time at this event was a big deal for me, and many people since then have said that the Los Angeles Jews of Color Hanukkah party was the first time that they were in a room where the guests were predominantly Jews of Color.

THE PARADOX OF VISIBILITY

For so long, many JOCs have felt like they were the only ones and didn't know that there were other Jews of Color. According to a study by the Jews of Color Initiative (JOCI), while 12–15 percent of American Jews identify as JOCs, that percentage of individuals is spread out geographically.[1] When people hear these statistics, there is still a lack of acceptance of these numbers. The Jews of Color Initiative gathered this data in partnership with Stanford University, and even though Stanford is a highly regarded institution, the study's credibility was still highly questioned because people are resistant to the reality that Jews of Color are an increasing percentage of the Jewish population. An even more recent study from JOCI in 2021 called *Beyond the Count* provided insights beyond the numbers, illustrating how JOCs experience the Jewish community.[2]

JOCI intentionally chose to partner with Stanford for a myriad of reasons. Not only is it one of the best institutions in the field for this sort of work, but collaborating with this organization would also mean that white institutions would have a more difficult time disputing the findings of a white authority institution. White people think there's no way that there could be so many JOCs. "If there are so many, where are they? We don't see them," they say. But that's the whole point. White Jews do not see us because they have built a community in which JOCs are not acknowledged, and so, if our existence is not acknowledged, why would we actually show up to participate in Jewish institutional life?

But now that Jews of Color do know that there are others out there, there is this feeling of "Where are you?" as we try to find each other. It's easier, though, for someone like me who lives in Los Angeles to find other Jews of Color, but what about someone who doesn't live in such a large city? A Black Jewish woman once reached out to me on LinkedIn. She was about 60 years old, living in North Carolina, and she told me she had never been in the same room with another Jew of Color.

Being a JOC unfortunately means that one is constantly subject to questioning, interrogation, and offensive assumptions. For example, I hear people say, "Sure, I know there are a lot of Jews of Color, but how did they become Jewish?" That's something you wouldn't say when you hear that your white friend's daughter is Jewish. You would never question or challenge her Jewish identity. At Jewish events, I have been mistaken for a valet guy, even though I'm in jeans and a blazer and not at all dressed like the valets. People have asked me where the coats should be hung or where the bathroom is, assuming that I'm the help, not the host of the event.

Another microaggression that might not seem like a big deal in isolation but that adds up over time is the dismissal of JOCs possessing Jewish knowledge. For example, a Jew of Color leads a prayer and a white person expresses surprise: "You knew that in Hebrew!" or "You know what that prayer means." There's a lot of chastising that happens with white Jews describing Shabbat or the points of Passover or the Yom Kippur War to me, as if I wouldn't know these things. What's amazing is that I've been to Israel 20–25 times, more than most people, and have also worked in the Jewish world for eight years, and while I'm more involved than your average Jewish person, people still say these things to me.

FACING HISTORY

The Jewish community is complex, beautiful, frustrating, layered, and filled with untapped potential. My friends who are not Jewish, particularly Black folk, often ask, "How did the Jews get to have such an organized and resourced community? How do Jewish communities have such infrastructure?" While Judaism and Jewish institutions have a lot to celebrate, it's important to name that the Jewish community also has deeply entrenched challenges around race, challenges that are endemic to simply being a part of American society.

Black people in this country have a very particular history. As much as oppression is oppression and racism is racism, it is undeniable that the racialized history of this country still very much informs modern-day society. As Jews, we talk so much about our history. We remember our history and we are proud of how that history has prevailed and stayed with us. The Dead Sea Scrolls are one of my favorite examples of the power of Judaism. We've somehow been able to sustain our story and keep it relatively the same even while there have been many expressions of Judaism over thousands of years. We see this when we compare modern-day Torah scrolls with the Dead Sea Scrolls.

But when we bring up the history of the United States, in terms of being a Black American, people often discount or diminish the role that history is currently playing. This country was built on the backs of slaves, of Black people, of African people. The United States' racist history is everywhere. In the U.S. Constitution, it is written that Black Americans are three-fifths human. Today's current issues around policing in this country, meanwhile, are very much rooted in the KKK and the other ways that slaves and Black people have been policed throughout history. As a Black Jew, I know that the pain and the everyday experience within and outside of the Jewish community is distinct from that of other races.

Given this history, institutions rub up against the fact that to undo deep-seated systems of oppression requires work that takes a lot of time and energy. When people change their racist behaviors, their psychology, and their understanding of structural racism, then we find the specific ways in which an institution or an individual can take actions to be more welcoming. The challenge for so many organizations, though, is that they've never done that work, or they're just starting to do this kind of deep work, or they don't know where to start. The work of dismantling racist systems takes time to manifest itself in ways that are meaningful. For example, during the recent racial justice movement following the murder of George Floyd, many people on the front lines of dismantling the system of racism said, "You're either with us here marching, putting out statements, posting on social media, and standing up for Black lives lost, or you're not." That's a hard line that people often draw, particularly during movement making, but changing people's ideas and belief systems, especially racist ones, be they conscious or unconscious, takes time. Often the people who are furthest away from understanding the root of racism become even more resistant and adverse to change. This does not mean we should not put pressure on others to change, but we need to allow for and lift up leaders and change makers who are willing to work with those who are not yet stepping into formation.

Yet rather than schooling people in how to change their ideas, sometimes individuals just need the space to come to realizations on their own. One day, at the end of a three-hour diversity, equity, and inclusion (DEI) workshop I facilitate called Diversity Gym, an older white gentleman who had a *kippah* on raised his hand. We had been having this reflective moment during the closing circle, and all the participants were feeling so much better about themselves by the end of the session. But as we drew to an end, this individual said, "Wait a minute, I have to say something." It's important to state that this man had been participating completely in the workshop and seemed to be getting a lot out of it. But now this same individual said, "I don't see race. I don't see color. I know we've been talking about this, but I just felt like I just had to say this truth, because that's where I'm at."

My jaw almost dropped, and I could see people of color in the room begin to fume; all their triggers were going off. I stood in the middle of the circle and invited the man to join me. I said to the man, "Please, can you put your hands on my hands?" and he did so. I said, "Do you want people to not see your *kippah*? Do you want them to not see that you're Jewish?" "Of course not," he said. "I want them to see that." I then responded, "Great. I'm Black, and I'd love for you to see me." I could see him processing this idea, and then he said, "Okay, I get it." He had an emotional moment, and we hugged, and then he went back to his seat. I think this story is a powerful one, because it is about having that moment to allow people to process and to think differently, as opposed to telling people what they need to believe.

It is very helpful for white-presenting Jews to continue to celebrate and grapple with their Jewish identity and what it means to be in the United States or part of other predominantly white-appearing societies. At the same time, we can no longer afford, when talking about racism, for white Jews to say both "Yes, I want to be inclusive" and "I am not white, I'm Jewish," or "I, too, am oppressed because I am a Jew." Any statements like these diminish the reality of Black racism in our country While Jews are still persecuted, discriminated against, and are the victims of antisemitism, even as recently as May 2021 in West Hollywood as Jewish diners at a sushi restaurant were attacked as a response to fighting between Israelis and Palestinians, the fact remains that unless you tell people otherwise, the majority of the population will see white-presenting Jews as white people and not as Jews.[3] Whereas, if you are of color, you do not have the opportunity or privilege to pick and choose when and how you communicate your racial identity.

THE CHALLENGE OF BEING WELCOMING

What would it look like to truly welcome Jews of Color into mainstream Jewish institutions? We need to create spaces that are conducive to change. We need environments in which the community has bought into an inclusive philosophy to tackle racism. We need individuals within institutions to receive training that is effective enough so that members of that community have the tools and language they need to do this work. We need spaces that will truly feel welcoming to anyone who enters them.

Being welcoming involves taking action, but it has to go beyond simply having door greeters. In fact, if not done correctly, the act of welcoming can backfire and even alienate people. For example, there is a large congregation in Los Angeles that has people who are called the welcoming committee, and their sole purpose is to say hello to people who walk through the door. It's a very beautiful concept, and the people are friendly and inviting. But what had been missing from people who had played that role was that they didn't realize that when they were going up to Jews of Color to say, "Hello, how are you? I haven't seen you here before," these words can be triggering if the JOC doesn't know that these individuals are part of this welcoming committee. "I've never seen you here before" is a pretty big statement for one person to make that can instantly feel alienating.

When I attended this synagogue, a member of the welcoming committee asked, "So, is this your first time here?" I said, "Yes." Then they said, "How'd you find out about us?" and I responded from a defensive and guarded place. Other times, people will ask, "Oh, so your mom is Jewish?" Yes, my mom is how I am Jewish to some extent; matrilineal descent is how I'm Jewish. But that question is just so dismissive, assumptive, and unnecessary. The intent behind some of these questions might not be malicious, but it still hurts. Some people will say things like "I'm just trying to understand. I'm just trying to learn," but these are not things you ask of white Jews whom you meet for the first time.

This experience I'm describing is sadly not unique. It happens every time I go into a new synagogue. I have a little bit of palpitation; I start getting nervous, and I'm on guard. I know that everyone has to go through security, and even when I go through security and the guards don't racially profile me, I'm so prepared for them to do that to me that it *feels* like I just did get racially profiled. Walking into a synagogue is not really a moment that is enjoyable to me, whereas other people are just so glad to be in that space and all it represents. From the time that you walk through the door and you take out your *tallis* bag and go into the sanctuary, all you want to do is exhale. So when the next interaction is someone essentially telling you, "Hey, I noticed you, you've never been here before, you look different," it doesn't feel very welcoming.

But the experience doesn't end there. Once I'm inside, now I've got to try to let go of that initial interaction and figure out where I'm going to sit in the synagogue. Since I'm not a member, I have to navigate the space. Where do I want to sit? And more important, where am I going to feel safe? Once I finally sit down, people start looking right in my direction, and again, because of previous experiences, I can never know what's going through people's minds as to whether they're looking because I'm a Jew of Color or because they just happen to be looking. But it feels like lots of people are looking and wondering, and I see people making certain faces and raising eyebrows. After all that, to then sit down and eventually to start *davening* and worshipping in this community, it's hard.

In order for this same experience that I just described to be more welcoming, consider the following: When you walk into the space, if there's a sign that says, "Look out for one of our greeters—they're going to welcome you. Let them know if you need help finding your way," that would give people some fair warning and some context for the questions that they're about to be asked. And it's not just the greeters. The security guards can also welcome people and say, "When you go inside, be sure to look out for one of the greeters who are here to welcome you into this sanctuary," which would potentially mitigate some of the tension that a Jew of Color might feel when they're going through security. It would help diminish some of that new harm or retraumatization of old harm that security screenings can bring up for JOCs. By putting up these signs and doing this sort of training for both volunteers and security guards, institutions can create a conversation and an awareness that would be extremely useful for people who are inhabiting these welcoming roles.

MORE THAN TELLING OUR STORY

As a Jew of Color, it is not uncommon for me to get calls where someone says, "We just want you to tell your story." Jews of Color, though, are more than their story of what it means to be a JOC. Some JOCs don't want to facilitate a conversation or workshop about identity. They don't want to participate in something where they have to explain to white people their challenges and their struggles or the simple fact of who they are. A lot of Jews of Color are not interested in that and don't think that it's their responsibility to do that work.

There are other people, myself being one of them, who actually, as a profession, have made the decision to do this sort of diversity and inclusion work. I have the patience to listen to some of the most absurd, racist things and still survive. I have the aptitude for helping white people work that stuff out so that they might be able to arrive on the other side at some point. I'm happy to share my story in the context of talking about leadership development, or board development, or systems change work. But when organizations only approach JOCs in this capacity, or when they have a panel with Jews of Color where white Jews can hear JOC stories, many Jews of Color are not going to have a positive reaction.

I told my Jewish story during the racial justice movement of 2020 when I was interviewed by a reporter from a national Jewish publication. At first, I was excited to be featured, but when I later thought about it, I realized they took out all of the substance that had to do with my professional experience, my perspectives on working in Jewish organizations, and my philosophy around leadership development. Instead of reducing Jews of Color to our personal Jewish stories, organizations need to capitalize on the multifaceted skill sets of Jews of Color, featuring them not just because they are Jews of Color but also because they are also experts on many topics. In an effort to be inclusive, majority white institutions instead make the mistake of reducing us to being "just" Jews of Color. It's important to have Jews of Color facilitate workshops that are not about race and that are not about inclusion but instead emphasize their strengths as individuals in other areas. Yet, looking at the professional Jewish landscape today, it's actually hard to think of Jews of Color who are hired to do work that is not about racial justice. Conversely, there are Jews of Color who are not really involved in the organized Jewish community, but who are consultants and professionals in other areas and who don't even have an idea that this conversation is going on within this organized Jewish world, and yet these individuals still very much identify as Jewish.

JOC-ONLY SPACES

While making Jews of Color feel welcome as part of the larger Jewish community is very much needed, Jews of Color affinity groups and JOC-only spaces are also vital. For decades, if not centuries, white people have tried to keep Black people from assembling. They thought that if a group of Black people was gathering, it was dangerous—that the Black people were either speaking negatively about white people or plotting something against them. But for minorities of all types, it's empowering to be with people with whom you connect and with whom you have an affinity. Women often share these types of experiences. For example, I have heard some women say, "I went to a women's conference, and just being in the room with all of these women and hearing our voices, feeling like we can support each other, just being in the room gave me power." I've heard similar sentiments from people who have gathered with LGBTQ groups and from so many other marginalized people. People gain power when we feel heard, when we have the experience of being seen, and when we feel that we are part of something greater, and that we belong.

Being a person of color in a leadership role in an all-white institution in the United States means that you are inevitably going to interact with and encounter racism. Having affinity groups is crucial, particularly in a space where an institution has not actually changed. Affinity groups are important because they allow people to process what's happening. I didn't realize how much I still need there to be other Jews of Color in leadership roles at Federation; there are things that happen in the institution that I need to process so that I can be better at my job. I benefit from being with people like me who can help me distinguish between experiences that are happening to me and perhaps I'm just taking the wrong way, and experiences that reflect real systemic racism. Even if these supports exist only to talk about something that happened that's negative, by talking about it, a lot of times the issue gets defused.

I've never had that sort of a cohort, and so it has been a huge burden, and really a part of my job, to manage that lack of other JOC peers. We know from psychology and emotional intelligence that the more we carry something with us, when we don't communicate it and get it out, then the more pervasive and detrimental it becomes to our emotional and mental well-being. Organizations and individuals need these support systems because it's an acknowledgment that structural racism exists and that power structures exist. I often have to find other outlets to communicate about these things that happen to me, but if I had JOC peers who worked at the organization itself, then I might not have to bottle things up as much.

Happily, Jews of Color spaces are now getting more visibility. The organized Jewish world is beginning to provide funding for Jews of Color projects. There are all sorts of pipelines that are emerging to support Jews of Color, including for Jews of Color who are not affiliated with any particular Jewish organization, which is key. Not having to prove that you're worth getting funding just because you're not a part of a Federation or another Jewish organization is a big deal. There are Jews of Color who are not at all engaged in the organized Jewish world, but who just happen to be people who are of color and happen to also identify as Jewish. They might go to synagogue a couple of times a year or celebrate holidays at home like Hanukkah or Passover. What would happen if we started to hold some of these people up? Just as much as there have been efforts to engage members of the Orthodox community into wider Jewish communal spaces, just as much as we seek to engage interfaith families into Jewish life, we need to make sure Jews of Color feel a part of the tent. At the same time, we have to make sure that we are not sensationalizing JOCs. When I hear people talk about Jews of Color, it's almost like there's a sense of fascination with them. The next phase of this work is to get beyond the sensationalism of Jews of Color and to simply engage them as we would, for example, young adults in the Jewish community.

There's an opportunity as well for there to be a much richer dialogue about how Jews of Color want to collaborate and partner with other Jews of Color and/or established white Jewish institutions. There are all kinds of emerging initiatives: the Jewish Multiracial Network; Dimensions; the JOC Mishpacha Project for LGBTQ Jews of Color in Washington, DC; the Jews of Color Initiative; Ammud: The Jews of Color Torah Academy; and the Mitsui Collective, to name just a few. Yet to connect with and benefit from what organizations like the Jews of Color Initiative are offering, you still have to be connected to organized Jewish life in some way. There are a lot of initiatives working toward creating a sense of centralization for JOCs, but the lack of a central address highlights the reality that there is not one singular vision for the JOC community. That said, there's also not one vision for the Ashkenazi Jewish community. That's a healthy tension point around organizing, collaboration, and centralizing efforts, and we need to figure out how to balance that tension so that each JOC leader can express their leadership and execute their vision for the community without being constrained or judged. There's not a right or a wrong way to do this work.

This collaborative approach contrasts with the larger organized Jewish community, which has often turned into an unhealthy competition among

organizations, and which often utilizes practices and approaches to community building that can be exclusive, damaging, and classist. My hope is that
as the JOC community evolves, it doesn't fall into that trap of competition.
Rather, many of the dollars that JOC organizations are receiving actually need
to be used toward the goal of dismantling structural racism and power. At the
same time, we need to be aware that the work is going to require multiple
strategies and approaches, and that just because you as an individual or an
organization have a particular approach, it doesn't mean that another person's
or organization's approach is not effective or not right.

GOING DEEPER

Well-meaning, established, predominantly white organizations are doing the
work of diversity and inclusion; however, oftentimes they are doing the work
in a vacuum. For example, they are not actually involving JOCs, or they're
engaging only one person of color, which does not allow for the full range
of JOC perspectives to be represented. An organization may do a couple of
trainings, but not continue them long term, or their leadership will not be
brought into the planning or participation. Organizations must put dollars
toward these efforts, which is often an organization's primary mistake. Their
stated goals or mission statement may talk about wanting to do the work, and
maybe they had one panel or a program about JOCs, but if they are not doing
any sort of systems change processes, then the changes won't be impactful.

Organizations bring in consultants to help them talk about race, and yet
many Jewish institutions are also still talking about how white Jews are an
oppressed people, which is not helpful, because that's not the issue at stake. It
is imperative for white-presenting Jews to be comfortable with talking about
race, racism, and Jews of Color (which are three distinct topics) without needing to mention the very real and current antisemitism and oppression that
Jews face both in the United States and around the world. If white Jews don't
understand that Jews are also Black, and that Jews are also Asian, and that Jews
are also Latino, that's a problem. If they don't understand that crucial fact,
then they often treat Jews of Color like "those people over there."

Another challenge white institutions must understand while doing JOC
programming is not to make Jews of Color feel othered or like second-class
citizens. If an institution is doing a program involving Jews of Color because
"we know we're supposed to be doing this" or because "somebody told us that
we're supposed to be doing this," but the organizers and participants are not
really understanding that this program is to actually bring Jews of Color into
the community in a meaningful way, that's a problem.

Some organizations, though, have really put in the work. When I go into
IKAR, an alternative Jewish community based in Los Angeles that is driven by

social justice values, I feel like I fit in there. I don't get nervous around security. They have done this deep work, and the environment has become inherently welcoming. From the sermons that Rabbi Sharon Brous, the founder and leader of IKAR, and the other clergy give to the inclusive content of podcasts and outward-facing panels they do, all this makes a difference in my experience. The security training that has happened there makes a difference. That they talk about Judaism and Torah in a way that is complex and multifaceted makes a difference.

IKAR started this work years ago with a five-day residency with Jewish DEI expert Yavilah McCoy, in which the entire community of IKAR attended sessions on a variety of topics. There were sessions for staff, for security, and for lay leaders, and the entire residency was designed *in partnership* with Jews of Color with whom the community had already been building relationships. These Jews of Color weren't necessarily members of IKAR, but they were members of the larger Los Angeles Jewish community. That whole five-day event led to a series of strategies, programming, and offerings that pushed the synagogue along its path of inclusivity. Then IKAR created a detailed leadership pipeline to get Jews of Color to join its board. They didn't just place these individuals on the board; existing leaders also prepared these new members in such a way that they were actually ready to be leaders. These strategies were both inward and outward facing. When an organization, like IKAR, does all this work, it has created a welcoming vibe that's energetic, inviting, and even spiritual.

Not all organizations are primed to do this work. IKAR was able to engage in this way because social justice is a part of its mission. If social justice isn't a part of an organization's mission (which it doesn't have to be), the question remains as to how an organization can leverage its commitment to Jewish values so that it can still do the work of dismantling racist structures. And when I say doing the work, I mean doing the work with its board and its staff, as well as doing the work of providing funding, building resources, and helping JOCs become self-sustaining.

To achieve this vision, this commitment to inclusion and racial equality starts at a leadership level. People need to read and have discussions around these issues. We are more likely to achieve this vision with more people committing to the longevity of the work; it can't be an episodic or one-time fix. If you gain anything from reading this chapter, I hope that it includes the following:

1. Center people of color when talking about racism within the Jewish community.
2. If you want to truly be an inclusive organization and community, put money into the budget and invest in doing the work.

3. There is no right way to address DEI needs, and the work will not be linear.
4. Do your homework. Research, be curious about, and actively engage people not like you. Then reach out to them and build relationships with them and get them involved in your process and your community.
5. Build multiracial communities. We can no longer think about DEI as a workshop, skill set, or episodic event. DEI should and can be integrated in all that you do. The outcome will be that you are not only more inclusive but also actively building and nurturing a multiracial program, staff, board, and—ultimately—community.

I'm interested in a vision of the American Jewish community in which the story that is being told is reflective of the people within the community, both those who are engaged in organized Jewish life and those who aren't. There needs to be a real allowance for the nuanced expressions of Judaism, leadership, and participation within this history, unlike the ways in which the story has been told over the past 100 or more years. Jews of Color have been in this country for a very long time, but they have been excluded from the white American Jewish narrative. My hope for the future is that the story of American Judaism, which includes Jews of Color, can finally be celebrated and told in its totality.

RESOURCES

Websites

Ammud (ammud.org) provides Jewish education for Jews of Color (JOCs) by Jews of Color.

Dimensions (www.dimensionsedc.com) is a women- and Jewish People of Color–led nonprofit that provides training and consultancy in diversity, equity, and inclusion.

Jewish Multiracial Network (jewishmultiracialnetwork.org) sets out to nurture and enhance Jewish diversity via capacity development, community development, community empowerment, and social capital.

Jews of Color Initiative (jewsofcolorinitiative.org) is a national effort focused on building and advancing the professional, organizational, and communal field for Jews of Color.

JOC Mishpacha Project (jocmishpacha.org) offers workshops, advocacy, outreach, and gathering spaces for Jewish People of Color and their families/allies/accomplices.

Mitsui Collective (mitsuicollective.org) is a new organization working at the intersection of Jewish wellness, spirituality, nature connection, and community building.

Books

Kaye/Kantrowitz, Melanie. *The Colors of Jews: Racial Politics and Radical Diasporism.* Bloomington: Indiana University Press, 2007.

Kendi, Ibram X. *How to Be an Antiracist.* New York: One World, 2019.

Oluo, Ijeoma. *So You Want to Talk about Race.* New York: Seal Press, 2018.

NOTES

1. Ari Kelman, Aaron Hahn Tapper, Isabel Fonseca, and Aliya Saperstein, "Counting Inconsistencies: An Analysis of American Jewish Population Studies, with a Focus on Jews of Color," Jews of Color Initiative, 2019, 2, https://jewsofcolorfieldbuilding.org/wp-content/uploads/2019/05/Counting-Inconsistencies-052119.pdf.

2. Tobin Belzer et al., *Beyond the Count: Perspectives and Lived Experiences of Jews of Color* (Jews of Color Initiative, August 2021), https://jewsofcolorinitiative.org/wp-content/uploads/2021/08/BEYONDTHECOUNT.FINAL_.8.12.21.pdf?utm_source=JoCI+website&utm_medium=PDF&utm_campaign=Beyond+the+Count+report.

3. Ruth Graham, "Los Angeles Mayor Calls Attack on Diners 'Anti-Semitic,'" *New York Times,* May 20, 2021, https://www.nytimes.com/2021/05/20/us/jewish-hate-crime-los-angeles.html.

CHAPTER 4

Disability Access and Inclusion

Gabrielle Kaplan-Mayer

When Adam Fishbein, now age 22, was going to Hebrew school at Congregation Kol Ami, a Reform Temple in Elkins Park, Pennsylvania, he recalls that attending midweek sessions after a day of secular school was particularly challenging. Fishbein, who holds a master's degree in public administration from American University and works as a nonprofit grants associate, has Tourette syndrome, a neurologically based tic disorder. As a child, the energy that it took Adam to participate in secular school and focus on his education while also trying to manage the tics that come with living with Tourette made him exhausted by 3:00 p.m. He simply couldn't do more after-school learning, although both Adam and his parents highly valued Jewish education and didn't want him to miss out on what his peers were experiencing in Hebrew school.

It took one of Adam's especially thoughtful Hebrew school teachers to come up with an outside-the-box solution for Adam: she offered to tutor him one on one at a time that allowed him to rest and restore his energy from the school day. This individualized approach to his Jewish education worked so well for Adam that, following his bar mitzvah, he became a *madrich* (teen assistant) in Kol Ami's school and focused on helping students who struggled with attention or learning issues.

While in previous generations, and certainly still in many congregations today, if a child wasn't able to access a synagogue's Jewish educational programming, that child often stopped participating in synagogue life altogether. Thanks to the collaboration among Adam's teacher, the school director, the rabbi, Adam, and his parents, not only did Adam feel valued in his community, but his whole family also felt supported by their spiritual community as they navigated the terrain of raising a child with Tourette Syndrome. In the years since, Adam's father has gone on to become a co-chair of the synagogue's Inclusion Committee, and Adam's mother and siblings have been active in the

53

congregation. Adam went off to college with a strong sense of Jewish identity, and he has gone on to participate in communal activities like the annual Jewish Disability Advocacy Day.

ONE-FOURTH OF YOUR COMMUNITY MEMBERS

The term "disability" is used for an incredibly diverse population—from someone who may be born blind or with a developmental disability like Down Syndrome, to someone who acquires a physical disability through an injury, to someone who has a mental health disorder that impacts their daily functioning. A disability may be physical, intellectual, developmental, learning, related to mental health, or any combination of these things.

Current statistics from the Centers for Disease Control (CDC) show that *one in four adults* has some kind of disability. In the United States, 14 percent of all public school children receive some kind of special education services.[1] The most recent studies in autism spectrum disorder (ASD) prevalence indicate that one in 54 children has an autism diagnosis.[2] The number of people with disabilities in the Jewish community may be slightly higher than in the general population because of the prevalence of Jewish genetic diseases.

What do these statistics mean in terms of our congregations? Understanding how common disability really is underscores the importance of creating warm and welcoming communities for those of us with disabilities and those who have loved ones with a disability. If your early childhood center has 100 students enrolled, you will likely have at least one student with an autism diagnosis. If your membership has 400 households and we know that it's likely that one-quarter of all adult members have a disability, consider the range of accommodations you may need to provide so that all of those people can fully participate in the life of the community.[3] Those of us who have neurotypical children may have grandchildren who have cognitive or learning disabilities, and we must remember that our need to accommodate extends beyond the immediate members of our congregation.

Consider how disability impacts us through the lifespan. When we can look at the incidence of disability in adults as it relates to aging, we see that many people need accommodations later in life that they didn't need at an earlier age. As people are living longer, the likelihood of experiencing disability related to aging increases, such as loss of mobility, hearing, vision, cognition, or some combination. Someone who has always sat in the sanctuary and been able to hear the rabbi speak without any problem may, later on in life, have a different experience when using a hearing aid. Many congregations are putting in hearing loop systems and/or providing captioning services. Making large-print *siddurim* (prayer books) or magnifying sheets that can go over sacred books available for congregants can be an effective way to address vision loss in the aging population.

Creating a ramp to a *bimah* (raised prayer platform) and/or an accessible Torah reading table for people with wheelchairs, walkers, or other mobility devices will improve accessibility for congregants with a variety of needs. These changes to your prayer space are equally important for both the child born with a disability that impacts mobility (like cerebral palsy, spina bifida, or muscular dystrophy) and an adult member of the congregation, or visiting grandparent, who can no longer walk up steps. None of us knows when an accident, illness, or injury could lead to a disability for someone in our family or for ourselves, but when we understand disability as part of the human lifespan and plan accommodations accordingly, we support the ability of all members of our communities to participate.

Every synagogue is concerned with membership numbers—both how to keep current members engaged and committed to the congregation and how to attract people who are not currently affiliated with a congregation. Taking measures to provide accommodations for people with disabilities means that a congregation can reach a segment of the Jewish community that has often felt outside of and even stigmatized by the Jewish community. Jennifer Laszlo Mizrahi, who is dyslexic and the president of RespectAbility, a nonprofit disability advocacy organization, knows what it means to raise a child with multiple disabilities. In words that hold true for every community and organization, she says, "We are our best when we are welcoming and respectful of all people."[4]

DISABILITY INCLUSION IS A MIND-SET

Our emphasis on creating inclusive and accessible communities begins with the mind-set that we can and should provide accommodations and modifications for people who need them to fully participate in all aspects of community life, including education (early childhood, religious school, youth group, adult education), life cycle events, religious rituals, social/cultural events, and leadership opportunities. One of the challenges that disability inclusion presents is that there is no one-size-fits-all model when it comes to accommodations. The successful solution described above for Adam Fishbein when he was a struggling student in Hebrew school may not have worked for a different student, whose priority may have been socializing with classmates. Coming up with the appropriate accommodations takes time and energy, and the process should always begin by listening to the person with the disability and/or any family member who serves as that person's advocate.

It was only with the passing of the Individuals with Disabilities Education Act (IDEA) in 1975 that school districts were required to provide an appropriate education to children with disabilities. One result of IDEA is that parents of children with disabilities were able to keep their children at home and raise them as part of their families and communities. In 1990, the Americans with Disabilities Act (ADA) was passed, which is our nation's most comprehensive civil rights law that prohibits discrimination against individuals with disabilities in all areas of public life. It is important to note that houses of worship were excluded from the ADA, meaning that synagogues do not have a legal responsibility to be physically accessible. It is, rather, a moral and ethical obligation. Just as people with disabilities have faced discrimination in our society in general for many years, we must acknowledge they have also faced those physical and attitudinal barriers right within the walls of our houses of worship.

Creating an inclusion mind-set in your congregation or organization means doing the *tikkun* (repair) of reversing years of stigma about disability so that you create a community in which everyone feels valued, whether or not they are personally touched by disability. Doing so takes ongoing work, but once you embrace the mind-set that doing so is possible, you set out on a path that will become more intuitive as you practice the inclusion mind-set. The pain of being stigmatized because of disability can be emotionally and spiritually devastating, and it will require ongoing education and awareness raising to end the unconscious prejudice that so many of us have internalized about disability.

Figure 4.1. Gabrielle Kaplan-Mayer with a participant at one of Jewish Learning Venture's "Whole Community Inclusion" programs.

NOTHING ABOUT US WITHOUT US

In the disability rights community, there is an important statement about working toward inclusion that is used in different contexts like housing, education, employment, and full community participation: *nothing about us without us*. For too many years, almost all decisions impacting the lives of people with disabilities were made *for* them rather than by and with them. In creating inclusive communities for people with disabilities, it's essential to talk with and listen to members of your congregation who have disabilities to learn about their experiences, and it is essential to involve people with disabilities in your inclusion and accessibility planning.

Wendy Elliott-Vandivier is an artist whose work explores issues of family, memory, and her experiences as a disabled woman who uses a wheelchair. Her autobiographical cartoons focus on attitudinal barriers and stereotypes regarding disabilities, as well as the microaggressions that disabled people experience while living their normal, everyday lives. Wendy has been a member of her Reconstructionist synagogue, Or Hadash, in Fort Washington, Pennsylvania, for 25 years. She joined the congregation's inclusion committee when it was first being formed five years ago. She is now the chair of the committee, which, in addition to hosting disability awareness speakers for the community, is working on a fundraising campaign with the goal of installing an automatic door in the synagogue and eventually creating an accessible *bimah*.

Though Wendy found a welcoming community at Or Hadash, she could have easily turned away from participating in Jewish congregational life based on her earlier experiences. When she and her husband, John (who was not Jewish at the time but later converted), were first married, they joined a large Reform congregation where she remembers that "no one talked to me," even after she and John were no longer newcomers to the community. Another barrier to Wendy's ability to feel at home there was that the sanctuary had fixed pews so there was limited seating available for her wheelchair, forcing her and John to sit apart from each other during services.

When Wendy and John decided that they had given that community enough of a chance, she started to explore other options. She was interested in becoming part of a much more intimate and intentional community and checked out a neighborhood-based *havurah* (independent prayer group) in which families met for services, Shabbat dinners, and holiday programs in one another's homes. But while the culture of the *havurah* was a better fit for them than the large Reform temple had been, Wendy quickly realized that there was no way that she could physically access the members' homes in her wheelchair. That option was out.

Fortunately, when they found their current synagogue, the welcoming attitude of both the clergy and the members convinced her quickly that they'd found the right home. People were friendly and got to know her as a person. She felt a sense of belonging. Still, because the synagogue is located in an old building that was once a mansion, it is has been a long, slow process to make all of the physical space accessible to her.

Her advice for any congregation working toward inclusion of people with disabilities is to bring stakeholders together to form an inclusion committee and to make sure that people with disabilities are represented there.

INCLUSION GOALS: HOW TO GET THERE

In directing Jewish Learning Venture's "Whole Community Inclusion" initiative, I have worked with many synagogues from all different denominations that are in the process of becoming more inclusive and accessible for people with disabilities. If you serve on a synagogue professional staff or are a lay leader who wants to work with staff to make your congregation or organization more accessible and inclusive, there are a number of steps that you can take to make your goals a reality.

Survey

It is challenging to set goals for your community if you aren't sure of what the needs of the community are. Remember that many disabilities, especially those related to mental health, chronic illness, and learning disabilities, are largely invisible. There are likely congregants or members of your organization who have never had an opportunity to share about their needs for accommodations, simply because they were never asked. Create a survey that invites people to share about their experiences and needs for support. One community I worked with was surprised by its survey to find out how many people had dietary restrictions that weren't being supported by the congregation because people didn't feel empowered to share that they needed gluten- or dairy-free food. As a result of the survey, these options were added to the weekly *oneg* (refreshments after services) menu, and more people were able to stay and enjoy the communal eating experience.

Come Together as Staff

Too often, our synagogue and Jewish communal professionals work in their own departments and may not be aware of the actions taken around inclusion throughout their institutions. A great place to begin is for professionals to come together as a team to learn from each other. How are children who receive early intervention services supported in the early childhood center? In what ways does the congregational religious school train teachers to support students with learning and cognitive disabilities? Is there a process in place to provide accommodations in the b'nai mitzvah process? Does the congregation do any outreach to adults with disabilities who live in nearby group homes or supported communities? Begin by learning from each other and noticing the places where your community needs to grow.

Inclusion Committee

An inclusion committee can be composed of professional staff and community members who are passionate about addressing the issue of accessibility, and such a committee should always include people with disabilities. You may also have congregants who have worked professionally in special education, policy advocacy, or therapeutic fields who would be happy to bring their professional expertise to your committee. The essential thing is that this committee involves both professionals and lay leaders working toward a common goal.

An inclusion committee's task should be to examine all of the different aspects of congregational life related to disability and accessibility, including the following:

- Synagogue culture: Are there attitudinal barriers to participation? Do people with disabilities feel welcomed, supported, and able to fully participate?
- Architectural accessibility: Does the structure of the building allow access for people with mobility issues? This includes getting into the building, having an accessible bathroom, and being able to access the *bimah* and all rooms in the building.
- Hearing and visual accessibility: Does your congregation provide American Sign Language (ASL) interpreters? What about captioning for services and/or adult education programs?
- Access to education: It is not a given that children who have an Individualized Education Plan in secular school can necessarily access a Jewish education. How does your congregational school provide supports for students who need accommodations? What kind of professional development is provided for your education director and teachers?
- Mental health supports: Is the topic of mental health addressed in your community? Is there a mechanism for those living with mental health challenges to reach out for support? Mental illness has long been an invisible disability, and communities require a proactive commitment to change that perspective.

Language and Communication

Because different people may need different kinds of accommodations to participate in congregational life, a simple but effective way to create better access to all services, educational opportunities, and social events is to include

a sentence on all communications: "For all accommodations, please contact
_____." The person who is named as the contact should, of course,
be someone who is aware of all of the accommodations that the synagogue
offers. Many synagogues share their inclusion statement on their website and
also feature a page that lists all of the available accommodations, which may
include items like elevators, sign language interpretation, accessible bathrooms, and inclusive religious education.

Set Attainable Goals

It may be overwhelming when a committee or task force comes together and
honestly examines all of the areas where an organization is not yet practicing inclusion. But accessibility and inclusion are a process, and some steps
will require time, energy, and money. When congregations identify physical
changes needed for accessibility, they may need to set up a fundraiser or search
for a grant or donor to fund that project. A committee can also look for low-
cost solutions to make their building more accessible in the meantime. For
example, one congregation wanted to create a Torah-reading table that was
accessible for people in wheelchairs, but they could not afford to purchase a
new table. They ended up purchasing a smaller drafting table that was placed
next to the larger Torah reading table, which worked perfectly for a Torah
reader who is a wheelchair user. Another synagogue inclusion committee led
a program for its Hebrew high school about physical inclusion and the synagogue. The result was that the high school students became so engaged and
excited about making their synagogue more accessible that they decided to put
their *tzedakah* (charitable donations) toward purchasing new *mezuzot* (small
decorative boxes containing Torah verses, which are hung on doorposts) to be
placed at eye level for wheelchair users.

Your committee should set one goal at a time and work toward that goal.
Communicate with your community about your work and engage constituents in your process, and you may find new supporters who can energize and
help move your work forward.

Financial Considerations

Because so many synagogues were built before there was consciousness about
physical accessibility, the greatest financial cost for congregations in becoming
fully inclusive is generally around architectural changes. Adding automatic
doors, creating accessible bathrooms, putting in ramps, and making your
bimah accessible may require a fundraising campaign. Some congregations are
able to find generous donors to support these changes, and others engage their
community in a grassroots campaign to raise the money that is needed, like
the examples listed above.

While the institution might question or balk at the notion of expensive physical changes to a building, consider the financial impact on families of raising a child with a disability. One of the greatest challenges that families raising children with any kind of special needs face is economic burden, as many therapies and educational supports aren't covered by insurance. Many families also need to hire lawyers just to get their children the appropriate education that is their legal right. Many times, these are the families who come to our synagogues and community centers and are then told that they need to pay more tuition if their child needs an aide for religious school or to participate in youth events. We should never put a tax on someone who has a disability. Work with your board to determine the cost for inclusion, and then fundraise to support all families.

Likewise, there may be adults living with disabilities (cognitive, physical, and/or mental health related) who might love to be part of a synagogue, but they never reach out to find out about membership because the cost is prohibitive if they are living on a fixed income. People with disabilities face unemployment at a much higher rate than nondisabled people, and so affording "extras" like synagogue membership may simply not be an option. By reducing or removing financial barriers, you can create a more inclusive space for everyone.

Program Ideas

A place to begin in any organization is with activities that educate and raise awareness around disability issues. Invite community members with disabilities and their family members to share their experiences, either during services or in a panel discussion. Read books about disability advocacy as a community or schedule a film night and screen a film like *Crip Camp*, which raises awareness about disability rights issues.

Our tradition teaches that we are inherently holy regardless of whether we happen to have a disability. Nearly every Jewish text can be studied and discussed through a lens that emphasizes the Jewish value of seeing every human being as created *b'tzelem Elohim* (created in the Divine image). We can remember together that our greatest prophet, Moses, had a speech disability (Exodus 4:10). There are also *midrashim* (interpretive stories) that depict Moses as someone who struggled to learn Torah.

While these texts may make it seem that the Jewish community has always been accepting and understanding of people with disabilities, in reality, this has not always been the case. In previous generations, when children with disabilities were sent away from their parents to live in institutions, the separation created both shame and loss for the parents and a complete lack of opportunity for the child with a disability to grow up with any sense of belonging to a Jewish community.

Commit to an Ongoing Process

Accessibility requires ongoing attention; as the needs of your community change, your efforts toward inclusion will grow and evolve. Empower and support leaders in your community who can keep the issue of accessibility front and center. For example, during the COVID-19 pandemic, issues of accessibility arose in new ways as people's life circumstances changed dramatically because of shutdowns and quarantines. Many congregations reported greater attendance and participation at live-streamed Shabbat services and educational programming, as compared to in-person services and programs that took place prior to the pandemic. In many cases, these online options created greater accessibility for people living with disabilities who find it challenging to get transportation to and from synagogue and/or for whom lack of access in the building makes it difficult to attend. Many congregational leaders are reflecting on what this experience has taught them about access and are thinking about what a more hybrid community could look like, with both in-person and online options for services, programs, and events, even after the pandemic ends.

The Goal: A Sense of Belonging

For too long, the stigma caused by disability has led to a sense of isolation and loneliness for people with disabilities and their family members. We now know that loneliness is more than an emotional state; it also impacts our health and well-being. Many studies have shown that both teens and adults with disabilities experience significantly higher rates of loneliness and isolation than their nondisabled peers.

Why do any of us join a synagogue? Certainly, it may be because we grew up as part of a synagogue community and doing so feels natural to us. We may want to raise our children with a Jewish education and see them become b'nai mitzvah. We may want to continue our own Jewish education as adults and are seeking cultural enrichment. We may join a synagogue to find emotional or spiritual support during challenging times in our life or when experiencing loss. Some of us may be seeking a spiritual community and join a synagogue to learn and pray.

As Jewish communities, we join together for all of these reasons and many more. *Belonging* plays a critical role in how we learn, experience life cycle rituals, comfort one another, and pray. But for people with disabilities, the barriers that we have discussed in this chapter—from not being able to enter a building to not being able to hear a service, to not receiving the educational supports that one needs, to feeling shunned or stigmatized because of one's disability—have prevented generations of Jewish people from feeling like they belonged in a synagogue or other Jewish communal spaces.

"Synagogue communities have focused attention and resources on how to be more inclusive. We need to turn our thoughts and actions toward why inclusion contributes to the well-being of individuals with disabilities and mental health conditions and to the synagogue community," explains Shelly Christensen, a faith-based disability advocate and the author of *From Longing to Belonging: A Practical Guide to Including People with Disabilities and Mental Health Conditions in Your Faith Community*. She writes, "All people want to belong. Yes, inclusion is a key to belonging, yet that precious sense of belonging that we cherish in our Jewish lives is something that all people want. When we belong, we are valued, respected, included, and we get to contribute our gifts and strengths to benefit others."[5]

In working toward inclusion and accessibility, we want to create communities in which there is space to get to know people of all different backgrounds and abilities, strengths and challenges, as well as to see everyone as belonging and adding value to our Jewish communities. In a world in which people with disabilities have been stigmatized, belittled, isolated, and even rejected, this is a radical action.

A PERSONAL STORY

We cannot assume, given the prejudice and stigma that still exists in our society, that we are raising children with the Jewish value of *kavod* (respect) for all people if we don't actively educate around disability awareness. I am the mother of an 18-year-old son with multiple disabilities (including autism, an intellectual disability, and bipolar disorder), and I can, unfortunately, share many experiences in which people stared, shushed, or shunned my son because, like many people with autism, his body and voice are not always regulated.

My family and I were sitting in a local kosher restaurant eating dinner one night. Across from us was a table with a family with six children of different ages. My son, who was 10 at the time, was really excited to be out to dinner at this restaurant and was bouncing up and down in his chair while we were waiting for his food. His hands were also flapping and clapping a bit. The children at the table across from us stared and giggled at my son. The parents of these children were engrossed in their own conversation, ignoring their children. I was disappointed that they had not educated their children that their behavior was rude, nor were they intervening in this moment. Though they had brought their children to a kosher restaurant, I couldn't help but feel that their meal was far from kosher.

While my son lacks the social awareness to be embarrassed by their staring, my husband, daughter, and I were all impacted by the children's rudeness. Yes, I could have left my table and gone over to the parents to say something, but I was feeling too vulnerable to do so and didn't want to break into tears in front of my daughter. It should not be up to the person with a disability or their family members to correct others' hurtful behavior. As a community, we should take responsibility for becoming more aware, more compassionate, and more welcoming.

Fortunately, our family has been overwhelmingly embraced with compassion and understanding in most Jewish settings, and this painful memory stands out as an exception. But I share it to emphasize how critical it is that whatever role we play in Jewish community, we should take it upon ourselves to become educated about disability inclusion and advocacy and to treat all community members with the Jewish values of kindness and respect. Your warm and welcoming community for people with disabilities becomes a more warm and welcoming community for all members. This important work is something that our Jewish values call us to do so that each and every one of us is regarded as holy and worthy of belonging.

RESOURCES

Websites

Gateways (jgateways.org/Resources) is a Boston-based organization that features many free downloadable resources for Jewish special education.

Inclusion Innovations (InclusionInnovations.com), the website of Shelly Christensen, includes all of the resource guides for JDAIM—Jewish Disability Awareness, Acceptance, Advocacy, and Inclusion Month.

jkidACCESS (jkidACCESS.org) is a virtual space for resources and information for families raising Jewish children with disabilities that includes social stories, videos, and more to make Jewish rituals and holidays accessible.

Matan (MatanKids.org) provides resources and disability inclusion training for Jewish educators.

RespectAbility (RespectAbility.org) is a nonprofit advocacy organization that has created many resources for faith-based organizations.

Whole Community Inclusion (jewishlearningventure.org/what-we-do/whole-community-inclusion) is an initiative of Jewish Learning Venture that features many resources for synagogues working on inclusion including Jewish values-based disability awareness lesson plans.

Books

Christensen, Shelly. *From Longing to Belonging: A Practical Guide to Including People with Disabilities and Mental Health Conditions in Your Faith Community*. N.p.: Inclusion Innovations, 2018.

Heumann, Judith. *Being Heumann: An Unrepentant Memoir of a Disability Rights Activist*. Boston, MA: Beacon Press, 2020.

Wong, Alice, ed. *Disability Visibility: First-Person Stories from the Twenty-First Century.* New York: Vintage Books, 2020.

NOTES

1. "Students with Disabilities," in *Condition of Education*, National Center for Education Statistics, May 2020, https://nces.ed.gov/programs/coe/indicator_cgg.asp.

2. "Data & Statistics on Autism Spectrum Disorder," Centers for Disease Control, September 25, 2020, https://www.cdc.gov/ncbddd/autism/data.html.

3. "CDC: 1 in 4 US Adults Live with a Disability," Centers for Disease Control, August 16, 2018, https://www.cdc.gov/media/releases/2018/p0816-disability.html.

4. Jennifer Laszlo Mizrahi, e-mail to the author, September 27, 2018.

5. Shelly Christensen, e-mail to the author, November 1, 2020.

CHAPTER 5

Millennials and Gen Z

Rebecca Bar

A small group of us were sitting on the beach at the Jersey shore on a warm Saturday afternoon. All in our mid-20s, we had walked the half block from the house we were staying in for Shabbat to the sand to hang out for a few hours. As it was getting a bit later, one member of our group, Mike, still lying face up on his towel, eyes closed, suggested we go back soon to get ready for *havdalah* (the religious ceremony that marks the end of Shabbat). Another friend, Josh, lying half propped up on his elbows, casually asked, "What's *havdalah*?" Mike shot straight up and startled all of us with an accusatory "*What's havdalah?!*" as if Josh had just asked, "What's a bicycle?" or "What's an apple?" As Mike rephrased his accusation to "How do you not know what *havdalah* is?" I tried, rather unsuccessfully, to pick my jaw up off my towel. As a Moishe House resident, I and the other residents were hosting a number of community members for a Shabbat weekend together at the shore with another organization—complete with lively Kabbalat Shabbat services Friday night; a beautiful Shabbat dinner where everyone was wearing white, singing, and enjoying each other's company late into the night; and yes, *havdalah* to close out the previous 25 hours and take us into Saturday night, before we headed home Sunday afternoon. We had all kinds of people in our community, and we liked it that way. In addition to those who were newer to certain Jewish experiences, we had people with robust Jewish backgrounds who were unfortunately less than welcoming and understanding to the broad swath of Jewish community we engaged.

Mike and Josh were both lawyers living in the city of Philadelphia, and both came to Moishe House looking for community, for friends, for companionship, and to further their own Jewish identities and journeys. Josh was only recently discovering more about his Jewish path and was very open to learning and exploring the many facets Judaism has to offer each and every one of us. Josh didn't know what he didn't know. Mike, however, grew up in a Conservative home, was day-school educated, and was very much a product of that system. Mike really only spent time with his Jewish friends, doing Jewish things like going to Shabbat dinners or attending synagogue, following a rather by-the-book Jewish upbringing, all in a very insular community.

Mike knew exactly what he knew and was rather elitist about it. He had been given an amazing education and grew up in a wonderful and giving community that taught him so many things about Judaism, Jewish culture, and Jewish history. But rather than taking this moment as an opportunity to share a beautiful teaching about the tradition and ritual of *havdalah*—how we take so seriously the separation between the holy and the profane, how we mark it with a ceremony that plays to all of our senses and is enhanced by sharing that ceremony in community—Mike made it very clear in that moment that he felt Josh was "less than." How dare he not know about *havdalah*, much less understand the time and preparation it took to put it together?

One of my favorite parts about being a Jewish communal professional working with millennials and Gen Z over the past 14 years has been being able to see in their eyes when something I believe is truly beautiful, meaningful, or extraordinary also appears that way to them. I'm thrilled when they are genuinely excited about learning more, delving deeper, or having a further conversation about their Jewish journey. Josh had that excited curiosity, and I could see it flicker in his eyes in that moment Mike questioned him. I quickly shared what I thought were some of the most compelling parts about *havdalah*, starting with the basics and adding in a few pieces I found particularly moving when I was first learning about it myself. Josh shook off however Mike had made him feel, and I saw that sparkle in his eye return as I was talking about the spices to wake us from our Shabbat stupor and watching our second soul leave our bodies through our fingertips in the light of the triple-braided wick.

In many ways, this interaction between Josh and Mike isn't much different from how many traditional Jewish institutions have also failed a whole segment of young, curious, but less traditionally knowledgable Jews. Josh needed something different from what Mike had been taught, and, as a product of those more traditional Jewish institutions, Mike couldn't meet Josh where he was at, take into account his prior life experiences, or show him a path to integrate "doing Jewish" into his full self. Similarly, instead of creating spaces for curiosity and wonderment, many institutions have become breeding grounds for the further separation of Jews who aren't sure where their place in the Jewish community is, institutions that are often undergirded by hierarchies of Jewish knowledge. Either you're a product of day school, Hebrew school, or another traditional Jewish institution, and therefore are on the inside of the community and know enough to participate, or you fall into the category of the unaffiliated and assumed uninterested. What we find so often with millennials and Gen Zers is that while their knowledge level of Judaism may be low, both their affinity and their capacity for deep knowledge is high. What is more, they're not interested in watered-down content or being talked down to.

The whole interaction at that New Jersey beach lasted maybe five minutes, but it left an indelible impression on me and the way I approach welcoming people and sharing Jewish traditions. Had Josh encountered more people and institutions like Mike, this interaction at the beach could have been the end of his Jewish journey. Fortunately, Josh kept coming back to Moishe House and meeting more people and organizations that put his needs at the center. He is now an active and staple member of the Jewish community. In preparation for this chapter, I asked Josh whether he, too, remembered the incident from that Shabbat afternoon. Sadly, he did; he remembered not being welcomed and, worse, being made to feel stupid for even asking his question. Rather than focusing on sharing a beautiful part of our tradition, welcoming in a new person to experience this piece of our culture, Mike, who was steeped in the world of traditional Jewish institutions, shut out an eager community member and didn't even realize what he was doing.

Many legacy institutions often don't even know when they're not being welcoming. It's not just about one off-putting person, but rather the notion of insider versus outsider that these institutions continue to perpetrate. This outdated thinking hasn't caught up with how millennials and Gen Zers integrate all parts of themselves into how they live their lives. These organizations think they know the answers to what millennial and Gen Z individuals want and need to become full participatory members of the Jewish community. But rather than putting these individuals, the "users," at the center, people in positions of power, often holding titles that include "community engagement" or "director of programming," decide what they think is best and most needed for young adults in their 20s and 30s, often without ever consulting a single person in that demographic.

And just who are these 20- and 30-somethings, the folks who are either millennials or Gen Z? While we don't yet have a definitive distinction between millennials (born between 1981 and 1996) and Gen Z (born between 1997 and the early 2010s), we already see differences in their attitudes around the stability of the world, how they engage with social media and technology, and where they focus their long-term goals. A 2019 report from Moishe House on Gen Z provides some helpful distinctions. Millennials were born into a fairly stable worldview, which was disrupted by the events of 9/11 and the subsequent economic crash in 2008. Gen Zers, however, were the inheritors of this new post-9/11 world. In terms of upbringing, most parents of millennials are baby boomers (born between 1946 and 1964), who appear more lenient in their parenting styles than Gen X (born between 1965 and 1980) parents were to their Gen Z children. As for their social media philosophies, millennials post with much more abandon as new technology continues to be novel for this generation, while digital native Gen Zers are much more careful with their personal brand. Millennials tend to be more focused on the present, yet still idealistic, while Gen Z is more future focused and practical in nature.[1]

What both groups share, though, is that they put themselves at the center of their personal paths and decision-making processes, with their individual experiences paramount. Given this focus on the unique individual, organizations and institutions designing programming for these demographics need new ways to address the particular needs of these generations, because there is no longer one way to "do Judaism."

DESIGNING COMMUNITY FOR MILLENNIALS AND GEN Z

My own work engaging young Jews has been deeply influenced by the principles of design thinking, which focuses on the end user of the product or service and starts with being curious enough to engage the user from the very beginning. Tim Brown, CEO of IDEO, a global design company founded on the principles of design thinking, says, "Design thinking is a human-centered approach to innovation that draws from the [traditional] designer's toolkit to integrate the needs of people, the possibilities of technology, and the requirements for success."[2] For the purposes of this chapter, there are five main stages of the design-thinking process that many organizations and institutions who have successfully welcomed millennial and Gen Z participants have employed. These stages are *empathize, define, ideate, prototype,* and *test.* Each stage in the process is crucial to coming up with solutions that work for the user. Unfortunately, many organizations and institutions skip one or more of these steps and then wonder why they aren't engaging the target demographics they're interested in serving.

The first stage in the process of design thinking is to *empathize.* Researching your users' needs is crucial to this work as it allows you to set aside your assumptions and gain real insight into your users and what they want. Not taking the time to talk directly to the group you are trying to engage is setting yourself up for failure, disappointing not just your organization but also, and more important, your intended user.

Once you've actually spoken to your target demographic and heard what some of their concerns are, you can begin to *define* the problem. Without doing this, you're trying to provide an answer to a question that might not need answering. To be clear, the problem to solve is not the organization's problem—such as "Why don't more people come to our events?" Rather, it's about solving challenges and issues in the lives of the users themselves.

Stages 3, 4, and 5 of the design-thinking process—ideate, prototype, test— all function in a cycle. You begin by coming up with some solutions in *ideation.* Don't focus on the details, just think broadly and widely. This is about generating ideas no matter how farfetched. Next, create a *prototype* of one or two of your leading ideas and *test* them out with some of your users as the intended audience/participants. But don't stop there! The whole idea of design thinking is to continue in this loop of ideation, prototyping, and testing, with user feedback built in, to make sure you are designing solutions relevant to your intended users and their needs. What follows are ways in which several organizations and institutions that serve millennial and Gen Z Jews have succeeded in the design-thinking process by focusing their efforts on one (or more) of these stages while following through with the entire process.

EMPATHIZE: CONNECTIONS AND USER-CENTERED EXPERIENCE

Looking at the 2013 Pew Research Center's *Portrait of Jewish Americans*, we learn that 24 percent of millennials were members of a synagogue and 16 percent were members of another Jewish organization, but the majority of millennials are completely unaffiliated with Jewish organizational life.[3] However, just because they aren't becoming members of Jewish institutions doesn't mean they don't want to spend time with their peers or participate in and even generate Jewish community themselves.

In the world of post-college Jewish engagement, one organization took the time to empathize with its potential users and, ultimately, provided them with a platform to spend time with their peers, participating in—and even creating—Jewish community. Moishe House, founded in 2006 by David Cygielman, began as a way for Jewish friends to spend Jewish time together and invite their individual friend groups to do the same. Cygielman said that his goal was to do something for Jews who were too old for college organizations but, in most cases, didn't yet belong to synagogues.[4] Fourteen years ago, opportunities for Jewish people in their 20s and 30s to connect with each other outside Hillels, synagogues, or Federations were few and far between. People weren't (and still aren't) getting married and having children right after college, further expanding the time between sites of young Jewish engagement like summer camp, youth group, and Hillel and joining a synagogue for the purposes of getting married and/or enrolling a child in religious school. Moishe House provided a way for Jews in their 20s and 30s to connect with one another while building community, often around, but not exclusive to, Jewish culture and ritual.

In the Moishe House model, two to five residents live together in an apartment or house in a given city and host between three and seven events a month for their friends and the broader community in which they live. Moishe House currently has 142 houses in 30 countries around the world. The residents themselves come up with ideas for programming, though Moishe House does offer broad categories as suggestions. By giving the reins to the residents, the Moishe House model puts the user—young adults in their 20s and 30s—at the center of the process. Moishe House is not telling residents how to connect with each other; rather, residents are telling Moishe House how they want to connect, and Moishe House is supporting them through regional guidance, learning opportunities, access to program guides, mentors, and the broad network of residents around the world. While the original idea for Moishe House centered on physical houses as places of community, perhaps leading people to think that Moishe House is "just another" Jewish institution, Moishe House is, at its core, all about *people*: the residents and community members who participate in the programming. You don't need to join or become a member of Moishe House to be part of the community; you just have to show up.

As a result of placing the emphasis squarely on doing and learning, rather than on things like dues or membership, Moishe House residents and participants alike have requested more opportunities to dive deeper into Jewish concepts, holidays, and rituals. Consequently, learning and peer-led retreats that now take place all over the world were created to provide supplemental immersive Jewish learning experiences for millennials and Gen Z that expand upon "one-off" events at Moishe Houses. This expansion of Moishe House programming—from initially just the houses to include learning, retreats, alumni programming, and more—is in direct service to the design-thinking methodology. Keeping the user at the center allowed Moishe House to be open to ideating on the idea of houses to prototype and eventually incorporate these other avenues of engagement.

For all of the complaints and laments from legacy institutions around these two generations not being interested in Judaism, the concept of immersive retreats should stop you in your tracks. In 2019 alone, Moishe House hosted 123 Jewish learning retreats, engaging 2,197 participants around the world. The young people participating in these opportunities were eager to connect with each other by diving deep into a topic they were exploring as part of their Jewish growth.[5] By *listening* to the end user, Moishe House discovered that these generations wanted *more* connection, *more* learning, and *more* exploration, not less. But the participants wanted to do it *their* way, and, paradoxically, it was only by letting these younger generations be leaders and handing over control to them that Moishe House, as a Jewish institution, became a leader itself in the field of engagement, meeting these individuals where they were and helping them further their own paths on their Jewish journey.

INTEGRATION OF THE WHOLE SELF

There was a time, not so many decades ago, when it was safer to separate out your Jewish identity from the rest of who you were. Jews didn't participate in the Sundance Film Festival; they went to their local Jewish film festival. They joined Federations and JCCs because the Union League wouldn't let them in. They supported the Federation's endowment fund because supporting the local food bank didn't necessarily mean their money went to Jewish families. Unfortunately, a lot of Jewish organizations still operate with this separatist mind-set, rather than recognizing all the ways in which people, especially younger folks, see themselves as full participants in the entire world and not just the Jewish world. Moishe House, by contrast, puts the participant front and center, but that's not the only key to creating a welcoming and engaging space. For Moishe House and similar organizations, it's not about finding a time to "do Jewish," but rather infusing Jewishness into all of the things that are already occupying an individual's life. Visit an art museum, but find a Jewish connection. Offer cooking classes, but teach people how to make traditional Jewish cuisine. And this needs to be done not in a kitschy or trite way but with content, substance, and relevance, taking into account the interests of the individual and recognizing that there are many ways to connect that aspect of someone's personality to their Jewish identity.

Moishe House isn't the only Jewish organization that focuses on the integration of the whole self. Challah for Hunger, where I am the current executive director, is an international social justice organization focused on teaching leadership development by inspiring and equipping communities of leaders to take action against college hunger. Challah for Hunger began in 2004 as a way for its founder, Eli Winkelman, to remain close to her Jewish identity *and* make an impact in the world with the proceeds from her challah sales. While that model has expanded considerably since its founding, the pillars of community, philanthropy, and advocacy housed in one single program remain a core component. The organization thrives on leaders being interested in making change in the world using a Jewish custom, baking challah bread, as a means to actualizing the social justice aspects of who they are.

Rather than baking challah in an exclusively Jewish space, with primarily Jewish people, for an exclusively Jewish reason, individuals who participate in Challah for Hunger get to ignite the many sparks of what makes them who they are—the Jewish spark, the interest in activism spark, the social justice spark—with others who may share one or all of those interests as well. It is this integration of self—the ability to be fully who you are *while* participating in Jewish activities—that is critically important to millennials and Gen Z. As Rabbi Lauren Grabelle Herrmann discusses in her chapter on social justice (chapter 9), individuals don't want to hang up their activist hat before walking into a Jewish space. Millennials and Gen Z desire to bring their full selves to the activities they take part in, and Jewish organizations cannot be the exception to that desire. We need to make space for, and cater to, an audience that wants to express their Judaism in myriad ways.

This integration of the whole self does not just apply to individuals; for couples there is a strong desire for connection to other like-minded couples at similar points on their life journeys. Honeymoon Israel, co-founded in 2014 by Michael Wise and Avi Rubel, seeks to provide an immersive Israel experience for couples that serves as a launchpad to localized, personalized community for cohorts of 20 couples at a time. The program sends the couples, two-thirds of whom have one partner identifying as something other than Jewish, on a 10-day, five-star trip to Israel where they are able to explore all aspects of their personalities as individuals *and* as couples. The couples travel with other couples who live in the same city and have similar interests, seeing the sights of Israel, all expertly guided by Israeli tour guides and city-specific Honeymoon Israel staff.

The trip, however, is just the catalyst for these couples. Through the bonds formed during the 10-day trip, couples report coming home and forming micro-communities with many, if not most, of the other couples on their trip. Not only that, but they are then connected to other cohorts from their same city, as well as to a national network of trip participants from all over the country. Hearing from couples about their disappointments in how they were treated in more traditional Jewish communal spaces and listening to what *would* interest them in terms of forming community has enabled Honeymoon Israel to continuously shape not only the trip details but also the Jewish experiences of trip participants once the couples are home again.

PLAYING THE GAME

Moishe House honed in on the idea of integration of self with its original residential model. Instead of asking participants to "be Jewish" only when they went to an activity, Moishe House literally made it part of the residents' day-to-day living. In this sense, participating in a Jewish activity wasn't a means to an end; rather, it was an end in and of itself. This stands in stark contrast to the outdated formula of attending many traditional Jewish events as offered by Federations or synagogues, which saw as its "end" the hope that participants would become members, meet Jewish people, marry a Jewish person, have Jewish babies, and enroll their children in Jewish institutions. Millennials and Gen Z are not content just playing the old-fashioned board game *Life*, following a set path and collecting degrees, jobs, marriages, and children along the way, all while filling the "expectation" of affiliating with traditional Jewish organizations like a Federation or a synagogue. Rather, the idea of being on the game board itself is the excitement—and hopping forward and backward and all around is part of the fun of the game. The reward is not some predetermined end point; it is being able to set your own path, and then prototype, test, ideate, and prototype again, all within an empathetic framework that sees each user as an individual with distinct needs. That's how millennials and Gen Z want to interact with Jewish experiences in 2021; that's what their journey looks like.

This individualized "game play" calls into question the quantitative metrics that are often used to measure the health of Jewish experience or participation from an institutional perspective. Typical metrics tend to be from a top-down, non-design-thinking perspective of success, and it's not working as a means to interpret successful engagement in Jewish life. If it were truly the case that the goals of these traditional institutions and organizations were about creating Jewish experiences in whatever forms they might take, it wouldn't matter how many people affiliated through membership or donated to the annual campaign. We need to find ways to measure Jewish experience from a quantitative *and* qualitative perspective, with opportunities for individualized expression, stories of impact, and network weaving in which participants bring other people into their experience to participate.

MAKING AN IMPACT

For millennials and Gen Z, simply participating in an activity or being part of an organization is not enough. Organizations that are going deeper—innovating on their original programming by utilizing the design-thinking methodology of centering the user and iterating on their prototypes with direct feedback from participants—are seeing more success with Gen Z. And instances when those organizations can pull back the curtain on the process provide Gen Z with much-needed transparency and vulnerability. I have seen that when you involve Gen Z in shared decision making, trust is built, and they become even more invested. They bring their full selves to programming, which also means organizations are then forced to address Gen Z's entire sense of self, including health and wellness. The singular program becomes much more of a vehicle for Gen Z to "improve themselves, their communities, and the world."[6]

And if you think that these changes are only about pleasing the user without any benefit for the organization, think again. Gen Zers will give their time and money as long as they know where their resources are going and it's a cause that matters to them.[7] If people they trust and respect are also giving to that cause or organization, their own desire to give grows.

The Challah for Hunger cohort model exemplifies the focus on Gen Z wanting to "give back." What may have started in one dorm room as a way to feel close to faraway family and support those fighting against genocide in Darfur has evolved into a robust advocacy organization focused on leadership development of Gen Z through chapter-based activities and smaller, more specialized trainings. Cohorts are made up of individuals from campuses nationwide, and members design a campaign specific to their college campus to focus on for the entire year they are in the cohort. In addition to training other student leaders, writing op-eds about hunger policy for local and national publications, and participating in the campus chapter bakes, cohort members go through a design-thinking process to define a problem on their campus to solve during their year, often with the help of administration and other stakeholders. Campaigns have included petitioning to add a clause on food insecurity to class syllabi, working to augment the campus bus route to include a stop in front of the only grocery store in town, and collaborating with administration to raise the funds to open and sustain a campus food pantry.

One Gen Z cohort member at an urban school in Philadelphia used the training he received to establish a food pantry on campus and help raise more than $15,000 to fund it. As he was advocating for the food pantry and continuing to participate in Challah for Hunger, he became increasingly more passionate about the work and impact he was making and still wanted to do more. The following school year, he won a campaign to serve as the school's student body president on a platform of further addressing food insecurity, which ultimately helped establish a meal swipe-donation program where students could donate their unused dining hall meal swipes to those in need. While serving as president, this individual met with state senators to discuss what he was able to do on his university campus through his cohort involvement. The student's successor also ran (and won) on a platform of fighting campus food insecurity. What started as an individual project to help others grew into a project that impacted his entire university, and it is now serving as a model for campuses around the country.

NEXT STEPS

With all of our design-thinking principles in mind—empathizing with the user to create connection, integrating the self as part of the ideation and testing process, making an impact through continued innovation, and returning to the user at the center—what can organizations do to serve this next generation of Jewish communal leaders and participants?

- **Start asking questions**, but, more important, *start listening when millennials and Gen Z tell you what they want (and what they don't want)*. This may mean giving millennials and Gen Z more, if not all, control over programming for their peers at your institution or organization. And if, for whatever reasons, you can't turn over all programming control to them, consider explicitly inviting millennials and Gen Z folks to be represented in rooms where decisions *are* being made, on boards and in working groups, enabling these generations to serve in leadership positions so their voices can be heard and listened to.
- **Make space for people to bring their whole selves, opinions, and identities into the program**. Provide opportunities for millennials and Gen

Z to share feedback from the start about a program—everything from the topic to the location, costs, and presentation style.

- **Redefine your picture of success.** Rather than Jewish communal participation looking like a specified path on a game board going in only one direction, embrace participants hopping all over the board. If your current model of success looks exclusively at statistics such as how many marriages come out of your programming, how many families you can get to enroll into your preschool, or how many millennials and Gen Zers you have in your top-tier donor programming, you are automatically eliminating a large swath of individuals who don't follow a particular (and often heteronormative) pathway. It might not be the ultimate goal for millennials and Gen Z to get married, have kids, or even affiliate with a large Jewish institution; therefore, those markers should not be your only reliable indicators for success. If you are able to keep the user at the center, you always have the opportunity to iterate on what's worked well in the past and give up on what has fallen flat. When the process of design thinking is working well, failure is inevitable. Failing forward—taking what worked and what didn't from one of your prototype attempts and iterating on that to try something new—will be the key to successfully engaging these generations. When you are able to recalibrate your goals to focus on connection, integration of self, and impact, you will see more millennials and Gen Zers participating in your programming.
- **Be authentic and transparent.** In a world that is full of spin, branding, and constant messaging, it's important to connect with people honestly and truthfully. Millennial and Gen Z audiences crave authenticity and don't want to be sold a bill of goods.

The techniques described in this chapter work specifically with the young adult demographic because these approaches appeal to a sense of individualism, address multiple identity categories at once, and break free of the expectations of what traditional models of success have looked like for Jewish institutions. These strategies can and should be applied to welcoming in other age demographics as well, but, in many cases, institutions assume that the way they currently engage their "core audience" must be working, even as that core group shrinks or becomes less engaged. Ideally, institutions will take what they've learned in this chapter and apply these ideas not only to individuals in their 20s and 30s but also (and equally) to longtime members who are typically not in their 20s or 30s as well as to people from a variety of backgrounds discussed elsewhere in this book.

Let's go back now to that same Moishe House in Philadelphia, to a different holiday, the holiday of Sukkot, and look at how each of the themes of serving millennials and Gen Z played out in their Sukkot Shabbat evening. The five residents planned an evening open to their friends and community members

Figure 5.1. Shabbat dinner in the Moishe House Philadelphia home with residents and community members.

that started with Kabbalat Shabbat, in partnership with another local organization, an independent *minyan*, Heymish, that met monthly at Moishe House for several years.[8] After services concluded with everyone crowded on couches, chairs, and stairs, participants made their way outside to the sukkah on the back patio for the blessings for sitting in the sukkah and shaking the *lulav* and *etrog* (ritual objects used during the holiday of Sukkot). Not everyone could fit in the sukkah, as there were more than 50 people in attendance for the evening, so they did the blessings in shifts, and everyone who wanted to had a chance to shake the *lulav*. A resident also made sure to stick close by if someone who expressed interest in the blessing wasn't sure of the words.

Both tradition and innovation were present throughout the evening. Since Sukkot is a harvest holiday, the residents' spin on a traditional Shabbat meal focused on food that was sourced from entirely local ingredients—nothing came from farther than 200 miles away—tying agricultural appreciation for the meal into the evening's activities. There were several speakers in attendance: a staff member of a local urban farm explained which parts of the meal came from them and why they chose to grow what at this particular time of year, a representative of a fledging mobile compost business discussed food waste and how to minimize it, and the head of the Jewish Farm School, located in West Philadelphia, shared the broader context of Sukkot within the Hebrew calendar and how Jewish holidays fit beautifully into an agricultural cycle. Each speaker stayed for the meal and shared their take on the holiday while participants talked and offered their own interpretations of Sukkot, while creating new, shared experiences at the same time. The entire evening was conceived by the residents. Moishe House never told them *how* to celebrate Sukkot, or even that they had to, but in conversations with each other, they were able to integrate pieces of themselves that were important to their identities—sustainability, Jewish text and ritual, delicious food shared with friends—while making meaningful connections with their peers and creating a positive impact on the broader community.

The residents did the work of planning and execution; Moishe House, the institution, was merely there as a resource and backbone if the residents needed direction. This structure holds for many of the organizations that are able to serve millennials and Gen Z in meaningful and user-centered ways. Recognizing the depth and intelligence of these new demographics and giving them the autonomy to design their own programming, institutions that purposefully stay in the background to provide assistance only if necessary exemplify how to give people the needed space to ignite that spark about Judaism that they are after. For these organizations, simply being there to celebrate that spark happening with no further expectations is all the success we need. While it may feel uncomfortable in the beginning, leading from the sidelines—and allowing the intended user to drive the programming—is the most empathetic, and ultimately successful, way to engage millennials and Gen Z.

RESOURCES

Challah for Hunger (challahforhunger.org) builds communities of leaders inspired and equipped to take action against hunger.

Honeymoon Israel (honeymoonisrael.org) provides immersive trips to Israel for locally based cohorts of couples that have at least one Jewish partner, early in their committed relationship, creating communities of couples who are building families with deep and meaningful connections to Jewish life and the Jewish people.

Moishe House (moishehouse.org) provides vibrant Jewish community for young adults by supporting leaders in their 20s as they create meaningful home-based Jewish experiences for themselves and their peers.

The Shift: A Discussion on Welcoming & Engaging Gen Z (moishehouse.org/the-shift/) serves as a springboard for an ongoing conversation to explore how we can best support and empower Gen Z in young adult programming and beyond.

NOTES

1. Jordan Fruchtman and Danya Schults, "The Shift: A Discussion on Welcoming & Engaging Gen Z," Moishe House, April 2019, 3, https://www.moishehouse.org/the-shift/.

2. "Design Thinking Defined," IDEO, https://designthinking.ideo.com/.

3. Pew Research Center, *A Portrait of Jewish Americans* (Washington, DC: Pew Research Center, October 1, 2013), 60, https://www.pewresearch.org/wp-content/uploads/sites/7/2013/10/jewish-american-full-report-for-web.pdf. In the updated 2020 Pew report, we learn that of Jews ages 18–29, 37 percent had someone in their house who was a member of a synagogue, and of Jews ages 30–49, 33 percent of respondents had someone in their house who was a member of a synagogue. Pew Research Center, *Jewish Americans in 2020* (Washington, DC: Pew Research Center, May 11, 2021), 82, https://www.pewforum.org/2021/05/11/jewish-americans-in-2020/.

4. Fred A. Bernstein, "The Four-Bedroom Kibbutz," *New York Times*, February 10, 2010, https://www.nytimes.com/2010/02/11/garden/11moishe.html.

5. *Moishe House 2019 Annual Report*, Moishe House, April 2020, 7, https://www.moishehouse.org/annual-quarterly-reports/.

6. Fruchtman and Schults, "The Shift," 3–4.

7. Alice Berg, "Gen Z: The Next Generation of Donors," Classy, https://www.classy.org/blog/gen-z-next-generation-donors/.

8. See chapter 12 in this volume for more about Heymish.

CHAPTER 6

A New Model for Jewish Institutions

Rabbi Mike Uram

Do you remember Blockbuster Video? It seems like ages ago that we lived in a world where Blockbuster peppered the landscapes of cities and suburbs across the United States. Watching a movie at home was a kind of outing. You had to drive over to the store and then wander around the aisles with your friends, debating which film to rent. It was both fun and infuriating. And, of course, you also had to return the video, and if you didn't do so on time, there were late fees. In the blink of an eye, companies like Netflix and other streaming services ended Blockbuster's dominance and the whole experience of renting videos. I remember occasionally visiting a Blockbuster Video during those last few years before its ultimate decline. It was a strange experience. The store was empty. Popcorn littered the floor. And yet the company kept trying anything it could to attract new business and make inroads with the younger, more tech-savvy consumers. It offered free popcorn, eliminated late charges, and devised new pricing models, but nothing seemed to work. Today it's hard to even imagine having to go out to rent a film rather than just streaming content instantaneously on an ever-growing list of services and platforms.

The story of the fall of Blockbuster Video and the current story of American Jewish organizations have more in common than we might imagine. They both controlled the dominant way that people could access content for their respective communities. They also had a huge physical infrastructure that was key to their business model and that was incredibly expensive to maintain. In the case of Blockbuster, they lost sight of their real mission: to connect people with video content that could enhance their lives. Somewhere along the way, they got stuck on brick and mortar stores, video cassettes, and DVDs—they were more focused on trying to maintain the status quo rather than look for new ways to connect people with video content, something that Netflix figured out quite quickly as it moved from a DVD-by-mail company to an online streaming service. That moment, when large organizations are focused on keeping things the way they've been, is often the moment when a new technology, a new way of organizing, or a new company can come and disrupt everything, frequently leading to the end of the older, slower organization. The organized Jewish community isn't in that moment yet, but it's getting close. As Jewish leaders, we are living through a time of disruption that is changing the whole way that Jews relate to community, identity, and organizations. If we aren't careful, if we are only concerned with trying to "sell" the status quo to the next generation of Jews, we may find ourselves where Blockbuster found itself once streaming services were already up and running. In this way, we are in a moment of tremendous opportunity, a moment of reinvention and reinvigoration, but only if we ask the right questions and have the courage to change and innovate.

JEWISH IDENTITY IS CHANGING

The 19th-century Russian Jewish poet Yehudah Leib Gordon said that a Jew should be "A person on the streets and a Jew at home."[1] There was, and has been for generations, a deep sense that Jewishness could and should only be expressed in spaces that are private and distinctly Jewish—the home, the synagogue, the ghetto, or the *shtetl*. But on the streets, in business, or any kind of mixed setting, it was safer and more tasteful to code switch to fit the norms of the host society where Jews lived. For most of the last 150 years, this dynamic made Jewish organizational affiliation a near given. Jews needed to show up at synagogues, Hillels, summer camps, and community centers because it was only in these public places where they could safely and comfortably enact their Jewishness. In this environment, large, centralized Jewish organizations flourished and, with it, an accepted set of norms around frontal leadership, community boundaries, and credentialed gatekeepers. Moreover, there was a set of implicit assumptions that saw Jewish identity as binary in nature. You were either in the community or outside of it.

The last few decades have witnessed seismic disruptions in the way Americans and American Jews understand identity and how they relate to organized religion, centralized institutions, and hierarchical leadership. These four changes in identity, which I explain below, are threatening to upend many of the norms and assumptions about organized Jewish life in the United States. In order for Judaism to remain relevant in the 21st century, understanding how people associate with organizations today and how such institutions must change their behaviors around engagement is crucial to reinvigorating the American Jewish landscape for the next generation.

Change #1: Jewish Identity Is More Fluid

For most of American Jewish history, there were significant boundaries for full Jewish participation and acceptance in public life.[2] While antisemitism still exists today, most of the structural boundaries that excluded Jews have dissolved over the last 50 years. What this means practically is that Jews don't need to seek out organizational affiliations in order to access special spaces to enact their Judaism, nor do they need to join religious organizations as a signal that they are "normal" just like their Christian neighbors.[3] Jews no longer need to only live in certain neighborhoods, go to certain colleges, or choose a certain set of professions as once was the case.

Another expression of the increasing fluid nature of Jewish identity is the rise of intermarriage. Between 1970 and 2020, the intermarriage rate increased from 18 percent to 72 percent.[4] But before there can be intermarriage, two things must first occur: (1) the bonds of ethnic cohesion among Jews have to become more malleable to allow people to marry out of the group and (2) the majority society has to become more open to marrying the minority group. This means that the boundaries both among Jews and between Jews and the larger world have to become more permeable. Moreover, once intermarriage occurs, then the definitions of who is a Jew, what is the nature of a Jewish family, and what is the essential character of a Jewish community must also all become more expansive and diverse. All of this is to say that while Jewish identity may never have been as fixed as we sometimes imagine it might have been, it is clear that Jewish identity is more fluid today than at any other time in American history.

Change #2: A Growing Distrust of Institutions

Another major factor in the shifting nature of how American Jews relate to Judaism and Jewish organizations really emerges from the same forces that are affecting legacy organizations and businesses throughout American society. According to Pew research, millennials are the least trustful generation in the history of generational research. When asked whether, generally speaking, people can be trusted, only 19 percent of millennials answered in the affirmative, down from 40 percent of members of the Greatest Generation.[5] At the same time, millennials are also the most collaborative and optimistic generation on record.[6] At first it seems hard to square these seemingly contradictory statistics: How can millennials be both distrustful and collaborative at the same time? For millennials, this "lack of trust" really boils down to a lack of confidence in large institutions. Whether we're talking about big business, government, political parties, or religious organizations, the younger you are, the less likely you are to believe that institutions have your best interests at heart or have the capacity to create the nuanced and personalized experiences you really want.[7]

When we think about it, this isn't really that surprising given the life experiences of millennials. Not that long ago, our world was filled with editors and gatekeepers who helped organize and sort the information and media content that we consumed. We once purchased music as curated albums with a specified order to the songs as envisioned and designed by musicians and music producers. Today, due to streaming services and mp3s, we can listen to almost any song we want, in any order we like. The essential point for leaders in the organized Jewish world is not whether this development to be able to curate one's life or interests is good or bad, but simply a recognition that these are important dynamics that are having profound influence on shaping how Americans relate to organizations and Jewish life broadly.

Change #3: A Major Shift from Joiners to Anti-affiliation

The third major trend is a shift of all Americans toward an anti-affiliation preference. In the 1970s, an average American attended 12 meetings a year. By 1999, that number was down 58 percent to just five meetings per year.[8] This trend has only continued to intensify in the 2000s. Americans today are less likely to be interested in joining organizations or to affiliate in many of the ways that are essential to the operating systems of legacy organizations. It doesn't matter whether we are talking about civic associations, the PTA, a non-evangelical church, or any kind of Jewish organization. What this means in practice is that even while younger Jews are genuinely interested in Jewish life, they are not looking to join an organization in order to participate; they are simply looking for a different style of experience.

The data bears out this shift. Only 35 percent of American Jews belong to a synagogue, only 15 percent of American teens attend Jewish summer camp, and only 45 percent of American Jews have visited Israel.[9] Even the time-honored tradition of many American Jews having a bar or bat mitzvah is reduced to just 51 percent of the American Jewish population.[10] However, we would be wrong to assume that these statistics that measure affiliation imply that folks who are choosing not to join today are in any way less Jewish than those who do identify as joiners.

On the contrary, both my personal experience through thousands of coffee conversations with Jewish students and the current research show that a significant percentage of the "unaffiliated" actually have a strong connection to their Jewish identity and positive feelings about Judaism in general. One of the hidden gems in the 2013 Pew study was that 94 percent of American Jews now report having positive or very positive feelings about Judaism.[11] For many younger Jews, being Jewish is an inalienable identity characteristic. Being

Jewish is something you are, not something you need to do.[12] It's about a set of values, smells, and tastes, but it has little to do with what clubs you join or what causes you donate to.

There are other forces pushing young Jews away from affiliation as well. There is a widespread belief that Jewish organizations are too focused on money, power, and politics.[13] Moreover, many of us carry with us a set of negative memories about the times when we did show up in a formal Jewish space and it didn't go well. Anytime a newcomer takes a risk and shows up in the organized Jewish community, there are real fears that they won't know anyone, that they won't be welcomed warmly, and that they will be revealed as Jewishly inauthentic or incompetent in some way.[14] All of these dynamics make it harder for Jewish organizations to reach new people if they are using the same models of programming and outreach that have worked so well in the past but no longer resonate with younger Jews today.

Change #4: A Shift from Macro to Micro

There has been a huge shift in the way Americans like to gather and how they like to interact with community and consumer products. For most of the 20th century, the key to connecting with people was through macro-communities that generated large gatherings and centralized organizations that had mass appeal, large events, and sizable memberships. Today, we are more drawn to micro-communities that are based on smaller, more intimate groups and that create experiences that feel less like mass-produced programs and more like customized and personal gatherings.[15]

A great example of how this shift has occurred in American life can be seen in the changing ways that Americans watch TV shows. In 1952, approximately 70 percent of Americans watched *I Love Lucy* on the same channel, at the same time, with the same commercials. As the decades have passed, "hit shows" have drawn an ever-shrinking share of the market. For example, in 1983, the final episode of *M*A*S*H* drew 45 percent of Americans. In 2004, the final episode of *Friends* only captured 18 percent of Americans, while the final episode of the hit HBO show *Game of Thrones*, with a huge audience base, drew only 3 percent of viewers.

Of course, it is easy to understand this shift. There are more programs to watch, more platforms creating content, and more ways to consume content than ever before. When we read these statistics, we can almost imagine the leaders of the major TV networks sitting in a board meeting or at a corporate retreat lamenting the end of TV as they know it. We can imagine them focusing on charts and tables that show that fewer Americans are watching their networks as they did in the past. This sounds a little bit like the conversations that many Jewish leaders have been having for the past few decades. Fewer young people are showing up at Jewish organizations because of the proliferation of choices. But just like those TV executives were wrong to assume that TV was dying—there are more high-quality shows and more viewers than at any time in history—we are wrong to assume that Judaism is dying just because memberships are shrinking. Judaism is changing, and just like with shows, these changes both threaten the status quo and create powerful new opportunities for new outlets and entryways to emerge.

FOUR RULES FOR ADAPTING IN THIS TIME OF CHANGE

We have inherited a set of Jewish institutions that are designed to serve a community of Jews with relatively fixed ethnic/religious identities, a community that expected to have hierarchical leaders and institutions that set boundaries and made decisions for the larger group, where programmatic offerings and a "client-server" relationship with a Jewish community was enough to sustain both Judaism and the organization's financial health. While the operating system for Jewish life worked so well for decades, today's Jews require something different. While it is beyond the scope of this one chapter to explore the many layers of what this operating system could look like, I want to offer four rules of engagement that I have learned over the years in my own work building Jewish communities and helping Jewish organizations to change. These rules, each of which builds on the next, will help leaders build a bridge between the organizations we have today and the organizations that we will need for the future.

Rule #1: End the Focus on Affiliation

So many of us as Jewish leaders are constantly thinking about ways to engage the next generation of Jews. We are constantly measuring and assessing how many members or participants we have and what we can do to ensure the long-term health of legacy organizations. While this kind of strategic focus is important and certainly a real part of our responsibilities as leaders, it is also part of a larger problem in the organized Jewish community—we are overly focused on thinking about, writing about, and measuring affiliation.

In talking with thousands of students, parents, and alumni over the years through my time as the executive director of the University of Pennsylvania Hillel, a constant theme emerged in my discussions with those Jews who identified as anything other than Orthodox. Many of these individuals expressed to me a sense of guilt around "affiliation." They talked about "not going," "not attending," "not belonging," or "not donating" to Jewish organizations the way they felt they should. All of these smart, successful, and passionate Jews, when they had a chance to talk about their Judaism, started by "confessing" to the rabbi all of the ways they were not living up to what the Jewish community wanted them to do. They had internalized this emphasis on affiliation as if it were one of the 613 *mitzvot* (commandments)! And herein lies one of the secret strengths of the model of engagement of Chabad, an Orthodox Hassidic movement of Judaism. Because of both its lighter institutional infrastructure and its ideology, Chabad Judaism invites you to join a Jewish experience without any expectation of membership or affiliation. It simplifies the relationship and the ask. It's about your Jewish experience more than it is the health and well-being of a preexisting Jewish institution.

One of the most impactful changes that Jewish leaders can make is to find ways to break Jewish organizations from our obsession with affiliation, programs, and attendance numbers. What many Jewish organizations often forget is that their mission is not about the continued survival of their organizations, even though, on a day-to-day basis, there are some very real organizational concerns, such as how many members we have, how many people attend our programs, and how we can raise enough money to keep the organization moving forward. The problem is that when we get stuck in these organizational concerns, we can end up inadvertently making a false equivalence between affiliation and Jewish identity, as well as mistaking what real success looks like. While both things are important, they are not the same, and when we confuse them, we run the risk of hurting not only the long-term health of our organizations but also the long-term success of Jewish life in the United States.

There are two strategies that can help Jewish leaders and organizations break our dependency on affiliation.

Strategy #1: Develop a New Vocabulary

At Penn Hillel, we actually went so far as to say that words like "affiliation," "attendance," "involved," and "program" are considered "dirty" words because each of them describes Jews based on their relationship to the organizations rather than a full expression of the ways people enact Jewish life. Figure 6.1 highlights some of the new and intentional language we adopted in place of those other terms. While some of this may feel like semantics, by consciously retraining us to think about the language we use, I'm encouraging us to refocus on what the *true* missions of our organizations are.

Strategy #2: Invert the Values Pyramid

Most leaders spend a great deal of time thinking strategically about how to sustain the institutions for which they are responsible. Just think about how many meetings we've all been to that focus on institutional needs like program attendances, membership retention, facility management, and policy debates. All of these are important concerns and essential responsibilities

Common Terms	New Vocabulary
Affiliated	Engaged—connotes an active process that is continuous rather than a passive and unchanging status determined by a membership.
Attendance	Active—connotes a measurement of ongoing Jewish activity that goes beyond measures of attendance at formal Jewish programs.
Involved	Connected—connotes dynamic and meaningful connections to other Jews, communities, and forms of Jewish life rather than measuring how much a person avails themselves of the organization.
Program	Initiative—connotes a three-dimensional strategy of how an organization fosters relationships, experiences, and communities that deepen a person's Jewish life rather than a one-off event intended to attract a large audience.

Figure 6.1.

of a board and professional leaders. We see this focus in figure 6.2, which places the needs of the institution at the top of the values pyramid. A focus on the needs of the institution does not imply that the leaders don't care about the loftier mission goals. Rather, it suggests a particular theory of change that assumes that if we can strengthen the organization, then we can build Jewish community, which will in turn positively impact Jewish individuals.[16]

The challenge with this model is that whatever gets placed at the top of the pyramid ends up consuming most of the time, money, and expertise of the

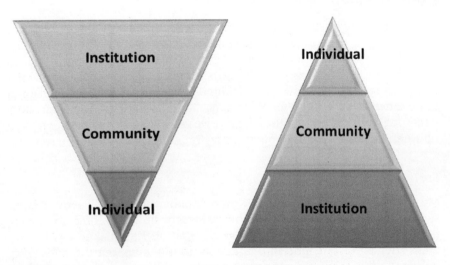

Figure 6.2.

organization, leaving less for the needs of the community or the individual. But what happens if we invert this values pyramid and shift our logic model to be more like the right side of the model? If we can create transformative Jewish experiences for individuals, they will form more powerful Jewish communities that will need and want a strong organization to support Jewish life for everyone. The irony is that the best way to strengthen any organization is to spend less time focused on organizational health and more time focused on fulfilling the mission.

Rule #2: Add the "Seeking Model" to the Existing "Receiving Model"

Most events offered by Jewish organizations today run on something that I call the "receiving model." This includes any event or service planned by leaders that is intended to attract the largest number of people possible. Nearly all of the programs and services offered throughout the year at Hillels, youth groups, synagogues, and Federations fit nicely into this category. Other popular but more specialized programs and organizations like Taglit Birthright Israel and OneTable, as well as independent synagogues or *minyans* like IKAR in Los Angeles and Kehilat Hadar in New York, also work on the receiving model. While many of these organizations offer highly innovative and deeply impactful programming, they rely again and again on a single and well-tested engagement strategy based on trying to attract the largest number of people possible.

To be clear, there is nothing inherently wrong with the receiving model. It is an important way of organizing Jewish life. The only problem with it is when it is overused by the organized Jewish community or when leaders assume that it is the *only* model available. That said, there are a few limitations baked into this model that leaders should be aware of and try to solve for: (1) It is very hard to design a larger event using the receiving model that makes it safe and easy for a newcomer to participate in the event. Trained greeters and good logistics can help, but in large events, group dynamics will take on a life of their own. No leader can control how any person at the event might greet a newcomer. The best we can do is try to create a warm and welcoming culture. (2) Any event that requires someone to sign up or show up means that nearly everyone there must also have a higher degree of Jewish self-direction: the motivation to seek out and attend Jewish events. This means that no matter the content, events that run on the receiving model are less well positioned to reach Jews who are less interested in organized Jewish life or who have fewer tools, such as Jewish knowledge or social connections to the Jewish community, that are required to access these types of events.

One powerful alternative for organizations to deploy is the "seeking model." Rather than trying to attract people to the organization, the seeking model starts by identifying people outside the organization and bringing Jewish life to them wherever they live, work, and play. When I ask groups to think of some examples of the seeking model that exist in organized Jewish life, folks have a harder time coming up with examples. They sometimes suggest "Torah on Tap," where Jewish learning happens in a local bar rather than in a synagogue, or "Guess Who's Coming to Shabbat," where folks can sign up to host or be hosted at smaller Shabbat meals. Yet each of these examples, while they represent creative and high-quality Jewish programs, still operate on the receiving model because they require people to show up or sign up. They still expect you to come to them, even if the event happens to be taking place in someone's house or a bar. Rather, consider these examples instead:

- Hillel programs like the Jewish Renaissance Project (JRP) at Penn Hillel and the Campus Entrepreneurs Initiative (CEI) throughout the Hillel system deploy student interns to reach out directly to their friends to work together to create Jewish events in dorms, fraternities, and off-campus apartments.
- Federation fundraising that seeks out high-net-worth individuals, by going out and actively and strategically building relationships with these individuals and finding ways to connect them to Federation.
- Chabad programs that bring Jewish life out to wherever Jews happen to be: at the mall, the park, or a city thoroughfare. For Chabad, this takes the form of setting up a table in a public space and asking anyone who is passing by, who they think might be Jewish, to perform a Jewish ritual, such as matzah delivery before Passover or offering people a chance to wave a *lulav* (a ritual object used during the holiday of Sukkot).
- The Jewish youth group BBYO uses a recruitment model in which members build lists of Jews in area high schools. Existing members are then assigned to go out and build relationships with their Jewish peers in ways that incrementally create deeper levels of connection and participation in the chapter's events.

Rule #3: Add the "Seder Model" to the "Yom Kippur Model"

Just like we may rely too much on the receiving model, we also rely too much on something I call the "Yom Kippur model," a method of event planning and community organizing that is most common in the organized Jewish community. In this scenario, a ticket, membership, or social connection to people inside the organization is required in order to gain access to the event. We are attracted to a particular service because of the reputation of the rabbi, the cantor, or the congregation itself. The experience is designed and run by a small group of leaders with formal titles who tend to sit at the front of the

	Yom Kippur Model	Seder Model
What gets you in	A ticket, membership, friends who belong	A personal invitation
What attracts you	The reputation of the rabbi, cantor, or congregation; other members who are like you; geographic proximity	The warmth of the invitation and the ability to know who will be there
Type of relationship	Institutional	Personal
Who's in charge	A small group of professionals, clergy, and formal leaders who sit up front	A host who is part of the group who facilitates a participatory conversation and experience
How success is measured	The number of people in attendance; the quality of the service	How the seder felt; how the food tasted; how the conversations flowed; the sense of connection with others
Strengths of the model	Everyone together in one place; mass shared experience; high degree of quality control	Small, intimate, and customizable experiences; lower barriers to entry; uses the power of social networks to engage people in Jewish life

Figure 6.3.

room, and success is normally measured by the number of people who attend and by the quality of the teaching and singing led by the professionals.

Nearly every program and service offered by the organized Jewish community functions on the Yom Kippur model: social programs like a BBQ or a speakers series, a new set of community service projects, a trip to Israel, or an immersive experience like summer camp or a retreat. They are designed and run by professionals, and the goal is to recruit a large number of people to the event. Just like the holiday of Yom Kippur is central to the Jewish calendar, this form of event planning is also essential to the organized Jewish community. It is a cost-effective way of reaching a large number of people with high-quality and meaningful Jewish experiences because it requires very little one-on-one personalized interaction.

However, there are other forms of organizing that could enhance and expand the work we do. The other option is something I call the "seder model." A Passover seder is just as Jewish and meaningful as a Yom Kippur service, and yet it is organized in a totally different way. We don't need a ticket or membership to be part of a seder; we just need a personal invitation. The seder is a more egalitarian model in terms of participation because while the seder is led by the host, there is a much smaller gap between the facilitator and the participants. A seder is also totally customizable, and the host can make changes during the seder based on the needs of who is actually in the room. While seders might lack the power that comes with being in a space with hundreds of people, people do have a shared sense that their smaller seder is part of something much larger, connected to Jews all over the world and throughout time who are partaking in these same traditions. Also, the success of a seder can be measured in a much more nuanced way than simply the size of the gathering. In relating their experience, people tend to talk about how the seder felt, the quality of the food, and the liveliness of the discussion.

What might this look like in practical terms if we could find ways to add opportunities for Jewish life built on the seder model, in addition to those already operating on the Yom Kippur model? (See figure 6.3.) At Penn Hillel, we focused on hosting large Shabbat dinners at Hillel that ran on the Yom Kippur model, but we also tapped dozens of student interns to host their own Shabbat dinners in their dorms, apartments, and fraternities, utilizing the seder model. Jewish Federations could strengthen the annual fundraising campaign that runs on the Yom Kippur model, and only reaches 15–20 percent of possible givers, while also establishing new ways to give that could run on the seder model.[17] For example, Federations could recruit 15-person cohorts made up of new Jewish leaders who have strong social capital among Jews who are not already connected to the Federation. Each leader would be tasked with building smaller giving circles within their social networks. Imagine the impact this could have over the years if each of these 15 ambassadors recruited 10 of their friends to join a new giving circle. In the case of synagogues, in addition to offering adult education classes and large-scale speaker events happening in the building, the synagogue could work with peer engagers who could create new book clubs to discuss the same topics being covered by the programmatic offerings in the building, but now offered in smaller, intimate environments where hosts would invite friends in. Just as the Jewish calendar is richer because it has both Yom Kippur and Passover seders, so, too, could Jewish organizations reach more people in more powerful ways by utilizing both methods.

Rule #4: Make It Relational

The final rule of engagement is to "make it relational." Thanks to the amazing work of Rabbi Ron Wolfson, the phrase "relational Judaism" has become a common concept among Jewish leaders.[18] What I have noticed in my work with various Jewish groups is that while terms like "relational Judaism" and even "engagement" have begun to permeate the strategic thinking of many Jewish leaders, what people mean by such words can end up being vastly different. In many cases, these words are left undefined, creating situations where they can mean everything and nothing all at the same time. That said, relational work is essential for building 21st-century Jewish organizations. For me, "relational Judaism" boils down to a very simple shift in how we talk, think, and act. Much of what establishment Jewish organizations do today can be called institutional Judaism, meaning that the primary focus of organizations is to attract and retain participants and members for the sake of an institution and its mission. It does this through the creation of programs and services that are promoted and provided by a centralized, professionally led organization. Much of this work is very meaningful and important for the community the organization serves.

Relational Judaism offers a contrasting and complementary approach. In this model, the organization's primary focus is to connect people with high-impact Jewish relationships, experiences, and communities in order to inspire people to live more vibrant and connected Jewish lives. The most important tool for an organization practicing relational Judaism is building relationships with a constantly expanding and more diverse network of Jews. In place of traditional forms of marketing, relational Judaism works best when people reach out directly to other people and tap them to become co-creators and active participants in an ever-growing and changing set of small, intimate, and personalized Jewish experiences. In practical terms, this means that when a group of leaders gets together to plan, rather than asking "What should we do?" the first question they ask is "Who should we speak to?"

We've already seen through our exploration of the other rules of engagement examples that work well here, too. Yom Kippur services function as expressions of institutional Judaism. Passover seders are relational. When Jewish professionals build one-to-one relationships, they start to learn of unfulfilled needs in the community. There are lots of people in their social networks who are looking to connect with Judaism in more meaningful ways, but many of them feel insecure about their Jewish knowledge, and they don't love the traditional programmatic offerings currently available. By focusing more on the individuals and less on the organization, some of the traditional barriers to involvement disappear.

Being a leader is often daunting, especially in a time of change. It is no accident that biblical leaders like Moses, Gideon, Jeremiah, and Jonah were all reluctant to accept the leadership positions that God foisted upon them.[19] The challenges that we face today will require outstanding leadership, courage, creativity, and fortitude to overcome. And yet it is not an overstatement to say that change is the greatest constant in the Jewish story. Abraham and Sarah, the parents of the Jewish people, began our story while they were uprooted from home, wandering through the Ancient Near East with only a promise of a Jewish future. The Hebrew slaves, after 400 years of Egyptian slavery, were freed and found ways to re-create their religion and sense of national identity. Imagine the innovation and change required to learn how to be a distinctive people after 400 years of subjugation and acculturation to the Egyptian way of life. More than a dozen times in the Torah, the children of Israel express fear about moving forward and even a desire to return to Egypt. Maimonides, in the *Guide for the Perplexed*, explains that some of the *mitzvot* were designed specifically to help the children of Israel adapt to this new situation and build a bridge between the religion they had seen in Egypt and a new Israelite religion that was yet to emerge.[20] As the period of the Temple in Jerusalem was coming to end some 2,000 years ago, Jewish life innovated, ushering in an age of personal prayer, rabbinic Judaism, and a whole host of new concepts, rituals, and textual repositories that could never have been imagined generations before. At each of these pivotal moments in our story, when Judaism faced a challenge, leaders found ways to create new vessels that could sustain and transform Jewish life in the new world that was emerging. Each time, our tradition didn't just survive; it deepened and became more profound.

We are living in a similar kind of moment today. Each of the challenges we face as leaders is really an opportunity for the renewal and revitalization of Jewish life. We may not know exactly where we are headed, which may make it hard to navigate our way. Yet I am still filled with hope that the essence of Jewish tradition and the Jewish people will emerge stronger through this process. The key to managing this moment successfully is to remain deeply committed to the key elements of Jewish ritual, study, values, and wisdom while remaining nimble and revolutionary in our willingness to experiment with new operating systems for those elements. If we can do that, I feel a deep sense of confidence that the Jewish future will be bright.

RESOURCES

Aron, Isa, Steven M. Cohen, Lawrence A. Hoffman, and Ari Y. Kelman. *Sacred Strategies: Transforming Synagogues from Functional to Visionary*. Lanham, MD: Rowman & Littlefield, 2010.

Chertok, Fern, Theodore Sasson, and Leonard Saxe. *Tourists, Travelers, and Citizens: Jewish Engagement of Young Adults in Four Centers of North American Jewish Life*. Waltham, MA: Maurice and Marilyn Cohen Center for Modern Jewish Studies, Brandeis University, March 2009. https://bir.brandeis.edu/bitstream/handle/10192/23170/com-study032309.com.pdf.

Crutchfield, Leslie R., Heather McLeod Grant, and J. Gregory Dees. *Forces for Good: The Six Practices of High-Impact Nonprofits*. 2nd ed. San Francisco: Jossey-Bass, 2012.

Gladwell, Malcolm. *The Tipping Point: How Little Things Can Make a Big Difference*. Boston: Back Bay Books, 2002.

Hoffman, Lawrence A. *Rethinking Synagogues: A New Vocabulary for Congregational Life*. Woodstock, VT: Jewish Lights, 2006.

Schwartz, Sidney. *Jewish Megatrends: Charting the Course of the American Jewish Future*. Woodstock, VT: Jewish Lights, 2013.

Wolfson, Ron. *Relational Judaism: Using the Power of Relationships to Transform the Jewish Community*. Woodstock, VT: Jewish Lights, 2013.

NOTES

1. The phrase comes from the penultimate verse of Gordon's poem "Hakit zah ami" ("Awake My People!"). Michael Stanislawski, "Yehudah Leib Gordon," *YIVO Encyclopedia of Jews in Eastern Europe*, accessed February 15, 2021, https://yivoencyclopedia .org/article.aspx/Gordon_Yehudah_Leib.

2. Jonathan D. Sarna, *American Judaism: A History* (New Haven, CT: Yale University Press, 2004), 214ff.

3. Isa Aron and Lawrence A. Hoffman, *Becoming a Congregation of Learners: Learning as a Key to Revitalizing Congregational Life* (Woodstock, VT: Jewish Lights, 2000), 16.

4. Pew Research Center, *Jewish Americans in 2020* (Washington, DC: Pew Research Center, May 11, 2021), 39, https://www.pewforum.org/2021/05/11/ jewish-americans-in-2020/.

5. Pew Research Center's Social & Demographic Trends Project, *Millennials in Adulthood* (Washington, DC: Pew Research Center, 2014), 7.

6. Claire Raines and Arleen Arnsparger, *Millennials @ Work: Engaging the New Generation* (Wichita Falls, TX: Claire Raines Associates, 2010).

7. Hartman Group, "Five Things You Need to Know about Millennials," February 26, 2013, https://www.hartman-group.com/newsletters/1643553096/five-things -you-need-to-know-about-millennials.

8. Robert D. Putnam, *Bowling Alone: The Collapse and Revival of American Community* (New York: Simon & Schuster, 2001), 42.

9. Pew Research Center, *Jewish Americans in 2020*, 82; this statistic is taken from a phone interview with the author and Jeremy Fingerman, the CEO of the Foundation of Jewish Camp, 2016; Pew Research Center, *Jewish Americans in 2020*, 138.

10. Theodore Sasson, Leonard Saxe, Fern Chertok, Michelle Shain, Shahar Hecht, and Graham Wright, *Millennial Children of Intermarriage: Touchpoints and Trajectories of Jewish Engagement* (Waltham, MA: Maurice and Marilyn Cohen Center for Modern Jewish Studies, Brandeis University, October 2015), 5.

11. Pew Research Center, *A Portrait of Jewish Americans* (Washington, DC: Pew Research Center, October 1, 2013), 13, https://www.pewresearch.org/wp-content/ uploads/sites/7/2013/10/jewish-american-full-report-for-web.pdf.

12. Steven M. Cohen and Arnold M. Eisen, *The Jew Within: Self, Family, and Community in America* (Bloomington: Indiana University Press, 2000), 184–85.

13. Pew Research Center, "'Nones' on the Rise," October 9, 2012, https://www.pew forum.org/2012/10/09/nones-on-the-rise.

14. Fern Chertok, Theodore Sasson, and Leonard Saxe, *Tourists, Travelers, and Citizens: Jewish Engagement of Young Adults in Four Centers of North American Jewish Life* (Waltham, MA: Maurice and Marilyn Cohen Center for Modern Jewish Studies, Brandeis University, March 2009), 27–28.

15. T. Scott Gross, "Portrait of a Millennial," *Forbes*, June 27, 2012, https://www .forbes.com/sites/prospernow/2012/06/27/portrait-of-a-millennial-2/#139c734cacf9; Chertok, Sasson, and Saxe, *Tourists, Travelers, and Citizens*, 2.

16. A theory of change is a strategic planning tool that helps organizations uncover their assumptions about how they think about change and how they understand the process of how the organization's work eventually leads to a set of intended outcomes.

17. This percentage is based on numbers that Federation leaders in key cities around the country have shared with me. There is a higher percentage of giving in smaller markets like Virginia Beach and a lower rate at big Federations in places like New York, Philadelphia, and Los Angeles.

18. In 2013, Ron Wolfson published *Relational Judaism: Using the Power of Relationships to Transform Jewish Community*, which launched a national conversation among Jewish leaders about how to integrate those techniques into community development work.

19. Moses (Exodus 4:10), Gideon (Judges 6:15), Jeremiah (Jeremiah 1:6), and Jonah (Jonah 1:3).

20. See Moses Maimonides, *The Guide for the Perplexed*, part 3, chapter 32. Moses Maimonides, *The Guide for the Perplexed*, trans. M. Friedlander (New York: Dover, 1956), 322–26.

CHAPTER 7

Arts and Culture Programming

Marilyn Levitch Hassid

Flashback to 2008: The Jewish Book & Arts Fair, or the Festival, as it's known, presented by the J (the Evelyn Rubenstein Jewish Community Center of Houston), is the largest annual Jewish arts and culture event in the City of Houston. The festival features authors, films, music, and theater and is open to the entire Jewish and general community. That year, the chairwoman and I had a plan to engage 20- and 30-somethings who were not regular attendees at the festival. The Jewish Federation of Greater Houston hosted successful events exclusively for people in their 20s and 30s, but they were more like singles meet-ups and always ended with the less-than-subtle punchline: "Donate."

Our goal, by contrast, was to create a no-strings-attached arts and culture experience. We felt young folks should determine their own programming, including author selection, and we wanted an event that would be open to everyone 21 through 35 years old. We identified Erin and Steve, two lifelong Houstonians in the 20s–30s demographic, based on their history with the J, their extensive circle of friends, and the fact that their parents were excellent role models for community leadership. They selected an author best suited for their cohort who was a TV and film personality, and I secured funding so the event would be free. As a bonus, each attendee would receive a copy of the author's book. It was essentially a done deal; all they needed to do was get their selection approved by the Festival Program Committee.

We invited these two new young leaders to be part of the larger Program Committee, which was diverse in every way except age, and whose task was to recommend the authors who would speak at the festival. We hoped that being part of this committee might stimulate Erin and Steve's interest and participation in the festival as a whole. We also thought that working alongside seasoned volunteers would make for a positive mentoring opportunity.

The meeting was a disaster. I watched Erin's and Steve's faces sink as one of the program co-chairs, a well-read, smart man in his 60s, chastised them about the author they had selected, deeming the author "trivial." It got worse as other committee members disagreed with him, but only because they thought the author was a great idea due to his popularity, and they wanted him to speak to a general audience. "Why should just the 20s and 30s get him?" they cried. But making the event open to everyone would negate the uniqueness of an exclusive program created and designed by the very age group we were supposed to be engaging. Erin and Steve were crestfallen.

We should have taken some time to have a serious conversation with the Program Committee co-chairs about what it means to bring on new voices and create an environment of consensus. What everyone seemed to miss was that the real goal in doing all this was not simply to bring a TV personality/author to Houston but to find new ways to create community that would be open and welcoming to all. It is one thing to want young people to get involved, but opening that door needs to be on their terms. Being "welcoming" needs to be more than creating a sliver of space for previously excluded people; rather, it often means rethinking current structures and committees completely so that all voices share space equally.

BRINGING MORE SEATS TO THE TABLE

Maybe it wasn't surprising that this initial attempt at 20s/30s engagement failed. Too often I hear arts and culture colleagues and their lay leaders say, "This is how we've always done it." Entrenched, seasoned leadership often bemoan that they want new voices but do not provide the creative, safe space to hear new ideas. Organizations that are interested in making changes to become more diverse and inclusive need to determine who is missing and why. Who is sitting on the board of directors and other committees, and what are their ages, backgrounds, affiliations, and interests? Does the organization have standing committees that broaden opinions, or are all decisions made by staff and maybe a handful of volunteers? Who is attending existing programs, and, most important, who is not? Only by asking and answering these questions is the organization ready for next steps.

Since 1973, the J's Jewish Book & Arts Fair has had a transition plan for leadership. Along with the executive director and board president, each chairperson identified a vice chair to work with, who would take over leadership the following year. While this leadership model worked well, we also struggled in finding the "right" people to take over. Like many organizations, Jewish and not, we were not unique in that we often had older individuals in charge, many of whom were resistant to bringing younger folks on board. As time went on, though, the lay leadership themselves realized the leadership transitions weren't following the most egalitarian of models and needed to include more diversity among the potential next generation of leaders. As a result, they restructured how author selection would take place, creating a focus group of mixed ages, backgrounds, and interests. This group focused on trends and areas of interest to their diverse peer groups—and thereby helped decentralize the decision-making process. Approaching programming this way expanded offerings that proved more interesting to a broader range of people.

Subsequent leaders pushed this decentralized model even further. New leaders created multiple, small peer-led planning groups to determine content and implement their ideas. For example, a group interested in parenting selected an author they thought would best speak to their fellow parents, while a group of 40- and 50-year-olds selected programs of interest to them. This removed the possibility of Program Committee members telling the special interest groups what they, the Program Committee members, thought was best. Furthermore, this model greatly expanded the marketing reach of these programs. Rather than relying on traditional marketing and PR, such as the local Jewish paper and the city's daily newspaper, we learned that the best way to attract new audiences was to have the special interest groups reach their friends and entice them to attend our events. This friends model of outreach served as a sort of *hechsher* (kosher certification)—that is, approval from someone they knew who believed a program was worth attending. This personal tactic to recruiting participants was a more welcoming and individualized invitation that, according to the special interest group leadership, would have far greater success than circulating general marketing messages of "You belong here," "We want you here," or "We know you'll want to attend this event." Circulating press from unknown individuals that lacked any personal touch would doom the program to failure from the outset. Instead, these leaders targeted their friends and friends of friends using their own preferred tools: social media, one-on-one calls, texts, e-mails, and even conversations in carpool lines or at other events. They also created on-site social events paired with the author talks and recruited individuals to gather friends at pre-event private gatherings in homes and local restaurants.

While there is no one way to structure leadership, diversifying committees and restructuring decision making in a way so that multiple people can contribute leads to fresh thinking and innovative programming that speaks directly to the diverse audiences they are trying to engage.

PARTNERSHIPS AND COLLABORATIONS

Why would any organization that is aiming to make a unique name for itself be interested in investing energy in creating partnerships? The answer is simple: going it alone limits reach and minimizes stature. Rejecting the idea that partnerships dilute brand, thoughtful strategic partnerships expand who an organization might engage and demonstrate that it is a player in the greater world in which it resides. Partnerships can be created within Jewish circles or branch out into the broader community. Any synagogue or organization that reaches out to another institution, seeking ways to work together, also sends an important message that it is not an island unto itself. Best of all, partnerships offer entry points to individuals who may have never walked through the doors of an organization in the first place.

Colleagues from other Jewish organizations around the country frequently ask me this question: What makes Houston different in that synagogues and organizations don't book major programs against each other or create similar and competing programs? I tell them: We like each other and work together. There exists a community culture that breeds cooperation and collaboration. This is true both within the Jewish community and between the Jewish community and larger community. It is reflected in programming from arts and culture to social justice to interfaith dialogue. Jewish communal organizations share a community calendar and organizations do their best to avoid conflicting programming. This offers an opportunity to maximize attendance as community members are comfortable entering each other's spaces.

Sadly, other communities do not enjoy this collaborative spirit. "It's all about *our* brand!" goes the battle cry. I realize every Jewish communal organization is vying for participation and survival, drawing from a finite number of individuals within a given community. In 2016, the Jewish Federation of Greater Houston conducted a population study of the Greater Houston Jewish community, collecting lots of demographic facts and figures for the first time since 1986 when the Jewish population was listed at 33,600 individuals. The study clocked the Jewish population at 51,000. What stands out is that 83 percent (42,330) of those surveyed said, "I have a strong sense of belonging to the Jewish people," but only 54 percent (27,540) were associated with membership at a synagogue, the J, or other Jewish organizations. The numbers are revealing: More than three-quarters of our community members feel they "belong to the Jewish people," but just a little more than half actually maintain some kind of membership. More than that, 17 percent (8,600) of Houston Jews seemingly have no connection or identity to the Jewish community at all.[1] These numbers tell me that our organizations do not need to worry about stepping on each other's toes as there are still many people out there who are not engaged at all. And because "a rising tide lifts all boats," even if an individual does switch allegiances within the Jewish community, we should be happy they belong somewhere. When Jewish communal organizations create program partnerships, they can increase participation, diversify audiences, maximize feelings of belonging, and strengthen community connections. When programming is presented collaboratively, it is possible that those Jews who do not maintain memberships anywhere may very well feel more comfortable attending an event that is not firmly identified with a single group or institution.

Figure 7.1. Israel Parade, Houston, Texas, 2008. *Source:* Mark Katz Photography.

In Houston, the J and the Jewish Federation served as the community's co-producers of Houston's annual Yom Ha'Atzmaut/Israel Independence Day community celebration. I had seen the Celebrate Israel Parade in New York City and thought we could do that in Houston, albeit not nearly as large. The idea that so many different synagogues, schools, and organizations could parade publicly together was exciting. I pitched the idea to my executive director and the Jewish Federation CEO as a unique way to celebrate Israel's 60th anniversary. I envisioned a full-out, collaborative community celebration that hosted a parade plus additional events over the course of three weeks involving all organizations. It would take significant dollars, but the Jewish Federation CEO was on board to raise the money, and we had 18 months to plan. He saw the potential for building community spirit and deepening Houston's connection with Israel. We called on every synagogue, organization, and school to recruit one or two representatives to come to the table to create what that year's Israel@60 would look like, and, with great energy, they did.

By bringing together such a large cross-section of the community to discuss potential programming, three weeks expanded to a full year of events. In the first announcement of this community-wide undertaking, the chairs of the Program Committee remarked, "Every Jewish organization and individual in Houston can have a role in this exciting benchmark of Israel's history." Lectures and scholar-in-residence programs were presented by various synagogues and organizations. The Jewish Federation's Yom Limmud Day of Learning was devoted to celebrating the diversity and unity of the Jewish people and the 60th anniversary of the State of Israel. A large Conservative synagogue hosted more than 1,000 people for a Cantors' Concert that featured *all* Houston cantors singing the best of the Hassidic Music Festivals. An Orthodox synagogue continued its tradition of hosting an Israel-themed *mincha* (afternoon service) and *maariv* (evening service) followed by a festive Israeli-style meal. The Idan Raichel Project, an Israeli world music ensemble that featured Ethiopian voices and songs in Hebrew and Amharic, appeared at a downtown hall populated on a regular basis by music enthusiasts. Houston's Israel Day Parade took place on a Sunday, and 3,000 people participated or attended, including all religious schools and their families. Houston's Israel@60 celebration had dramatically increased in scope, production, and participation due to the collaborative spirit built on shared goals and enthusiasm to embrace a variety of ideas brought to that initial meeting.

GOING BEYOND THE JEWISH COMMUNITY

Partnerships don't have to happen just within the Jewish community. Arts and culture partnerships with organizations outside the Jewish community create different opportunities for diversification and inclusion. These partnerships might (1) find "unengaged Jews," those who, as the Houston demographic study indicated, feel they "belong" but don't maintain a formal relationship with any organization; (2) welcome those who do not identify as Jewish; (3) increase the reach for all organizations involved; and (4) raise the profile of the Jewish organization, thereby taking us out of our proverbial *shtetl*. Depending on the program, it might also create a new experience for Jews who limit their participation to specific types of events.

The J's Dance Month at the Kaplan Theater began in 1980 presenting performances, master classes, and lecture/demonstrations that featured Houston-based, national, and international choreographers and ensembles. No organization in Houston at the time was presenting emerging dance companies. A few members of the J who were dance enthusiasts saw this as an opportunity to fill an artistic void as well as gain stature in the general arts community. One of those members was the wife of the senior rabbi at a major synagogue who had her own dance company and welcomed the opportunity to showcase her work. Another reason that launching Dance Month made sense was that the J had a vibrant adult dance class program and its students wanted the opportunity to perform publicly.

When Dance Month was first created, audiences were solely from the general dance community. Members of the J and general Jewish community, including our own arts and culture donors, rarely attended. They viewed it as an "outsider program," not really a JCC program. Even when presenting big names in the dance world like Ohad Naharin, the Jewish community was just not responding. We needed to change the perception of the program in a big and accessible way—we needed to take a risk.

Naomi Goldberg, a Los Angeles–based choreographer, had collaborated with the world-famous music ensemble the Klezmatics for KlezDance, a community-based dance performance. For this project, Naomi had worked with various adult and student ethnic dance troupes, choreographing their traditional dances to klezmer music. Bringing Naomi and her project to Houston meant the J could more meaningfully connect with some of Houston's ethnic dance ensembles who were already involved with Dance Month and create an opportunity for them to learn about a Jewish music tradition. Plus, with the klezmer theme, members of our Jewish community who had never attended a dance performance before might finally attend. In 1998, Naomi spent two weeks in Houston working with Irish, Mexican folkloric, Indian, and African dance troupes, setting klezmer music to their traditional dance movements. When her own company arrived, they put together a seamless concert of culturally specific dances, traditional costumes, and modern dance. The concert culminated in a grand finale where all the dancers formed a moving line that wove across the stage to one of the most famous Klezmatics songs, "Shnirele Pearle" ("String of Pearls"), a hopeful song that speaks to the coming of the Messiah. This sold-out performance was the most diverse audience ever to attend a Dance Month event. And for the first time, Jewish attendees made up 60 percent of the house. From that year forward, Dance Month welcomed more and more members of the Jewish community to many concerts. The success of KlezDance inspired the committee to take risks each year presenting other Jewish and Israeli ensembles while still offering the modern, tap, and ballet performances the larger dance community loved.

The arts are inherently collaborative in nature. Partnerships and collaborations create more programming opportunities; give rise to creative thinking; generate greater exposure through larger, diversified audiences; and can create sustainable economic models through shared expenses. Organizations that allow themselves to be pigeonholed, stuck in their own world, limit their capacity for growth. Reaching out to create partnerships, to collaborate on the production or presentation of a mutually meaningful and advantageous program, is by nature being warm and welcoming.

BAD JEWS: RISKS AND REWARDS

In my time as the assistant executive director of the J whose portfolio was primarily arts and culture, I was involved in many partnerships with non-Jewish community arts organizations, but one that stands out was 10 years in the making. The details are relevant because they involve not only organizational collaboration but also personal relationships between the professionals involved in the partnership, both of which are key to this model of programming. When Kenn McLaughlin, the new artistic director for Stages, a professional theater company, arrived in Houston in 2005 from the Great Lakes Theater Festival in Cleveland, Ohio, he called to meet with me and shared that he wanted us to work together one day. Flash forward to 2015: Stages, the J, and Black Lab Theater, an alternative, start-up theater company, created a partnership to stage Joshua Harmon's off-Broadway hit play, *Bad Jews*. Harmon's work is a dark comedy about a beloved grandfather who dies, leaving behind a precious piece of religious jewelry that he succeeded in hiding during the Holocaust. Three self-absorbed cousins fight over this heirloom with battle lines drawn based on their personal observance of Judaism, level of assimilation, and even romantic interests.

A conscious decision was made to stage the show at the J's facility. Kenn wanted to grow Stages' audience beyond its base, and the J's theater offered a larger stage and more seating. Black Lab, by contrast, was still emerging and needed all the exposure it could muster. The J wanted to grow and diversify its audiences, and partnering with two very different but recognized professional theaters offered the J theatrical "street cred." In addition, that year, the J was in the process of relaunching a theater season that had been dormant for 20 years, and this project was a real boon to reestablishing our program.

Each organization was able to further its own goals through the partnership, and each organization's strengths and resources helped pull the project together. Jordan Jaffee, who grew up at the J, was the founder of Black Lab and would direct Harmon's play. Stages' staff provided artistic, technical, and box office support. In addition to the theater itself, the J provided maintenance staff as well as technical and front-of-house support. Income, after expenses, was shared. Mailing lists were combined to publicize the show, and we agreed that each organization could use the actual attendee lists to publicize future theater events. Audiences were diverse in age, gender, and religion. Black Lab attracted a younger, hipper crowd, while Stages, like the J, attracted a more traditionally older theatergoing audience, but one that also drew from the LGBTQ community.

Kenn, Jordan, and I made it a point to be present at the performances to welcome attendees. This not only added a personal touch to patrons' experiences but also granted us the opportunity to learn more about who they were and what inspired them to attend this event. One night, a couple who exercised daily in the J's fitness center walked in. In all my years, I had never seen them in our theater for anything. When I asked what brought them there, they told me, "We go to *all* Stages events." After this initial experience, the couple attended other arts and culture events at the J.

Presenting *Bad Jews* came from a meaningful partnership, but it wasn't without risk. Programming without taking risks leave seasons stale; however, organizations that are willing to take calculated gambles, whatever they may be, need to be prepared for failures, challenges, and sometimes even loss of donors. Successfully taking risks involves (1) garnering buy-in from boards, committees, supporters, and partners; (2) creating strategic scaffolding for potentially controversial programs, in which the organization constructs a framework of information and reasoning to explain why the event is being presented; and (3) adding learning opportunities when appropriate. When those steps are taken, a potentially dicey program, even one of merit, can be effectively presented and risks can be mitigated.

For me, an arts and culture programming risk is presenting something that has never been done before and that has the potential to be misunderstood or be perceived as offensive by some members of the community. Presenting *Bad Jews* offered up just such dangers. One day, a woman stopped me in our lobby after the initial publicity for the show went out and asked why we were doing a play that would show how terrible Jews are. This was an important moment, but rather than giving a quick, dismissive answer, I took the time to have a real, personal conversation that included listening to her concerns. It was an opportunity to engage with a person I did not know. I explained the play to the patron, and I even offered her two free tickets so she could see it for herself. Creating open and inclusive spaces takes time and effort and should be invested in, even if that investment of time only affects a single person.

Our theater committee also acknowledged the need to create a framework for explaining the play to the community. Both Stages and Black Lab understood our concerns and supported our plan. Our theater committee spent an entire meeting discussing how we would buttress the production by pre-empting confusion and criticism. I had learned the concept of "scaffolding" and being proactive about potentially controversial events when the Houston Contemporary Arts Museum (CAM) scheduled a showing of a photograph that had garnered virulent universal criticism.[2] CAM staff came to the J to meet with me and with other clergy and staff leaders in the community to let us know they were exhibiting this art, in what context, and why. The respect CAM showed, particularly for the non-arts community, was a lesson learned. To have not taken that time and energy, to have not shown that kind of sensitivity and respect, would have not only exhibited a great deal of hubris on their part but also demonstrated a disregard for the sensitivities of some members of the community. That to me was a real illustration of what it means to be a welcoming voice—showing interest, care, and concern for others, especially around difficult material.

Using that experience as a model, we decided to reach out to all rabbis and Jewish organizational presidents first in writing and then with follow-up calls to educate them about the play prior to any publicity being released. Each committee member selected who they would communicate with, making it a very personal approach. Additionally, we organized a series of post-performance talkbacks with rabbis, as well as the play's director and the actors, so audience members would have an opportunity to wrestle with the tricky themes about Jewish identity that the play explores. In the end, all this hard work paid off: *Bad Jews* played to sold-out performances.

INVESTING IN THE FUTURE

Let's return to 2008 and the book selection meeting that didn't go so well. The author whom Erin and Steve, our 20s/30s representatives, had selected for the festival was Evan Handler, who had gained fame as Harry on the TV show *Sex and the City*. Handler's book, *It's Only Temporary: The Good News and the Bad News of Being Alive*, was a witty (yet deep) memoir about his battle with cancer and other personal challenges. It also met the Book Festival's criteria of presenting Jewish authors or Jewish topics. After the meeting, we sat down with our new young leaders to hear their frustrations and recommendations for the future. Despite their initial disappointment, I ended up negotiating a compromise with them and the committee: there would be a private event for 20s and 30s participants and a second, separate program for a general audience. Lucky for us, Erin and Steve stayed on, created a new series called *Inside the Author's Studio*, recruited friends to volunteer with them, and remained active for many years until we transitioned to new leaders who they recruited from the active participants.

Our initial intentions had been in the right place, but we didn't think through the details, including potential stumbling blocks, in welcoming and activating new leaders to create an innovative program designed for their cohort. We were committed to their program idea and were dedicated to see it come to fruition. It took time to get this right, but the investment paid off.

Inside the Author's Studio continued for years, providing exclusive book and author programs for 20s and 30s patrons on the J campus. Each time, participants gathered for a pre-talk reception in the pop-up bookstore. "Closed for a private event" signs were placed on the auditorium doors. Participants received a book upon arrival, and staff "bouncers" were at the doors to politely control access. After the author presentation, attendees regathered in the bookstore to meet the author and get their books signed. The exclusivity of the event was clearly stated in all publicity, and only a handful of people who were not eligible due to age attempted to attend, telling us it was discriminatory against older people. While this move might seem counterproductive and counterintuitive to all I have discussed about how to positively welcome in participants, sometimes we need to keep others out precisely to create a more welcoming environment. In her book *The Art of the Gathering*, author Priya Parker explains that a good gathering is not afraid to leave people out. She writes, "Isn't exclusion however thoughtful or intentional, the enemy of diversity? It is not."[3] If the goal is to create spaces that are more welcoming to young people, then sometimes dedicated, exclusionary space needs to be made for such purposes.

Bringing in new voices, including potential future leaders, means rolling off those who, as wonderful as they are, have served their time in an effort to make way for the future. I did this succession work many times during my years at the J, and it can be a painful conversation for the staff person and the volunteer if not handled well. This process takes time and needs to be an in-person, one-on-one conversation to explain the goals of the organization and the reasoning for making these changes. When these delicate discussions are handled with care and respect, the seasoned folks will often appreciate and embrace what the organization is trying to achieve. In fact, they become part of the purpose-driven plan of action, feeling invited into a process to ensure their many years of hard work have laid the groundwork for the continuation of everything in which they invested their time and energy.

Through arts and culture programming, I have shared techniques we used to create a more inclusive organization. The tactics I described here can create a framework for creating a diverse and welcoming space in any organization no matter what type of programming it presents or the position it occupies in the communal life of a community. Putting into practice opportunities for open, honest, and respectful dialogue, bringing new voices to the table, and nurturing feelings of ownership and belonging from diverse constituencies will make an organization stronger. Creating partnerships and collaborations both within and outside an organization will widen an organization's reach and impact. The biggest challenge is the willingness to take risks, but with perseverance, patience, and drive, new ideas that seem scary might turn into your biggest success yet.

RESOURCES

Brown, Brené. *Dare to Lead: Brave Work. Tough Conversations. Whole Hearts.* New York: Random House, 2018.

Gladwell, Malcolm. *Talking to Strangers: What We Should Know about the People We Don't Know.* New York: Little, Brown, 2019.

Harlow, Bob. *Taking Out the Guesswork: A Guide to Using Research to Build Arts Audiences.* Wallace Studies in Building Arts Audiences. New York: Bob Harlow Research and Consulting, 2015. https://www.wallacefoundation.org/knowledge-center/Documents/Taking-Out-the-Guesswork.pdf.

Parker, Priya. *The Art of Gathering: How We Meet and Why It Matters.* New York: Riverhead Books, 2018.

NOTES

1. Ira M. Sheskin, *The 2016 Jewish Federation of Greater Houston Population Study: A Portrait of the Houston Jewish Community*, Jewish Federation of Greater Houston, January 2017, 6-25, 7-2, https://www.houstonjewish.org/wp-content/uploads/2020/03/Houston20Main20Report20Volume20.pdf.

2. The artwork that CAM brought to Houston was *Piss Christ* (1987) by Andres Serrano.

3. Priya Parker, *The Art of Gathering: How We Meet and Why It Matters* (New York: Riverhead Books, 2018), 45.

CHAPTER 8

Music

Rabbi Josh Warshawsky

To say that I was lost would have been an understatement. I wandered through the narrow alleys and winding streets of Jerusalem in search of the Belz Yeshiva, the school of the large Hassidic dynasty from Ukraine, which was famous for its music. I was told that their *tischen* (Yiddish for "table")—Friday night gatherings filled with music, Torah learning, and food—were beyond compare. I finally arrived at a building that could only be described as a full-scale model of what the Temple would have looked like, and I tried to find a way in. I followed the music down into the basement into a room larger than a football stadium with a massive table in the middle surrounded by bleachers. Hundreds of *Hassidim* mingled all around the hall. It was 11:30 p.m., and I thought I had missed it. But suddenly the *rebbe*—their spiritual leader—entered, and a mad rush up the bleachers ensued. There were more than 1,000 men crowded into the room, all wearing the exact same black robes. Even in my Shabbat white shirt and black pants, I very clearly stuck out as an outsider. But then it hit me. At first barely a whisper, then suddenly it was everywhere: a haunting melody I had never heard before, sung by 1,000 voices in unison. As the *rebbe* took his seat at the table, I found myself being carried away by the melody. I listened as the melody transitioned from section to section, each more complicated than the last, before cycling back on itself to the beginning. And though I had never heard this tune before, I found myself being carried away and began to sing along. We were all singing just the melody line, but I could hear phantom harmonies reverberating around the room, and the sound felt like it had weight, hovering above and around us and lifting us up along with the notes.

Six months later and on the other side of the world, I found myself at Hava Nashira, a song-leading conference founded 40 years ago by prominent singer/songwriter Debbie Friedman, Cantor Jeff Klepper, and others, put on by the Reform movement every spring at a Jewish summer camp in

Oconomowoc, Wisconsin. The five-day conference, which featured an open mic event that tended to last the whole night given the sheer number of people who signed up for four-minute slots to perform, was nearing its end. It was close to 3:00 a.m., and the number of people in the room was dwindling when I asked the emcee how much longer until my turn. It turned out I was the very last slot. By 3:30 a.m., my turn had arrived, and I realized that, being last, with no one waiting to perform after me, I did not have to abide by the rules of the open mic, including sticking to the four-minute time limit. I made my way to the center of the room, turned my chair around to face the row behind me, and asked all those around me to do the same, forming concentric circles in the center of the room. I shared the meaning of the piece I was about to sing from Psalm 59, how the words teach us the power of our voices coming together, and what it feels like to find your own voice and sing out. We sang the melody, lifting up as the refrain repeats the words, "Uzi eilecha azamerah" ("My own strength I will sing out"). There were only 30 people in the room when we began to play, but suddenly, as we repeated the phrase over and over, people appeared as if from thin air. I looked around and the room was full, and as voices and harmonies came together, I again felt the sounds become tangible, filling up every corner of the room.

CAN MUSIC BE WARM AND WELCOMING?

Communal singing is a powerful tool at our disposal in the quest for meaning. Singing together allows us to be a part of something greater than ourselves, our voices blending together to form something beautiful that no single person could create on their own. You feel this power at a concert, standing shoulder to shoulder with hundreds of people you have never met, belting out the words to your favorite songs along with the band. Music and the experience of communal singing can turn strangers into family. In Jerusalem at the Belz Yeshiva, I was a total outsider feeling very lost and out of place, but suddenly the music and the way it was built by the insiders that filled the space pulled me along, so much so that I forgot I was on the outside. And in Oconomowoc, the way I set up the space and set intention around the meaning of the melody and words allowed the group, who might otherwise have been immediately turned off by the complicated Hebrew and unfamiliar tune, to let go of their feelings of discomfort and allow themselves to be pulled along with the melody. The music we use when we gather together to pray can help create and foster a warm and welcoming space.

I have spent much of the last six years traveling to synagogues, schools, and communities across North America to explore ideas of prayer and music, helping to build musical intentionality into our prayer gathering spaces. It has been fascinating to experience communal gathering in Jewish communities like

Omaha, Nebraska, as well as in Chicago and Los Angeles. Across the board, three constants have become clear: (1) people of all ages are seeking community and gathering opportunities, (2) synagogues and Jewish organizations are trying everything they can to bring people into their institutions, and (3) when people and institutions meet, music is usually essential to those gatherings.

In organized Jewish settings, we encounter music most frequently in prayer. But for many, prayer has become mundane, rote, and meaningless, or perhaps it was first encountered that way and never changed. Prayer can be complicated and hard. When we pray, we are trying to accomplish varied and conflicting goals at the same time. Prayer connects us to God and to the community around us. Prayer allows us to look inward into ourselves and outward at the world as a whole. Prayer is meant to center us and guide us through all we may encounter that day. Prayer helps us better express what we are feeling in the moment. Prayer is a moment of quiet gratitude, a moment for requests, a moment of joyful noise.

It seems almost impossible for prayer to fulfill all of these aims at the same time, so we must think strategically and practically about how to create a space for prayer that is intentionally directed for each individual person and still engaging and meaningful for the broadest subset of our community. Every generation of Jews has attempted to solve this problem, and in every generation, prayer has been molded and changed in order to incorporate the practices and rituals of Jews in every time period and all over the world. Today, so many people are searching for meaning and spirituality in their lives, but for some, the teachings, practices, and rituals of Judaism still seem foreign and out of touch. Many Jewish seekers have turned to Buddhism, Yogi teachings, and even the "religion" of SoulCycle to find spaces where they feel connected and included. Yet Judaism can be such a beautiful place for many seekers to come home to if only we could effectively communicate and share its beauty. I believe music is the way to do that. What follows is an attempt to bring forth some of the questions and solutions that arise for me when considering how we create an inclusive community through music.

How Can Prayer Be Meaningful and Accessible If It Is All in Hebrew?

Hebrew, the eternal language of the Jewish people, is an increasingly foreign language to most Jews. It has tragically become one of the biggest impediments to people feeling welcome and at home in traditional Jewish spaces. According to the 2013 Pew study, only half of Jews (52 percent) said they know the Hebrew alphabet, and far fewer (13 percent of Jews overall) said they understand most or all of the words when they read Hebrew.[1] When many of these people walk into a Jewish prayer space and hear Hebrew, they feel immediately out of place and, by no fault of their own, erect a wall between themselves and the communal prayer experience happening before them.

Prayer leaders, then, have the responsibility to create prayer experiences that are meaningful and fulfilling with or without prior knowledge of the Hebrew language, to create opportunities to interact with the prayers in modes beyond specific Hebrew words, and, if participants want it, to provide the educational access to learn the prayers in their original language. In preparing for and thinking about the people assembled for our services or other musical or prayer experiences, leaders may provide resources to make the Hebrew more accessible, such as line-by-line transliteration and translation. Leaders can also pause during services to provide intentions before specific prayers so that if the words themselves are unfamiliar or not directly accessible, the *kavanah* (the intention) may reach everyone who is gathered together to pray.

Fixed prayers in Hebrew have the potential to unite Jews with their past and unify them no matter where they live. However, over and over again in the Talmud, the main body of Jewish law, the rabbis return to the idea that prayer is empty unless it comes with intention and from the depths of the heart. Therefore, to be truly meaningful, prayers need to be understood and should reflect that person's particular need at a given time. The Talmud says, "Recite the Shema in any language you understand."[2] Perhaps that means we should recite and sing prayers in other languages, and give pray-ers permission to engage with the prayers on their own terms. But perhaps we don't need word or spoken language at all; we can use the language of music, a universally understood language. Judaism has a long and rich history of *niggunim* (wordless melodies). Rabbi Abraham Joshua Heschel wrote, "The wave of a song carries the soul to heights which utterable meanings can never reach. Such abandonment is no escape, for the world of unutterable meanings is the nursery of the soul, the cradle of all our ideas."[3] *Niggun* is a powerful and accessible way to lower the barriers of entry to prayer, but it cannot be the only means at our disposal. As a rabbi and a pray-er, the words of our *siddur* (prayer book) are constantly finding new ways to open me up to the words that are in my own heart, but only if I can find a way to internalize what these words are trying to say and the emotions they are trying to express.

How Can Different Musical Modes and Differing Musical Taste Cut across Generations?

I once was a visiting artist-in-residence at a large synagogue in New York. Usually when I prepare for Shabbat residencies, I work with the clergy and lay leaders to plan our prayer experience together. This community had a clergy team who recognized the power of music in prayer and had been slowly cultivating the congregation into a strong singing community. I thought the weekend was going really well and that the melodies we were sharing were resonating with the community. On Shabbat afternoon, I co-led a session on singing as a spiritual practice, and about halfway through the session, an older woman raised her hand. She was furious. This had been her synagogue since childhood and she had grown up with melodies that stayed with her as she aged, and she did not like these new ideas and melodies. Though the words were familiar, they felt strange to her ears. She felt lost and alone, as if this place was no longer her home. In that moment, I was stuck with two opposing thoughts: I would never want to cause anyone pain through my choice of music. At the same time, I believed this new music truly lifted up the liturgy and opened up a whole new generation to the power and depth of the words of our tradition. In that moment, I chose to validate the woman's experience. It is so hard to be made to feel like a foreigner in your own sanctuary! I hope she noticed that throughout our service that morning, we had interwoven traditional melodies fluidly with some of my newer pieces in order to find the balance between tradition and change.

Music grounds us. If you were a Jew who grew up going to synagogue on Yom Kippur, and you walked into a synagogue 25 years later and didn't hear your traditional melody for "Avinu Malkeinu," you might feel like you were at a concert with your favorite band and they didn't play your favorite song. Jewish prayer is chanted with *nusach* (musical cantillation), which changes depending on the service and time of year, and even depending on the time of day. Along with the specific *nusach*, for hundreds of years, Jews have infused their prayers with new melodies, taking musical themes and traditions from the times and places in which they have resided. As a result, the musical needs of different generations vary dramatically. This brings up an important point. Because we are attempting to create diverse spaces, we have to understand that we will not be able to please every person at every moment. And that is okay! But we should strive to intentionally make musical choices that create moments of connection and love for multiple audiences and communities within our gathering spaces. This requires forethought and strong musical leadership in our institutions.

What Does Strong Musical Leadership Look Like?

Music has a way of reaching beyond what even words and language can express. My teacher Rabbi Elliot Dorff once shared with me a teaching he learned from Rabbi Stuart Kelman. Kelman suggests that perhaps the reason why the Book of Psalms—and the psalms that we use in our daily liturgy of *Psukei D'zimrah* (verses of praise)—ends with Psalm 150, which speaks of praising God with musical instruments, is because after 149 attempts to express ourselves in words, we finally realize that some things cannot be expressed that way but can only be captured musically.

Jewish prayer is both individual and communal. Sometimes it is led and chanted by an individual, and sometimes the entire congregation is invited to sing along. We can trace the lineage of music in Judaism back even before

Figure 8.1. Rabbi Josh Warshawsky leading participants in song at Hadar's Rising Song Institute in 2019 at B'nai Jeshurun in New York City. *Source:* Aleya Cydney Photography.

the endeavor of prayer. The prophets in the Bible needed music to prophesize. According to the Talmud, King David would wake up in the middle of the night to the sound of his harp strings stirring in the wind.[4] Music was essential to the sacrificial cult in the Temple, and after the Temple was destroyed, music played a central role in the transition from sacrifices to the prayer practice we have today.

No matter what Jewish denomination you identify with or where in the world you are, if you enter a synagogue, you will be greeted by music in some form. But what we cannot agree on is how that music should sound and how it should be led or performed. Cantor Merri Lovinger Arian, who teaches at the HUC-JIC Debbie Friedman School of Sacred Music, explains what congregations are looking for in terms of their musical prayer experience. She writes:

> There was a time when people yearned to be spoken to and sung to! People flocked to Carnegie Hall in large numbers to hear great orators like Rabbi Stephen Wise, and great *chazzanim* like David Kousevitsky. They were lifted and inspired by these experiences, and they walked out of these great halls having transcended their mundane, day to day existence. . . . Those times are long gone. People want to be involved in a very different way . . . they want to be part of the conversation. . . . They, quite literally, want a voice in prayer.[5]

If someone is brave enough to walk into one of our spaces, it behooves us to consider how we welcome them and how we help their voices to be heard. Some may enter just to be filled up by listening, experiencing prayer, and being uplifted by the voice of the leader. Some may be seeking connection but are in need of guidance and want to be led through a moment of prayer and song. Still others want an opportunity to sing out and add their voices to a harmonious cacophony of prayer. For all of these potential joiners, it can be music that helps them connect inwardly with themselves, with the community around them, and with the Divine, holiness, and the world around them.

This connecting looks different for each person. Those Hassidic Jews in Jerusalem learned those complicated melodies as if by osmosis, just by being present in the building late Friday night after late Friday night, swaying and praying together. In my synagogue growing up, there was a rotation of *shlichei tzibbur* (service leaders, literally "messengers of the congregation"), who would weave in and out of the *nusach* with their favorite melodies, and they guided me through the words of our liturgy as I fell in love with the music of Jewish worship.

A Jewish prayer leader takes the community along with them on a musical journey through the *siddur*. That journey must be intentional. The leader must know where they are beginning, where they intend to go, and how they plan to get there. And they must not leave the community behind on that journey; they must lift them up and carry them with them. Without a strong plan, music can be a prime detractor from the experience, especially if it is not crafted with intention. More than once, I have visited communities that call themselves innovative and welcoming and have musical leadership teams and greeters but have neglected to craft the musical arc of the experience with intention. The service will begin with a complicated and beautiful melody for a prayer early in without teaching or preparing the community for it, and when it finally seems like people may be catching on, they will jump jarringly into an upbeat dance, followed by moments of silent prayer, leaving many in the room with musical whiplash.

Musical leadership takes planning. The person in charge of such leadership might be a cantor, but they don't have to be. The Jewish Theological Seminary has been investing and ordaining cantors for more than 60 years, and the Hebrew Union College's cantorial school was founded back in 1948. The time of the cantor in American Jewish worship is not over; however, the time of worship as a hands-off, concert experience might have come to an end. As Cantor Arian wrote, people want an ownership stake in their own spiritual and prayer journey. They want to make their voices heard. In 2021, we need to live our prayers. We pray-ers today need interaction, so whoever the musical leader of the community may be, it is essential that they spend time preparing their congregation for worship.

What about Musical Instruments on Shabbat?

The ultimate goal of using musical instruments in prayer, on Shabbat or oth-erwise, should always be to better and more intentionally engage the commu-nity in prayer. The question of musical instruments on Shabbat as it relates to Jewish law predominantly applies to traditional Conservative and/or Ortho-dox congregations, where a strict interpretation of Jewish law may prohibit instruments on Shabbat. Reform, Reconstructionist, and Renewal movements have already embraced musical instruments on Shabbat and holidays. Here are a few facts and thoughts about these *halachically* minded (Jewish law–minded) Conservative and Orthodox communities.

According to a 2013 survey conducted by Rabbi Paul Drazen on behalf of the United Synagogue of Conservative Judaism, of the 365 congregations who responded to the survey, half of the congregations use instruments in some capacity on Shabbat or holidays.[6] Rabbi Drazen notes that "use of instrumen-tal music" is not a technical term. Of the synagogues that use musical instru-ments on Shabbat, 25 percent use them all the time, and 85 percent use them on Friday nights. No matter when instruments are being used, the survey was clear that instruments were used as a draw to make services more lively and more engaging for their communities. Twenty-five percent of synagogues used musical instruments as part of a scheduled service or series rather than as part of a standard weekly service. These services drew in a much larger crowd, espe-cially on a Friday night, than a typical Friday night worship service.

In response to a final prompt in the survey, one synagogue commented, "Our shul is not made of 'daveners.' Without instruments, they would simply sit there and watch a traditional service. Instrumental music brings *ruach* [spirit] to the congregants, and provides a spiritual environment that traditionally comes from hearing the sounds of people davening to themselves."[7] At the same time, it is important not to downplay the power of a cappella and non-instrumental *davening* (prayer). I grew up at a synagogue that did not use instruments, and I was always struck by the power of 250 voices singing along together on Shabbat without any accompaniment. I remember when I interviewed at Temple Beth Am in Los Angeles to be their artist-in-residence in 2013. I led *davening* on Friday night without instruments, and we brought a few singers from the congregation up to surround the *amud* (lectern). They were all strangers to me, but a few sec-onds after I sang the first notes, the room filled with music and I was engulfed in harmonies, that same feeling I felt in the Belz Yeshiva in Jerusalem.

As rabbis Elliot Dorff and Elie Kaplan Spitz wrote in their *teshuvah* (respon-sum) on the question of musical instruments on Shabbat, "it is important to note the educational value of music when there is a critical mass of unison singing from the congregation balanced by quiet time. The varied moods and volume of music are a commentary on the text. That commentary is lost if people do not join in."[8]

Where Do We Find Music and How Do We Keep It Diverse and Inclusive?

Jews have been accompanying their worship with music since the very outset of communal prayer. Rabbi Lawrence Hoffman, a renowned scholar of Jewish liturgy, explained, "At its core, prayer was radical. It was revolutionary. It was an entirely new form of worship, and leaders of prayer communities continued to renew it daily with improvisation and personal petition."[9] As a result, the music and intention changed wherever it went in order to reflect the makeup of the community. As early 20th-century German rabbi Ismar Elbogen wrote about Jewish liturgy, "Because its performance required no more than the will of a relatively small community, it was able to spread easily throughout the world."[10]

As Jewish prayer practice traveled, the musical traditions of prayer changed and were impacted by the surrounding cultures and societies in which Jews were living. Different ways of chanting the liturgy emerged and circulated. In addition to the *nusach* differentiations, new melodies for specific prayers were written and sung by numerous composers and cantors over the last 200 years. Many of those melodies are still in use today. If we learn where these melodies came from, we can continue to make intentional choices and reach and utilize the music of Jews all over the world, past and present.

Melody choices matter a great deal and can carry with them great emotional baggage. For example, using Rabbi Shlomo Carlebach's music has become controversial in many communities after it came to light that he sexually assaulted numerous women. Carlebach's music is a large part of the soundtrack of my and many people's Jewish upbringing, but, like many other worship leaders, I now often seek other artists and melodies to supersede his musical offerings when I can, in order to prevent trauma resurfacing for anyone who may be gathering with me to pray.

Replacing Carlebach's melodies with other songs is much easier now than it was in the 2000s or 2010s due to a huge surge in compositions of Jewish worship music in the United States. In the 1970s and 1980s, Debbie Friedman led this new birth of American Jewish music, and her melodies are still the basic canon for many Reform and Conservative synagogues today. Her *havdalah* (ritual ceremony that marks the end of Shabbat) melody is sung far and wide all over the world, even by ultra-Orthodox Jews who most likely have no idea that it was written by a lesbian Jew in the United States. I already mentioned Hava Nashira, the Reform movement's music song-leading institute that they founded in 1992, and in 2010 Rick Recht created a new conference called Songleader Boot Camp, both of which have led to an explosion of new Jewish composers seeking to write melodies for worship.

Joey Weisenberg and the Rising Song Institute have also contributed in a major way to the proliferation of a new generation of Jewish music. Let My People Sing is another organization that has served as a transformational space bringing Jewish music from around the world to Jews all over. Their mission is based on the belief that any person can be a leader of song, and their vision is for more people to learn how to embody and lead Jewish music and tradition, transforming us individually and transforming Judaism as a whole. This has led directly to more People of Color and queer Jews crafting and sharing new Jewish music as well.

There are now many people like me who serve as itinerant Jewish musicians and teachers full time, traveling to communities across the country attempting to build intentional prayer spaces. In order to really create warm and welcoming musical spaces, we must look outside of our own local communities to incorporate music that speaks to and lifts up people from all walks of life. All this music is out there if we choose to look for it and learn it.

What about the Pandemic?

It should go without saying that the world looks entirely different now than it did in 2020, and therefore the way to build inviting spaces has necessarily changed, too, especially when it comes to the ways in which we use music. As of this writing, it is still nearly impossible to sing together while video conferencing or streaming. However, we can and should still strive to infuse our virtual gathering spaces with music, too. We can sing and be led by engaging musical leaders virtually, especially if we choose engaging and interactive melodies. We can share these melodies before we gather, sending them out to our communities via e-mail or social media beforehand and afterward.

The amount of preparation, organization, funding, and technological assistance that so many synagogues put into their High Holiday services provides a great example of the effect preparation and intention can have on our spaces. Communities all over the world had to find new ways to connect safely for holiday services since many could not gather together in person. Rabbis, cantors, and synagogue prayer leaders all over the world spent months crafting meaningful worship experiences for their communities. In some ways, if the pandemic had happened in the 1980s but with today's technology, they wouldn't have had to work nearly as hard. The cantor could have gotten up onto the *bimah* (raised prayer platform) and belted out the gorgeous arias of the High Holiday prayer liturgy in all of their miraculous glory, with sporadic interventions from the rabbi. The Jews of that moment might have sat on their couches feeling completely fulfilled, because that's what prayer was like in much of the liberal American Jewish world at the time.

If there is one major takeaway from this time period for crafting inclusive spaces, I hope it is the fact that preparation is so important. Synagogues sent out holiday participation baskets, with intention-setting stickers to put on people's computer screens with words like *hineni* (here I am) or *mikdash* (holy space). They put up slides with quotes related to the themes of the service and retranslated prayers to connect to our feelings, needs, and desires of the moment. And musically, congregations recorded virtual choirs and found ways to include hundreds of congregants in the experience both before the holidays and during the days themselves. The dreaming and planning and intention that went into so many of these musical and worship experiences shined through. The more we prepare ourselves and those we are bringing together for the experience we are about to have in our spaces *before* the experience itself, the better and more meaningful that experience will be for all of us.

WHERE DO WE GO FROM HERE?

When I visit a community for an artist-in-residence weekend, I always arrive on a Thursday so that I can gather before the Shabbat experience itself with anyone who is interested to sing and prepare ourselves for Shabbat. We enter into many of the new melodies we will be using so that by the time Shabbat arrives, it feels like the melodies are coming from within the community as opposed to from the outside. A community can also create a music committee featuring diverse members and gather semi-frequently for prayer or *niggun* circles, or other musical happenings. We need to understand each other's needs and desires when it comes to music and prayer—and to deepen our relationships to each other and to our tradition through this process. In prayer, the liturgy itself gives us a built-in structure. Think about the musical arc of your prayer service with an eye toward emotion, energy, and tone.

Music is incredibly powerful. When done right, singing together instantly helps us form invisible yet tangible bonds with the people around us, connecting us intimately through shared experience and shared energy. Music is what stays with people when they leave our synagogues and gathering spaces. It comes back to them when they hum as they're walking down the street. Music can be the guide, the connector, the string that draws people in. Once a person finds their way to your community and has opened the door to enter into these spaces, what is happening in that space has to matter. Something meaningful has to be going on there that makes them want to stay. Something musical and magical and memorable.

Music is the vehicle, so we need to remember to make intentional musical choices. When we are dealing with music for worship, this includes understanding the liturgy in order to help the music better express what the words are already trying to say. One specific suggestion is to create a "PrayList." The work that goes into preparing yourself and your community before the moment itself makes all the difference, and the music can spread the message beyond the walls of your space, too. Share your music, and use music as a platform to reach the people who aren't showing up in your space. If the music matters and has something to say, if it is beautiful and catchy, then perhaps it will draw people into everything else your community has to offer.

To make the music you sing appealing to the broadest possible audience, gather community input and buy-in. In 2019, I spent time over the course of four wonderful weekends at synagogue Adas Israel in Washington, DC, composing a new melody for the *Musaf Kedushah* (the additional morning service sung on Shabbat) with members of the congregation. These were congregants suggested by the cantor who happened to be interested in music but would not have thought of themselves as composers, especially not for prayer. We explored the meaning and the context of what is happening in the *Musaf Kedushah*, and we crafted a melody that we hoped would be engaging and meaningful for this community and that came from the community itself. When people feel invested in and feel ownership over the music, they'll continue to use it and be inspired by it. The more people we involve in this process, the more the music changes from frontal leadership to being sown and grown by the community.

In Psalm 59, the psalm we sang for the first time together at 3:30 a.m. in Oconomowoc, Wisconsin, we sang about raising our voices and using music to sing our strength. "Va'ani ashir uzecha" ("And I will sing Your strength"), it says. "Ki hayita misgav li" ("For you have been a haven for me"). The right music brings us home, makes us feel safe and warm and connected, and lifts us up. The psalm closes with the words "uzi eilecha azamerah" ("My strength I will sing out"). Though we might start out singing someone else's song, by the end of the experience we have found our own voices, and we sing out our own strength. I want to bless us that we are all able to find warm and welcoming communities that lift us up and see us for who we are. May you find your own voice and use it to help others find theirs. *B'hatzlacha* ("Good luck").

RESOURCES

Websites

Hadar's Rising Song Institute (risingsong.org) cultivates Jewish spiritual life through song. It is a meeting place and incubator for creative musicians and prayer leaders who hope to reinvent the future of music as a communal Jewish spiritual practice.

Jewish Rock Radio (jewishrockradio.com) strengthens Jewish identity and engagement for youth and young adults through the power of music.

The Kol Isha Collection (tinyurl.com/4rywna9s) is a spreadsheet of melodies for worship written by female-identifying composers.

Let My People Sing (letmypeoplesing.org) brings together singing traditions across Jewish time and space—from ancient to contemporary music, and everything in between, in Ladino, Hebrew, Yiddish, Judeo-Arabic, Aramaic, and other languages from around the world.

Milken Archive of Jewish Music (milkenarchive.org/resources/useful-links) documents, preserves, and disseminates the vast body of music that pertains to the American Jewish experience.

Songleader Boot Camp (songleaderbootcamp.com) provides powerful Jewish leadership training opportunities led by nationally renowned Jewish leaders, educators, and music artists.

Books

Weisenberg, Joey. *Building Singing Communities: A Practical Guide to Unlocking the Power of Music in Jewish Prayer.* New York: Mechon Hadar, 2011.

NOTES

1. This question was not asked in the 2020 Pew study. Pew Research Center, *A Portrait of Jewish Americans* (Washington, DC: Pew Research Center, October 1, 2013), 16, https://www.pewresearch.org/wp-content/uploads/sites/7/2013/10/jewish-american -full-report-for-web.pdf.

2. Berakhot 15a, Babylonian Talmud.

3. Abraham Joshua Heschel, *Man's Quest for God* (Santa Fe, NM: Aurora Press, 1998), 39.

4. Berakhot 3b, Babylonian Talmud.

5. Bruce Kadden and Barbara Binder Kadden, *Teaching Tefillah* (Denver, CO: A.R.E., 2004), 162.

6. Paul Drazen, *Use of Musical Instruments on Shabbat / Yom Tov*, United Synagogue of Conservative Judaism, January 2013, 3, http://www.cantors.org/wp-content/ uploads/2016/02/uscj_instrumentusesurveyresults_20130219.pdf.

7. Drazen, *Use of Musical Instruments on Shabbat / Yom Tov*, 14.

8. Elie Kaplan Spitz and Elliot N. Dorff, *Musical Instruments and Recorded Music as Part of Shabbat and Festival Worship*, Voting Draft, November 2011, 12, https://drive .google.com/file/d/168cvbq-c0kgzj4sZT3SxLRpBuMx_6baK/view.

9. Lawrence Hoffman, *My People's Prayer Book* (Woodstock, VT: Jewish Lights, 1999), 3:96.

10. Ismar Elbogen, *Jewish Liturgy: A Comprehensive History*, trans. Raymond P. Scheindlin (Philadelphia: Jewish Publication Society, 1993), 3–4.

CHAPTER 9

Social Justice

Rabbi Lauren Grabelle Herrmann

I sat in my office with Hannah, a 24-year-old who had been regularly attending Kol Tzedek in West Philadelphia, a newly created, progressive Reconstructionist congregation I founded in 2004 alongside a group of lay leaders. Hannah told me how surprised she was to be meeting with a rabbi to talk about her Jewish journey and potential community involvement. She had felt alienated from the suburban synagogue of her childhood, where her parents had been active and served as board members, because she felt the congregation was removed from the world around them. She described the congregation's engagement with social justice as white, affluent Jews "doing good" for poor people of color, without engaging in any more complicated narratives about race, class, privilege, or history. The synagogue culture did not value or even speak about the Jewish obligation of *tzedek* (justice). When Hannah went to college, she refused to engage in Jewish life on campus because she did not believe that the organized, mainstream Jewish community spoke to her Jewish values.

Hannah attended Kol Tzedek's High Holiday services out of a sense of obligation to be in a synagogue during the Days of Awe. She was surprised and moved to find a community where social justice lay at the foundation and center of communal life. She heard sermons that connected Torah to issues of injustice in our city and spoke of our obligation to fight for what is right. She learned of the congregation's work with POWER, an interfaith group of Jews, Christians, and Muslims working to make the city of Philadelphia a more just place. She saw a diverse group of people, including Jews of Color and queer Jews, as participants and leaders in the service.

In our conversation, Hannah said to me, "I honestly thought I would never walk into a synagogue again. But that's because I never knew that a synagogue like this could exist. I feel like I have come home again."

Nearly a decade later, I sat in my office at SAJ (historically known as the Society for the Advancement of Judaism), the synagogue in New York City founded by Rabbi Mordecai Kaplan nearly 100 years ago, with Barbara, a recent empty nester. Though Barbara is a generation older than Hannah, the two women share a similar story of Jewish disconnection and alienation that was transformed when they experienced a Judaism integrated with justice. While Barbara is a long-time member of the congregation, she has been a self-described "High Holiday Jew," attending only those services each year, especially since her daughter's bat mitzvah. She felt obligated to be a member of a congregation, but she wasn't compelled to engage beyond that because she did not see it as relevant to her life. Barbara asked to meet to discuss a new effort around racial justice that I introduced to the congregation on *Kol Nidre* (the night when Yom Kippur begins), a few days prior. On that evening, I had spoken about systemic racism and why we as a Jewish community should care and be involved in this issue. I outlined specific actions we would engage in this coming year as a community, including a visit to the newly opened National Museum of African American History and Culture, a speaker series featuring voices of Jewish people of color, and the launch of a monthly racial justice reading and discussion group.

Barbara said to me, "I have been attending High Holidays for 25 years. I have heard many wonderful sermons. But this is the first sermon where I feel inspired to not just listen but do something: to learn, to change, and to make the world and our community better."

Barbara became involved in the racial justice reading group and an active participant in an ongoing partnership we established with Grace Congregational Church, an African American church in Harlem. A year later, she co-chaired the planning committee for a congregational Civil Rights Journey to the South. She continues to lead initiatives related to race and racism in the congregation. Barbara went from being a three-time-a-year synagogue attendee to an active leader in the synagogue. More significantly, the trajectory of her life had been changed because the synagogue gave her a way to grow and act on her Jewish values.

POLITICS VERSUS SOCIAL JUSTICE

As described in the above stories about my congregants, in my 15 years as a rabbi, I have served two different types of communities: a new congregation predominantly composed of young adults, and an established synagogue with people of all ages, but primarily families with younger children and older adults. In these two very different settings, I have seen how social justice animates and energizes congregational life, invites those who have been on the margins to find a home in the Jewish community, deepens engagement among long-standing members, and builds community. I have also seen the profound impact we can make when we act on issues we care about and partner with others in the fight for justice.

I know there are those who do not believe politics have a place in Jewish communal life and/or worry that being engaged in political issues as a synagogue or Jewish organization is divisive and unwelcoming. Let me be clear that social justice is not the same as partisan politics. Synagogues and communal institutions should not be endorsing candidates, which they cannot do according to their nonprofit status. But this does not mean that we cannot speak out about the Jewish spiritual values that are central to our tradition and dictate a vision of a just and equal society. It also doesn't mean we cannot work in solidarity with others toward fundamental social change.

There are those who worry about upsetting congregants if we speak out against issues of privilege or address societal and economic structures of inequality, especially if those realities benefit the members of our own communities. But we must not forget: when we go gently so as to not ruffle any feathers, we also exclude those seekers, like Hannah, who are hungry for a Judaism that speaks to the issues of inequality and works in the name of Jewish values and tradition toward ameliorating them. Or we might fail to motivate and inspire long-term members like Barbara whose Judaism newly comes alive when they see the possibility to contribute toward a better world through their Jewish community. Furthermore, we must also remember that our Jewish communities are diverse and contain within them those in marginalized groups. When Jewish leaders of all backgrounds refuse to speak out against issues including racism, homophobia, transphobia, misogyny, and poverty, Jewish communities are no longer safe for the full range of Jewish experiences and diverse individuals who are a part of the Jewish world. We must not leave behind our own Jewish community members; rather, we must fight for justice alongside them and follow the lead of our fellow Jews who are directly impacted by systemic oppression.

The need for congregations to engage in this work, even with the hesitations expressed above, has felt more urgent since the election of Donald Trump. Trump's emboldening of white nationalists; the neo-Nazi rally in Charlottesville, Virginia; the shooting at the Tree of Life synagogue in Pittsburgh; and the separation of children and their parents at the Mexican border are now part of our national conscience and identity. These are inflection points for the Jewish community, and demand that congregations reject neutrality and work, each in their own way, to address antisemitism, racism, xenophobia, and more. Regardless of who occupies the White House in future years and decades, the hatred that has risen at this time cannot be overlooked or overstated: the mandate to act is clear.

SOCIAL JUSTICE VALUES ARE CENTRAL TO JUDAISM

Building Jewish communities infused with a commitment to social justice is not a fashion or a trend; it is the fundamentally Jewish thing to do. Rabbi Chiya bar Abba teaches in the name of Rabbi Yochanan, "One may pray only in a space with windows."[1] As has been interpreted by so many, this rabbinic mandate offers a profound statement on the way we should live our spiritual lives. We do not leave the world or worldly concerns outside at the door and enter into an entirely spiritual space when we pray. We connect our prayers to the outside world, which we see through the synagogue windows, allowing the concerns and challenges of the outside world to impact and direct our prayers and our actions. In the words of Rabbi Claudia Kreiman on this verse, "When we come together, we must not disassociate ourselves from the larger world; instead, we must realize the depth of our interconnectedness."[2]

The diary of the Jewish people—the Torah—is itself a political (nonpartisan) text. It is a document of a particular people, and yet it starts with the fundamental teaching of *b'tzelem Elohim*—namely, that every person, whether of our tribe or not, is created in the image of the Divine and, therefore, should be treated with dignity. The Torah revolves around a promise of an end to oppression and a commitment to forming a society that is more compassionate and just than the one we left behind. In the words of Rabbi Jill Jacobs:

> The Torah is political because it lays out a vision for a just civil society. It is political because it forms the basis for a social contract. It is political because it concerns itself with relations among human beings as much as with relations between human beings and God. It is political because a liberation struggle stands at its core. It is political because it demands that those with more wealth take responsibility for those with less. It is political because it forbids those with more power from taking advantage of those with less. And it is political because it is a document meant to be lived.[3]

Not only our texts but also our history call us toward the work of transformation and liberation. In the United States, Jews have been at the forefront of the labor movement of the early 20th century, and Jewish leaders have been among those to champion and make possible the extraordinary gains for society through just labor laws. Jews showed up in disproportionate numbers in the civil rights movement. Many Jews of a certain age grew up with the image of Rabbi Abraham Joshua Heschel marching arm and arm with Reverend Martin Luther King Jr. in Selma and hearing the echo of Heschel's famous statement "my feet were praying."[4] This legacy of Jewish activism and impact on American society invites us to consider how we, in the moment in which we are living, can bring Jewish values into the public square. In fact, according to the 2020 Pew study on American Jews, 59 percent of Jews believe that working for justice and equality is part of what being Jewish means to them.[5]

THE CHANGING CHARACTER OF THE AMERICAN JEWISH COMMUNITY

The need for people to integrate concerns for the world with religious practices is especially important as the Jewish community's demographics and dynamics change. One study in particular is illuminating: the 2012 Jewish Values Survey, conducted by the Public Religion Research Institute (PRRI) for the Nathan Cummings Foundation, which sought to understand "Jewish values, culture, and experiences, and their connections to Jewish political beliefs and behavior."[6] The study found that 84 percent of American Jewish respondents said that pursuing justice is a very important value that informs their political beliefs and activities. Seventy-two percent said that *tikkun olam* (repair of the world) and welcoming the stranger are important values.[7] If our congregations do not respond to this reality and build communities that can integrate social justice and respond to the world in meaningful ways that people cannot do alone, they are failing to meet the needs of *the vast majority* of the Jewish community.

Outside of synagogue life, there has been a proliferation and strengthening of Jewish nonprofit social justice organizations over the past 15 or so years as well as an increase in the number of opportunities for young Jews to engage in Jewishly rooted social justice experiences. These programs include JOIN for Justice, Repair the World, Avodah, Hillel alternative spring break programs, Etgar 36, Tivnu, and more. Further, the growth and success of Jewish social justice organizations like Jews for Racial and Economic Justice (JFREJ) in New York City and Detroit Jews for Justice, among others, demonstrate the hunger—especially among younger Jews—for communities that seamlessly integrate Judaism and justice.

Jewish communal leaders would be wise to pay attention to the changing attitudes and experiences of members of the Jewish community and change our institutions from the inside out. If we do not, we risk our organizations and congregations no longer being relevant or seen as welcoming places. After all, congregations are meant to be places where people can bring their whole, authentic selves. They are places to address spiritual, educational, and social needs. Why should they not also be places where people can bring their care for the world around them, their hopes, and their dreams and commitments for a better world?

A PATHWAY TOWARD INCORPORATING SOCIAL JUSTICE IN YOUR ORGANIZATION

In Deuteronomy, we read, "It [Torah] is not in heaven . . . neither is it beyond the sea . . . no, this thing is very close to you, in your mouth and in your heart, to observe it."[8] This statement certainly applies to the Jewish values of social justice. Whether you are looking to start a new organization or to change an entrenched organizational culture, there are steps you can take to create vibrant communities where a commitment to social justice is palpable and a shared value among congregations. The following are some best practices for bringing social justice forward in your organizations.

Be Explicit: Name Social Justice as Part of Your Mission and Vision

In the very first verses of the Torah, we learn that speech constitutes creation. Just as God spoke before each act of creation, so, too, do we utilize our words to create and shape who we want to be in the world. To that end, it is vital that we speak our intentions and be explicit about our organization's commitment to social justice. This in turn constantly reminds us of our intentions and enables those who are seeking a way into Jewish life to be able to find us and join us as co-creators.

When I, alongside a core group of community members, founded a new synagogue in West Philadelphia, we knew that a commitment to social justice would be central to our work. As an emerging congregation, we had the opportunity to choose our name, and we democratically chose "Kol Tzedek: Voice of Justice," making our intentions extraordinarily explicit. In March 2005, when we were only about 30 member units, we created our first mission statement:

> Kol Tzedek is a Reconstructionist Synagogue committed to creating a diverse and inclusive community that cultivates the opportunity for people to experience Judaism through prayer, education, spirituality, and Jewish activism; we are dedicated to community building and *tikkun olam* [repair of the world] both within and beyond our local neighborhood.

Being explicit about our aspiration to be a voice of justice enabled us to draw many unaffiliated Jews (and allies) who longed for a community that could integrate their passions for social justice and for Judaism, without compromising one for the other. Many of them were people on the margins of Jewish life, including many young Jews, LGBTQ folks, and interfaith couples and families. Whether you are creating a new mission statement, rebranding, or creating material for your organizational website, consider how the words themselves can manifest your vision into reality. What words will help inspire your community and also hold you accountable to that vision? What words are true for the present of your organization while also serving as an aspiration for a future that looks different from today? How can you create commitment and buy-in for your social justice vision through your message?

Center the Pursuit of Social Justice

After leaving Egypt, the Hebrew people are instructed by God, "Make Me a Sanctuary that I may dwell among them."[9] In building contemporary sanctuaries, past generations focused primarily on our synagogues as places for prayer, learning, community support, and celebration. Social justice has been delegated to the periphery of congregational life, and yet social justice is not a peripheral idea in Judaism. It is one of the core principles of Jewish life, according to both the text and the lived history of the Jewish people. We must build and restructure our organizations to reflect social justice as an integral part of Jewish life, equal to those other fundamental Jewish experiences.

At SAJ, we went through a conscious process to center social justice as part of our vision and identity. This process involved working with lay leaders to set a vision for SAJ's next organizational iteration that highlighted the centrality of social justice, implementing new, diverse initiatives that gave people the opportunity to see their congregation as a place of inspiration and action, and building partnerships with organizations that aligned with our commitments.[10] In a short time, especially by the standards of congregational life, social justice had gone from a smaller part of organized congregational life to a significant part of SAJ's identity and culture. It played such a central role that when we engaged in a rebranding process to help us better articulate who we are and are becoming as a synagogue, the committee chose "Judaism that Stands for All" as our new tagline, to indicate both radical hospitality internally and our commitment to standing for what is right and just in the world.[11]

Centering social justice means that it is valued equally alongside all the other pillars of congregational life. Take a look at your organization. Are there specific allocated resources assigned to social justice, in terms of your overall programming budget or even staff budget? To build institutions that can respond deeply to the issues in the world, we need to allocate staff and financial resources toward that end. Is your organization highlighting the achievements of those individuals engaged personally or communally in the work of social action as much as we are those involved in prayer and learning? If you work at a synagogue, what is the balance of topics in sermons and congregational learning? Are new members introduced to the various social justice activities in the congregation? If not, what conscious shifts can you make to ensure that activism and wider-world volunteerism is equally valued as all other parts of the organization or congregation? Social justice is not a peripheral idea in Judaism—let's ensure our organizations reflect its centrality. We should also offer diverse opportunities for *tikkun olam* (repair of the world), *tzedakah* (charity), *gemilut hasadim* (good works, direct service), and *tzedek* (advocacy, system change).

Integrate Social Justice into All Facets of Organizational Life

On Yom Kippur, we read the words of the prophet Isaiah (58:1–14), who chastises the people, on God's behalf, for fasting while simultaneously exploiting their workers. Isaiah teaches us that the fast that God desires is one in which we break the yoke of oppression and share our bread with the hungry. Isaiah's stirring words come to teach the universal lesson: religious acts without care and compassion are empty gestures; our spiritual life should be integrated with our commitment toward the world.

Isaiah's vision is one we should take to heart in building welcoming congregations committed to social justice. Social justice isn't something we do on Tuesdays and Wednesdays, while prayer is something we do on Fridays and Saturdays. We.should instead strive to have our justice commitments and our values woven into the fabric of all aspects of Jewish life, from prayer to *divrei torah* (words of Torah) to holiday celebrations, life cycle events, religious school, and adult education.

When introducing or pursuing areas of justice that your organization wants to prioritize, map how this commitment can manifest in the various areas of your organization. Here is an example: A few years ago, SAJ endeavored to consider how we could be even more embracing of LGBTQ Jews, especially those who are transgender or gender nonbinary.[12] We pursued this effort by engaging with outside speakers to facilitate community education, including speakers whose words inspired new practices that enabled us to be more inclusive. We planned guest speakers and lesson plans in several grades in our religious school. We examined the language we use for life cycle moments and looked at our liturgical practices, all of which ultimately led to concrete changes toward more inclusive language, which has in turn enabled young people in the community to feel very safe being open and expressive about who they are.

When you are considering an issue you are working to bring to your organization, examine how that work can be integrated into every facet of congregational or organization life. In a congregation, how might the issue become not only the work of a committee or task force but also an issue "owned" by the entire organization? In a congregational context, you can integrate core issues like antiracism, immigrant rights, and others into services through speakers and *drashot* (sermons) or through age-appropriate lessons for your Hebrew school classes and family education. When we integrate social justice across the many activities of a congregation, it enables people to see that the pursuit of justice is not something relegated to the side, but rather informs all aspects of Jewish life.

Engage the Youngest Members of Your Congregation

In the *Ve'ahavta* ("and you shall love") that we say as part of the central *Sh'ma* prayer, we say, "Take to heart these words . . . repeat them to your children."[13]

These words we pray each day remind us to take those values we hold dearest and share them with the next generation. As we form new congregations or shift existing organizations, it is vital that we consider how our hopes and values are transmitted to our youngest members.

We can and should teach the Jewish values of social justice and infuse an understanding of the integration of Judaism and caring for the other, in age-appropriate ways, throughout all stages of our children's educational programs. This is both proactive and responsive to the world around us. For example, when anti-immigration sentiments are enflamed, as they have been in the past years and will likely be again, education can bring the values of caring for others and *hachnasat orchim* (welcoming strangers) to young children. Without talking about the complexity of issues or policy, we can nonetheless promote the values that underscore our commitment to justice. With older children, we can more explicitly acknowledge injustices in the world such as racism and homophobia and aim to offer practical ways of living Jewish values in their day-to-day lives. Teens are ripe for complex conversations about inequality, power, and justice infused with Jewish sources. Additionally, we can equip teens through offering hands-on experiences including service-learning, teach-ins, interfaith conversations, and service trips or historical tours, which help them better understand themselves as Jews in a complex world and inspire them to utilize their particular tradition toward the freedom and justice and dignity of everyone.

When we share Jewish values with children and demonstrate the ways Judaism speaks to the world around us, Judaism and Torah become relevant resources to their lives. And whatever path they pursue in their lives and regardless of how much a role Judaism plays for them in the future, they will forever make the connection between their Judaism and the obligation to make the world better than how they found it.

Follow and Support the Passions of Your Members

The *Sh'ma*, the foundational prayer of Jewish faith, is one that invites us to *listen* and *pay attention*. In the pursuit of justice in our Jewish organizations, this is wise counsel. Community organizing, with its emphasis on listening and building power through self-interest, is an incredible tool to grow and expand social justice in organizations. I have approached building congregational life from this approach: by listening to the concerns and passions of members and empowering them to work on the issues they most care about with others who feel similarly.

At times, this has led to successes beyond my wildest imagination. One example from recent years at SAJ was in the area of reproductive rights. In a gathering a few months after the Trump election, several members expressed concern over the threats this election would pose to abortion rights, for

Figure 9.1. Rabbinic intern Sarah Brammar-Shlay (left) and two lay leaders escorting as a community at the Bronx Abortion Clinic.

themselves and for the next generation. The issue of reproductive justice had not been identified as a priority area for SAJ in the past, and yet it was clearly a unifying theme for a core group of members. I connected these members with each other and encouraged them to form a task force to find ways to engage the congregation, which they did by hosting educational forums and attending the Planned Parenthood Lobby Day in Albany, New York.

After some time, the group felt it was time to take their work to the next level. The members began organizing fellow SAJers to become trained abortion volunteer escorts at an abortion clinic in the Bronx, where right-wing protestors were all too common, threatening the safety of those seeking to exercise their reproductive rights. This program, supported by staff but driven and organized by members, became transformative for the congregation. SAJ members ranging in age from 30 to 70—new members and longtime members, and those who were active in the congregation and those who were not— became regular volunteer escorts. This initiative became even more powerful for our members when we integrated the volunteer escorting program into Shabbat morning services, by offering an *aliyah* (a chance to say the blessing before and after the reading of the Torah) for anyone who had volunteered that morning before services began. This program has been transformative for those who participated in this volunteer work and for the congregation itself, building deep connections and serving as a model for the kind of powerful work we can do when we come together.

When looking to build powerful campaigns or social justice engagement, begin by listening. Once coalesced around areas of shared passion and self-interest, empowered organizations, with the support of their leaders, can transform institutions and the world.

Promote Your Values While Making Space for Disagreement

The Talmud recounts that there was a three-year debate between Beit Shammai and Beit Hillel, two early schools of Jewish thought. Ultimately, a Divine Voice came down and said, *Eilu v'eilu divrei Elohim hayim* ("These and these are the words of the living God").[14] This is the example par excellence of civil and respectful disagreement in Jewish tradition. In the climate we live in, many Jews raise concerns that integrating social justice into our congregations and organizations is welcoming to some, while alienating others who may hold more conservative political views. While every community is different, and every rabbi and spiritual leader is different, and there is no one model that can work for everyone, I do believe that we as leaders can be strong and vocal about Jewish values in light of the inequality and racism in our world, while still making space for those who do not agree with us.

In creating an organizational culture with a focus on undoing racism and fighting corruption and inequality while also honoring a diversity of voices, I use the following four guidelines, especially when speaking with congregants who may disagree with me, that I hope are helpful to others seeking to promote social justice leadership which makes space for opposition: (1) speak about issues and values from a particularly Jewish lens, with texts and traditions that illuminate the larger point or commitment; (2) educate the community on these issues, including sharing diverse resources; (3) acknowledge potential points of disagreement; and (4) remind people that they are free to disagree with me and that I welcome people to speak to me about their concerns.

These guidelines have served me well while working with my community on what might be considered controversial issues. The threats to noncitizen immigrants living and working as our neighbors has been of particular concern since 2017. From the beginning, I raised up Jewish texts that support the immigrant and the stranger while reflecting on Jewish history around immigration. I also introduced the SAJ community to volunteer opportunities with the New Sanctuary Coalition, an organization dedicated to supporting immigrant friends at risk. While I knew that many congregants supported immigrants, I was aware of others who did not look favorably on or did not understand those who were noncitizens. As I spoke out, I included in all of my communications a variation of this phrase: "Jewish tradition teaches us that human beings are created in the image of the Divine (*b'tzelem Elohim*). While we may disagree about the details of immigration policy, we can all agree that every single person should be treated with *kavod* (dignity and respect)." Throughout the years, several congregants have taken me up on invitations to discuss issues connected to the Women's March, the Black Lives Matter movement, and immigrant rights movements. Those conversations provided healing, trust, and growth for me as the rabbi as well as for my congregants.

One of the most challenging issues for civil disagreement and healthy discourse is on Israel/Palestine. While Rabbi Toba Spitzer's chapter in this book offers more in-depth resources and ideas for expanding the conversation on this issue in your organization or congregation, for now, I will share briefly from my experience as a rabbi in congregations with diverse perspectives on Israel, including views that did not match my own. The more space we can make for a wide range of views deemed "acceptable" in communal discourse on Israel/Palestine, the more welcoming a congregation will be, especially to those on the margins. If we do impose limits and lines in our communal discourse, let us consider who we might be excluding from the conversation as a result and make sure we are comfortable with that decision. As we determine the terms of organizational and congregational discourse, we must understand that we are in the midst of a seismic shift within the Jewish community around Israel and Palestine, often played out along generational lines where younger Jews—resentful of an upbringing that taught them to love Israel and did not expose them to the realities of war and conflict and the different narratives of allegiance to that land—are walking away from organized Judaism entirely or choosing to affiliate only in explicitly non-Zionist and anti-Zionist settings. If we want this group of folks to also see itself part of a larger Jewish community and to have a home there, we must—at the very least—be open to their perspective and assume integrity and care in their approach.

BE STRONG AND HAVE COURAGE

There are so many people, especially younger Jews, who have not connected with Jewish organizations or who refuse to affiliate, but who are hungry for a passionate, authentic Jewish community that honors and integrates Judaism and the commitment to work for a more just world. There are many individuals in our organizations who are present but uninvolved and uninspired. These individuals need Jewish experiences that can help them see that they have a meaningful place within the Jewish landscape. They need leaders who are willing to be bold and do the necessary and hard work of building new institutions or working within existing ones to make our organizations relevant and responsive to the world around us. The world in which we live is broken in so many ways, and it is in great need of people to champion truth, justice, and equality. By committing our institutions to the Jewish work of social justice, we are both providing meaningful entry points for otherwise unaffiliated or hesitantly affiliated individuals and continuing the ongoing work of redemption that our ancestors began. This is sacred work. In the words of the biblical leader Joshua, "Be strong and have courage!"[15]

RESOURCES

Websites

American Jewish World Service (www.ajws.org) is the leading Jewish organization working to fight poverty and pursue justice in Africa, Asia, Latin America, and the Caribbean.

Bend the Arc (www.bendthearc.us) is uniting progressive Jewish voices across the United States to fight for justice for all.

Dayenu (www.dayenu.org) works to secure a just, livable, and sustainable world for all people for generations to come by building a multigenerational Jewish movement that confronts the climate crisis with spiritual audacity and bold political action.

Hazon (www.hazon.org) is the largest faith-based environmental organization in the United States and is building a movement that strengthens Jewish life and contributes to a more environmentally sustainable world for all.

Jewish Social Justice Roundtable (www.jewishsocialjustice.org) is a network of 70 organizations that strengthens and aligns the Jewish social justice field in order to make justice a core expression of Jewish life and help create an equitable world.

JOIN for Justice (www.joinforjustice.org) is building a powerful field of Jewish leaders capable of effectively organizing for justice, both inside and outside Jewish communities in the United States.

Repair the World (www.werepair.org) mobilizes Jews and their communities to take action to pursue a just world, igniting a lifelong commitment to service.

T'ruah: The Rabbinic Call for Human Rights (www.truah.org) brings together rabbis and cantors from all streams of Judaism, together with all members of the Jewish community, to act on the Jewish imperative to respect and advance the human rights of all people.

Books

Jacobs, Jill. *There Shall Be No Needy: Pursuing Social Justice through Jewish Law and Tradition*. Woodstock, VT: Jewish Lights, 2010.

NOTES

1. Berachot 34b, Babylonian Talmud.

2. Rabbi Claudia Kreiman, "If Not Now When?" 2015, https://images.shulcloud .com/1288/uploads/Documents/Spiritual-Life/High-Holy-Days-Sermons/If-Not-Now -When.pdf.

3. Rabbi Jill Jacobs, "The Torah Is Political: Rabbis Can Be, Too," *HuffPost*, November 26, 2011, https://www.huffpost.com/entry/rabbis-and-political-sermons_b_980423.

4. Quoted in Susannah Heschel, "Following in My Father's Footsteps: Selma 40 Years Later," last updated December 17, 2008, http://www.dartmouth.edu/~vox/0405/0404/ heschel.html.

5. Pew Research Center, *Jewish Americans in 2020* (Washington, DC: Pew Research Center, May 11, 2021), 66, https://www.pewforum.org/2021/05/11/jewish-americans-in -2020/.

6. Robert P. Jones and Daniel Cox, "Chosen for What? Jewish Values in 2012," Berman Jewish Databank, 2012, 5, https://www.jewishdatabank.org/content/upload/ bjdb/584/N-Jewish_Values_Survey_2012_Main_Report.pdf.

7. Jones and Cox, "Chosen for What?" 2.

8. Deuteronomy 30:12–14.

9. Exodus 25:8.

10. For additional information, see SAJ Vision Statement for 2016–2021: https:// images.shulcloud.com/793/uploads/SAJ%20Vision%20Statement%202016%20-%20 2021.pdf.

11. I explain the meaning of our new tagline in two High Holiday Sermons. See Lauren Grabelle Herrmann, "Becoming a Judaism That Stands for All," *Medium*, September 11, 2018, https://rabbilauren.medium.com/becoming-a-judaism-that-stands-for-all -489762a7e69; Lauren Grabelle Herrmann, "Judaism Standing for Justice: A Conversation with Rashi," September 20, 2018, https://rabbilauren.medium.com/judaism -standing-for-justice-a-conversation-with-rashi-e5c880bcb16a.

12. Gender Nonbinary: "A gender identity that specifically rejects the notion of binary gender. Can sometimes be used interchangeably with genderqueer." "LGBTQ Terminology," Keshet, November 30, 2020, https://www.keshetonline.org/resources/ lgbtq-terminology/.

13. Deuteronomy 6:6–7.

14. Eruvin 13b, Babylonian Talmud, https://www.sefaria.org/Eruvin.13b?lang=bi.

15. Joshua 1:9.

CHAPTER 10

Israel/Palestine

Rabbi Toba Spitzer

INSIDE AND OUT

In spring 1985, I was a senior in college, a few months away from graduation. My best and oldest friend was preparing to become the director of the summer camp where she and I had met more than a decade earlier. Habonim-Dror Camp Moshava in Maryland was more than a summer camp to me; it was my entrée into the socialist Zionist youth movement that profoundly shaped my teen and early adult years. Beginning in ninth grade, I attended weekly gatherings in our *ken*, our "nest," the local Habonim chapter. And it felt like a nest: a cozy space where my politics and my personality developed together with people who remain some of my closest friends. After high school, 60 of us from across North America headed off to live on a kibbutz in Israel for a year. When I got to college in 1981, I became involved in progressive Zionist activities with local Habonim friends and others, and I returned to Camp Moshava the following summer to work as a counselor.

But something had shifted by that final semester. When my friend was hired as camp director, she was told by the local camp committee that they had very serious concerns about her hiring me as her assistant director. Another friend who had been hired to run the movement's leadership training camp for 11th graders had similarly been told by the national movement staff that he was not allowed to hire me. I knew all of this, and it was excruciatingly painful. Habonim-Dror had been my home, the place I could fully be myself, where I had learned to become a leader. What had happened?

Beginning at the age of 11, I had been raised by Habonim-Dror to be a left-wing Zionist, part of a movement to create a socialist paradise in the Holy Land. During the year on kibbutz, I, along with my entire cohort, was exposed to a more complex reality. I developed a deep personal connection to the land and its people, and I gained a broader, more complex understanding of Israel as a society, warts and all. During my second year in college, as the Lebanon War raged, I discovered the local chapter of the New Jewish Agenda and joined its nascent Middle East Task Force. We spent much of 1983 debating whether we could include the three letters *PLO* in our mission statement, knowing that to even suggest that the Israeli government negotiate with the Palestine Liberation Organization could get us banned from the organized American Jewish community.

When increasingly anti-Israel demonstrations in Harvard Square erupted in response to the Lebanon War, a couple of friends and I organized a two-day teach-in on the Israeli-Palestinian conflict, trying to bring a greater level of sophistication and complexity to a painful topic. Around that time, when I went to a national Habonim-Dror gathering, I asked one of the *shelichim* (Israeli representatives) if perhaps there were issues from Israel's founding in 1948 that we needed to wrestle with. He told me that was a question I was not allowed to ask.

I drifted away from Israel activism in my later college years, coming out as a lesbian and getting more involved in feminist politics. But somehow word had gotten around that "Toba's not a Zionist"—hence my apparent banishment from the Habonim-Dror movement. The fact that I had never uttered those words, and honestly didn't know exactly how I would characterize my beliefs on Israel, seemed to be irrelevant. In the end, my friend convinced the camp committee just to call me and ask me my views, and once we had that conversation, I was hired. But the episode has stayed with me, 35 years later. How was it that I could be so hurt by the community I loved so much?

THE WIDENING GAP

That question is, unfortunately, one that too many American Jews have had to ask when it comes to the role of Israel in our larger community. Over the years, I have heard from many Jews about their ambivalence in joining a congregation because of the rhetoric over Israel they heard there and the not-so-subtle message that those who did not unconditionally support the Jewish state were not welcome. The 2020 Pew Research Center study on the American Jewish community makes clear that there is a wide range of sense of connection with and opinions about Israel. While 58 percent of American Jews say that they feel very or somewhat attached to Israel, 82 percent say that caring about Israel is either essential or somewhat important to their sense of Jewish identity.[1] This discrepancy between feeling "attachment" to Israel and the importance of "caring about" it suggests that across the demographic and political spectrum, American Jews are concerned about what happens in that region of the world, while differing greatly in how they express that concern.

While I do not know of any studies that have specifically explored congregational affiliation and mainstream messaging about Israel, I wonder how many American Jews drifted (or ran) away from the organized Jewish community over the past 50 years, alienated by misguided attempts to foster Jewish "unity" by banishing any and all progressive criticism of Israel. Being effectively told that one is a "bad Jew" or a traitor to the Jewish people for critiquing Israeli policy is existentially painful. It is not that people holding views that are critical of Israel have rejected Judaism, but rather that they have felt rejected by a community that refused to accept them.

Those who have remained engaged—including many rabbis and other Jewish communal leaders—have learned to keep their own views and questions to themselves, fearful of losing jobs and/or dollars. Until very recently, the result has been an American Jewish community incapable of having reasonable, nuanced discussion about a country that is home to half of the world's Jews. Whether from the active banishment of dissenting voices or the effective silencing of those who—like 19-year-old me—wanted to ask some hard and important questions, the American Jewish community has been immeasurably weakened by a half century of failure when it comes to dealing with Israel.

Over the past 10–15 years, the American Jewish conversation has shifted, and these shifts have brought new challenges as well as new opportunities. J Street was founded in 2007 as the first significant alternative Israel lobby to the American Israel Public Affairs Committee (AIPAC). The level of nervousness in the organized Jewish community about this development was such that I—then the president of the Reconstructionist Rabbinical Association—was the only current president of any national Jewish organization who signed onto J Street's founding Advisory Committee (there were a number of prominent past presidents). In the years since its establishment, J Street has created a powerful Jewish voice on Capitol Hill in support of a two-state solution as in the best interests of Israel, and it has been remarkably successful in broadening the conversation around acceptable critique of Israel both in the U.S. Congress and in the American Jewish community.

In more recent years, active and engaged Jews who are more militant in their criticism of Israel and its occupation of the Palestinian territories have further expanded the communal discourse. Jewish Voice for Peace (JVP), founded in 1996, gained prominence when it signed onto the Palestinian-led "Call for Boycott, Disinvestment and Sanctions (BDS)" against Israel in 2005. If the letters *PLO* functioned during my young adulthood to demarcate who was barred from the mainstream Jewish conversation, then, in recent years, the letters *BDS* have functioned in the same way. Even when it was officially agnostic about supporting a two-state or one-state solution to the Israeli-Palestinian conflict, and before it declared itself explicitly anti-Zionist in 2019, JVP was barred from the "establishment" Jewish communal world due to its support of the BDS movement. At the same time, JVP has been effective in providing an organizational home for Jews who have felt they had no place in the larger Jewish community.

IfNotNow, founded in 2014 in response to Israel's war in Gaza, is a movement of young Jews focused on ending the occupation and confronting the American Jewish establishment on what it sees as immoral positions regarding Israel. IfNotNow—which has no stance on either Zionism or BDS—has similarly become an important home for active, engaged young Jews impatient with the reluctance of the mainstream Jewish community to actively oppose the occupation. The rise of these further-left-wing Jewish organizations has widened the discourse, positioning a group like J Street much closer to the center of American Jewish opinion (regardless of the continued demonization of J Street by Jews on the right).[2] These groups have also become an important means for young progressive Jews to maintain a connection to their Jewish identity without sacrificing their political convictions. Both J Street and JVP claim 200,000 supporters, and both have rabbinic/cantorial cabinets (there are 900 Jewish clergy associated formally with J Street and approximately 50 rabbis on JVP's Rabbinical Council).

While in general it is a healthy sign that our community can contain such a wide array of views and voices, the unfortunate reality is that we have a profoundly difficult time dealing with one another. Demonization of unacceptable views now takes place on both the right and the left, and we even lack a shared nomenclature. Many on the left use the phrase "Israel/Palestine" when referring to that area of the world, acknowledging the claims of both peoples to sovereignty in biblical Israel/historical Palestine. Many on the right reject the term "occupation" in reference to Israel's relationship to the Palestinian territories of the West Bank and Gaza. While for some on the left, support of BDS is a moral stance in line with Jewish values, for many in the mainstream community it is synonymous with antisemitism.[3] Perhaps most controversial of all is the word "Zionist"—a claim to the land of Israel and to Jewish nationhood that is foundational to many Jews' identity, and anathema to others. Whether we are on college campuses that have become battlefields between the left and the right when it comes to Israel or are trying to create safe, welcoming places in our congregations, Jewish communal leaders face a profound challenge in trying to make room for the plethora of views across a widening divide.

TWO NARRATIVES

In trying to both understand and overcome this divide, I have found it useful to distinguish two dominant narratives that shape much of the American Jewish discourse around the state of Israel and its relationship with the Palestinian people.[4] I call these the "existential narrative" and the "justice narrative." They each go something like this:

In the existential narrative, the core conflict is between the Jewish people and those who seek to displace or destroy us. Israel was founded as a haven for Jews in response to European antisemitism, and threats to its existence continue to this day. The Israeli-Palestinian conflict raises existential fears for many Jews: fears that we will never be accepted as a nation among nations and fears of physical annihilation. These fears have only increased in the years since 9/11 and the rise of violent Islamic extremism. In this frame, the conflict between Israel and the Palestinians is inextricably linked to worldwide antisemitism and to the failure of much of the world to understand, or sympathize with, the Zionist project.

This "us versus them" existential narrative evokes a long history of Jewish struggles for survival, centuries of Jewish suffering at the hands of those who tried to destroy us. In the existential narrative, the state of Israel is not only felt to be key to the survival of the Jewish people but also takes on the symbolic power of standing in for the Jewish people. Thus any kind of attack on Israel—whether physical or verbal—becomes an assault on Jewish existence. To be "anti-Israel" means, ipso facto, to be antisemitic. By extension, a person who is anti-Zionist threatens the well-being not just of Israel but also of all Jews.

By contrast, in what I call the "justice narrative," the binary is not "Jew versus enemy" but "oppressor versus oppressed." In this narrative, the state of Israel—and by extension the organized Jewish community—is the oppressor, and Palestinians (and their supporters) are the oppressed. Categories used to analyze other global struggles are used to frame the situation: narratives of colonialism and national liberation, narratives of racism and the fight against racism. Allying with the struggle for Palestinian liberation from Israeli occupation is, thus, at its core a matter of morality, of choosing to be on the side of justice versus injustice. Zionism, by definition, becomes an ideology of colonial oppression. This narrative has been strengthened in recent years by a deepening sense of connection between African Americans working for racial justice with Palestinian activists both in the United States and in Palestine, as well as the embrace of a right-wing Israeli agenda by American white nationalists and conservative evangelical Christians.

Both of these narratives contain some truth, and it is theoretically possible to have a reasonable discussion about elements of each. But in practice, inhabiting one of these narrative frames makes it difficult, if not impossible, to have a real conversation with someone inhabiting the other. There are simply no terms in common.

From one perspective, if you disagree with me, then you are hostile to the very existence of the Jewish people. From the other, if you disagree with me, then you are immoral. There is very little room left for productive discourse. What tends to happen is that a person from one narrative, when confronted with someone inhabiting the other, pulls out a barrage of "facts" to bolster their position. Each person sees the other person and the other narrative as disconnected from reality. I have heard many people with a deep love of Israel who are convinced that those who criticize it simply do not know history. Similarly, many who are deeply committed to the well-being of Palestinians believe that if they bring to light the realities of Palestinian suffering, then others will change their stance. Both arguments miss the point. Our narrative frame defines what to us is accepted as a "fact," and it is rare that exposure to historical and contemporary realities alone will shift us out of that frame.

It is also possible to experience both of these narratives within oneself. This internal cognitive dissonance may explain why some American Jews find the whole issue of Israel too painful to engage with at all. My own desire is to construct an entirely different narrative, one in which we can acknowledge the pain and suffering, the hopes and aspirations, the humanity of all who reside in Israel/Palestine. This would be a narrative that allows us to wrestle honestly with both history and current realities, and in which no one needs to choose a "side"—except, perhaps, the side of truth and love and justice, for all.

Until such a time as we can arrive at that all-encompassing narrative, the task for American Jewish institutions and congregations is to figure out how to make room for all Jews who want to join us, without creating litmus tests defining who is in and who is out. Explicitly political organizations—like J Street, IfNotNow, JVP, or AIPAC—are completely within their rights to stake out a position and welcome as members those who agree with their stance. But it is not only self-defeating but also ethically problematic for any organization that purports to represent a local or national Jewish community, or for a congregation or denomination that proclaims itself welcoming to all, to question either the Jewish commitment or the morality of fellow Jews. Being anti-Zionist doesn't mean a person wants to undermine Judaism or the Jewish people, and loving Israel doesn't mean someone is innately unjust or immoral.

Our congregations and our Jewish communal institutions have to be places that do not automatically exclude significant segments of our community based on their political beliefs. Rather than creating enough distinct, ideologically pure organizations to house all members of the American Jewish community, let us strive to create Jewish spaces in which we can coexist without erasing or vilifying one another.

TOWARD INCLUSIVE COMMUNAL SPACES

My own experience comes from being the rabbi of a Massachusetts congregation whose members largely identify as progressive, and whose views on Israel range from disengaged to centrist and liberal Zionist all the way through non- or anti-Zionist. The congregation also includes a few explicitly right-wing members. While my community certainly does not represent the entire swath of American Jewish opinion, it is diverse enough that we, like most American

Jewish institutions, have had to navigate the difficulties of conversation around Israel. We have members who were born in Israel or who have lived significant parts of their lives there; members who identify strongly with the Palestinian struggle for self-determination and freedom from the occupation; and members who grew up in Zionist movements and are now questioning much of what they were taught. We also have many members who have never been to Israel and see no real reason to want to go, given what they hear on the news and the general controversy aroused by these conversations.

When I began serving my congregation in 1997, I was aware that we were one of very few Jewish spaces in greater Boston where people holding left-wing views on Israel would be welcomed and not shunned (happily, we are not so alone anymore!). This was not explicitly stated in any of our materials, but my personal involvement in work for Israeli-Palestinian peace was known, and the absence of activities found in more traditional synagogues—like Israel Bond drives or participation in local Israel Day parades—marked us as different. And while we have hosted a variety of Israel-related programs over the years, from Israeli dancing to films to adult education classes, I have been saddened to find that creating a space where everyone feels seen and heard is really hard to do. In an unfortunate mirror image of the mainstream Jewish community, some of my congregants who are more traditionally supportive of Israel have felt that their voices are not represented and that their views or experiences are not welcomed by the majority of the community. The reasons for this are complex, and we are working to correct this perception as I write this chapter. But part of the reality is that the toxicity of the conversation in general is such that anyone who assumes they are in the minority view finds it hard to fully express themselves. And I admit to my own failure in not entirely knowing what kind of positive programming can replace the unquestioned celebration of Israel—and the attendant erasure of Palestinian experience—that has for too long dominated American Jewish discourse.

While I am still very far from having all the answers, I have become increasingly committed to figuring out how our congregation—and the American Jewish community in general—can become spaces where a larger range of experiences and views can coexist, and where we can learn with and from one another.[5] The following are a few examples of first steps toward that goal.

Education: Creating a New Narrative

In 2013, I taught a class at my congregation called "Israel and Us: Creating a New Narrative." Following a High Holy Days talk in which I laid out the two narratives described here and my desire to create a new narrative, roughly 40 people signed up for the class. Here is how I described what we would be doing:

This is not a "history of" class, even though there will be historical elements. We are not aiming to get at "what happened" or "what's really going on." Rather, we will be exploring some of these questions:

- What are the narratives that Jews throughout history have brought to all of the issues relating to Israel? What about other narratives involving that land?
- What values, concerns, and assumptions lie behind those narratives?
- Which elements of those narratives are important to us, that we might want to incorporate or reshape for our own narrative?
- In the class, we will mindfully explore the following:

  - **Ourselves.** How do I react when certain views are expressed? Where does my own passion/pain/confusion live? What is difficult for me to hear?
  - **Others in the community.** How might we allow ourselves to fully hear opinions/beliefs/assumptions that feel alien or dangerous? What happens when we do hear?
  - **Jewish narratives around Israel.** What has the land of Israel meant to Jews across the centuries? What were Jewish reactions to the advent of Zionism? How do Israelis today understand the country? What have been the dominant narratives surrounding Israel, and how have those narratives affected us?
  - **Palestinian narratives about both the land and the establishment of the Jewish state.** How do Palestinians understand themselves and their history? What do their narratives add to ours?

The class was a wonderful experiment. While we did come not up with the new narrative I had hoped for, we did create a space in which no question was taboo and in which people who were previously afraid to speak in typical Jewish settings—for fear of being attacked from either the left or the right—found their voice. The class was an important first step in creating a broader space for dialogue and discussion. By abandoning any attempt to teach the "real" history or to push one approach to the topic, I was able to bring a variety of historical and contemporary voices into the room. Most important, I created a space in which participants could explore their own assumptions and fears when it comes to talking about Israel.

Exploring Hard Topics

Responding to a desire for more conversation about Israel/Palestine from a progressive perspective, our congregation created a dedicated listserv called "I-PPeace," open to anyone interested in exploring the history of and solutions to the Israeli-Palestinian conflict. The listserv soon became a working group creating educational opportunities for members of the listserv and the broader congregation. One of the most successful programs was a presentation about

BDS, the Boycott, Divestment and Sanctions movement, organized and led by congregants who were both knowledgeable about the topic and skilled in facilitation. The I-PPeace group's program was neither an endorsement nor a condemnation of BDS, but rather an opportunity for those who had heard about the controversy around BDS to learn about the issue in a safe and open discussion. The facilitators had participants read a range of Jewish responses to the BDS movement, both critical and supportive. The program was so successful that it was offered again, and we even got inquiries from other congregations about how to hold similar events in their communities. I heard from many who had participated how useful it was to learn about the topic in more depth than it was usually presented, as well as to be able to engage with such a complex issue with other members of the community.[6]

What I took from the experience was that we should not be afraid to host conversations about volatile and controversial topics. Jewish communal leaders need to trust that members of our communities are mature and thoughtful enough to explore important issues if the issues are presented in a thoughtful way. Also important to the success of this program was that an outside speaker was not brought in to argue for or against; this was a conversation by and for our own members, and, as such, the program was a safe (and well-facilitated) place for conversation.

Dual-Narrative Tour of Israel and the West Bank

I have, as of this writing, led two congregational trips to Israel. The first was relatively straightforward, a combination of sightseeing and engaging in conversations about important issues facing Israeli society. While I had hoped to attract people who had never been to Israel, in the end the group was largely composed of folks who had visited before, including a few people who had lived there.

When it was time to organize a second trip a few years later, I decided to take a different approach. I invited a representative of the MEJDI tour company, which believes that "tourism should be a vehicle for a more positive and interconnected world," to speak with a group interested in going to Israel.[7] MEJDI specializes in "dual-narrative" tours of Israel/Palestine, giving each tour group a Jewish Israeli and a Palestinian guide. When it came time to recruit for the trip, more than half of the group had never been to Israel before, and a number of the participants made clear that they would not have considered going on a more conventional Israel tour.

The trip was wonderful on many levels. Both for the experience and to save money, we stayed at hotels in areas—the Israeli Arab city of Nazareth in the Galil and East Jerusalem—where Jewish tourists rarely go. Having a Palestinian guide along meant that when we visited sites that are commonly visited on Israel tours—like Tzippori in the north—we heard about not only the ancient Jewish and Roman history of the site but also the painful story of the destruction of the Arab village that was there in 1948. We got to see the spot in Jerusalem's Old City where our Christian Palestinian guide had grown up, and we also heard him speak about his incredibly painful decision to leave Israel, so as not to subject his children to the discrimination that he had faced.

In addition to the challenging experiences, we ate wonderful meals, visited tourist spots, and met with Jews and Palestinians doing amazing work for peace and reconciliation. Those who came on the trip suspicious of Israel discovered that the reality on the ground was far more complex than they had ever imagined. Those who had never heard the Palestinian perspective gained new insight. And perhaps most important, the Palestinian experience was not an "add on," undermining an otherwise rosy picture of Israel. Rather, our group was trusted to embrace the whole complex, messy reality all at once, which actually made it easier to integrate. I am now committed to only doing these kinds of dual-narrative tours when I take groups to Israel/Palestine, for the sake of getting as full a picture as possible and in order to do fuller justice to the stories of all those who live in that land.

Resetting the Table

As one step in bringing together people of diverse opinions in our congregation, we brought in the group Resetting the Table (RT) to facilitate a workshop enabling dialogue across difference.[8] Resetting the Table is an invaluable resource to the Jewish community, bringing a straightforward methodology and expert facilitation to difficult conversations about divisive topics. Based on the understanding that once someone feels heard, defensiveness lessens and opportunities for conversation expand, they teach people both how to hear and then how to articulate back the view of someone they don't agree with.

Before bringing RT to my community, I participated in a workshop organized by our local Federation for Jewish communal leaders. First, we were asked to line up along a spectrum from "strongly agree" to "strongly disagree" in response to a number of statements. One of these was "I believe that settlements in the West Bank are a major obstacle to resolving the Israeli-Palestinian conflict." I was one of the people on the "strongly agree" side, and I volunteered to dialogue with an Orthodox colleague who had stood on the "strongly disagree" side. When it came time for each of us to articulate our reasoning, I realized that we weren't actually having the same conversation. While I was thinking of geopolitics and on-the-ground obstacles to achieving a viable two-state solution, my dialogue partner was thinking about the people he knew living in those settlements, good people whom he admired for fully realizing their commitment to the land of Israel. Once we had truly heard each other, it was clear that, while neither of us was going to change the other's mind, an actual conversation could result.

For a Resetting the Table workshop to function properly, people with a variety of opinions need to be in the room. In planning our congregational workshop, a few congregants and I reached out to members of the congregation whom we knew had felt alienated from community discussions about Israel in the past, and we did our best to invite potential attendees who represented diverse views. While one workshop can't transform a community all at once, that experience was an important first step toward bridging divisions in our community. In its wake, a small group of left-wing members of the I-PPeace group began meeting intensively with a group of Israeli and Israel-identified congregants, and together they have begun to help me and the rest of the congregational staff articulate a new vision for how we engage with Israel in our community.

MOVING FORWARD

When we in the United States talk about Israel, we often are actually talking about something else. As the only place in the world where Jews exercise power as Jews, and where Jews are visible in such a distinct way, Israel and its policies become repositories for much of the Jewish "baggage" that diaspora Jews carry, from the legacy of the Holocaust to ambivalence around Jewish identity to conflicted feelings about Jews and power. At the same time, Israel symbolizes much of what makes many people proud as Jews. Given the weight that the topic of Israel carries, it makes sense that it has become the third rail of Jewish communal life. For the health of all Jewish communities, it is imperative that Jews don't allow disagreement over Israel to rip us apart.

If we are sincere in wanting to foster full participation for American Jews of all backgrounds and beliefs, regardless of their feelings toward Israel, then we need to become mindful of the messages we are sending as rabbis and communal leaders about Israel. First, it's important to understand that we don't need to abandon our own commitments and beliefs in order to be welcoming to those with whom we deeply disagree. One step toward that understanding is to examine our own biases and become aware of what pushes our buttons. Leaders may benefit from acknowledging which of the two dominant narratives explored earlier we feel most comfortable with and examining how our beliefs affect our attitude toward those who reside in the other narrative. We must check our impulse to label others as "bad Jews" or "bad people" for holding opinions that we may regard as misguided or even dangerous. When that temptation arises, I would suggest treating it as an opportunity to ask questions. Why does this person think this way? What is their understanding of the situation? Most important, what are the life experiences that undergird their opinions? It is far easier to relate to another person's story than it is to connect with their politics.

It is also time to acknowledge that we cannot talk about Israel today in a "nonpolitical" way. For too long, the "nonpolitical" meant promoting a narrative that erased the Palestinian experience. Just as white Americans are more fully engaging with the enduring legacy of genocide and slavery in the United States, we in the American Jewish community must take up the challenge of acknowledging the Palestinian suffering that accompanied the founding of the state of Israel. However we understand that history, the fact that what Israelis celebrate as Independence Day is mourned as Nakba/Destruction Day in the Palestinian community means that we cannot avoid "politics" when it comes to talking about Israel. This does not mean that we can't engage with Israeli history and culture or that every program about Israel needs to be critical. It is simply a reminder that pretty much any program about Israel is bound to rile someone up. We will be more successful as Jewish institutions if we can be honest about that than by pretending that all Jews feel the same.

I want to encourage all those in leadership of congregations and community organizations to take whatever next step is right for you in creating open, brave, and inclusive spaces in your community. What "brave and inclusive" looks like may vary greatly community to community and may change over time within a community. Mistakes are inevitable—I have made my own share over the years. But you do not need to be an expert on Israel/Palestine or have a degree in conflict resolution to take on this transformative work. Because the nature of this work is so difficult and potentially polarizing, if you have the resources and the energy to do so, consider hiring those who are experts to help guide your community through the process of addressing these issues.

We Jews have never been entirely unified, and we have never all agreed on anything. Far from being a weakness, our ability to engage in "machloket l'shem shamayim" (debate for the sake of heaven) has been at the core of our spiritual and intellectual life. The Talmudic tradition of preserving minority opinions—on the grounds that today's minority might one day be the majority—is a wonderful guide to us as we navigate the difficulties of our Israel discourse. If we can create communities where those in the minority—whether on the left or on the right—can feel validated and not silenced, we will have succeeded. If we can replace nostalgia for a mythical time of "Jewish unity" around Israel with a healthy respect for diversity and debate, our communities will be far healthier. If we can equip our young people with a capacity to grasp the complexities of the situation in Israel/Palestine, so that they do not feel betrayed when they discover it on their own, we will prevent a lot of heartbreak and alienation. If not now, when? And if not us, then who?

RESOURCES

Websites

Encounter (encounterprograms.org) is an organization dedicated to fostering deeper understanding among American Jewish leaders of Palestinian experiences in the West Bank and East Jerusalem. They do programming both on the ground in the Middle East and in the Unites States (and increasingly via webinar) that allows for learning, difficult questions, and deep listening.

MEJDI Tours (mejditours.com) offers dual-narrative tours of Israel and the West Bank that incorporate diverse perspectives on Israeli and Palestinian history and experience. Each tour can be customized for your organization.

Resetting the Table (resettingthetable.org) offers workshops and consultation on having difficult conversations about Israel. Their methodology is straightforward, and their facilitation is incredibly compassionate and expert.

Books and Articles

Adwan, Sami, Dan Bar-On, Eyal Naveh, and the Peace Research Institute in the Middle East. *Side by Side: Parallel Histories of Israel-Palestine*. New York: New Press, 2012.

Spitzer, Toba. "A Guide to Talking about Israel in Your Congregation." Reconstructing Judaism, April 19, 2016. https://www.reconstructingjudaism.org/article/guide-talking-about-israel-your-congregation.

NOTES

1. Pew Research Center, *Jewish Americans in 2020* (Washington, DC: Pew Research Center, May 11, 2021), 139, 141, https://www.pewforum.org/2021/05/11/jewish-americans-in-2020/.

2. For information on American Jewish opinion about a two-state solution, BDS, and U.S. policy toward Israel and the Palestinians, see chapter 7, "U.S. Jews' Connections with and Attitudes toward Israel," in the Pew report *Jewish Americans in 2020* (https://www.pewforum.org/wp-content/uploads/sites/7/2021/05/PF_05.11.21_Jewish.Americans.pdf). Another 2021 poll of American Jews commissioned by the Jewish Electorate Institute asked specific questions about Israeli policy reflected in left-wing critiques and found that 34 percent agreed that "Israel's treatment of Palestinians is similar to racism in the United States"; 25 percent agreed that "Israel is an apartheid state"; and 22 percent agreed that "Israel is committing genocide against the Palestinians." Jewish Electorate Institute, *Survey of Jewish Voters*, 2021, 8, https://www.jewishelectorateinstitute.org/wp-content/uploads/2021/07/JEI-National-Jewish-Survey-Topline-Results-July-2021.pdf.

3. In my article "Beyond Erasure: A New Look at Antisemitism and Anti-Zionism," Evolve, October 29, 2018, http://evolve.reconstructingjudaism.org/beyond-erasure, I explore this debate in the American Jewish community.

4. I explore these narratives in "Israel and Us: Creating a New Narrative," Evolve, March 7, 2018, http://evolve.reconstructingjudaism.org/israel-us-creating-a-new-narrative.

5. One very successful program is Brown RISD Hillel's Narrow Bridge Project ("Narrow Bridge Project: Jews Reaching across the Divides on Israel, Activism & Antisemitism," Brown University, https://www.brown.edu/campus-life/spiritual-life/chaplains/programs-projects-and-events/narrow-bridge-project). Founded in 2018, this is a groundbreaking student program that, in their words, "is a radical strategy for addressing a diminishing sense of Jewish peoplehood, rising bilateral antisemitism and the flammable subject of Israel/Palestine on campus. It is rooted in a belief that positive developments in any of these realms necessitates Jews discussing the interconnectedness of all of three subjects, together, across divides."

6. While overall there is more opposition to the BDS movement than support across the American Jewish community, more than 40 percent of American Jews say they have heard very little about it. Pew Research Center, *Jewish Americans in 2020*, 151–52.

7. MEJDI Tours, "About," https://www.mejditours.com/about/.

8. I am deeply grateful to the Combined Jewish Philanthropies of Greater Boston for making the expertise of Resetting the Table available to congregations in our area.

CHAPTER 11

Education

Beverly Socher-Lerner

What does it take to truly entice a family and a child to Jewish education? When does the experience of Jewish learning become irresistible and highly anticipated? Let's begin with the story of a time it certainly wasn't.

I first met Cheryl when she moved to our area for a new job. She was a single mom with an eight-year-old son, Sam. Cheryl grew up attending Hebrew school, and she remembered the great pride her parents expressed at her having a bat mitzvah. She wanted to have that kind of pride in her son and to share it with her parents, in their role as grandparents. Looking for a Jewish education for Sam, she called the closest synagogue to her house. The secretary who answered the phone shared that their Hebrew school met for 90 minutes twice a week, one day after school and on Sunday mornings. Upon hearing her son's age, the secretary gushed about how much time students spent in class learning to do rote Hebrew reading and prayer recitation and bragged that they were practically "prayer robots" by the time they got to bar mitzvah. Cheryl shuddered a bit at the idea of so much focus on rote learning and didn't really like the idea of her son becoming a "robot." Her son attended a progressive school and loved to ask big questions and pursue them in research and collaboration, so she wasn't sure this program sounded like a good fit for her child.

But as it was the only option anywhere near them, she turned to logistics. "I work full time, and there's a gap between the end of his school day and when Hebrew school starts. Do you offer transportation or have a homework space available where he could work until Hebrew school starts?" Cheryl asked. The secretary informed her that they were not a day care to cover the gap between school and Hebrew school, but she could ask around and see whether other families who lived nearby could help with a carpool. But the secretary never called Cheryl back. She meant well. She was committed to the synagogue and loved connecting with kids and families in the school. She certainly didn't

151

mean to be off-putting, but for Cheryl, it came off this way. Cheryl was disappointed but determined to connect. She found two other congregations, a bit farther away, but it was the same thing there. The learning was focused on bar mitzvah prep and the rote practice of prayer and ritual with the occasional element of art or service learning. Most frustrating, there was no accommodation for her as a working parent.

The message Cheryl heard was clear: "Your needs as a working, single parent without strong social networks in this area are not our priority. We'd love to give you access to Jewish community, as long as what we have to offer works for you. We'd love to see you come back if our offerings are a fit for you in the future! Have a nice day." Cheryl was hurt and felt resentful of the Jewish community, a community that she loved dearly, for excluding the family she worked so hard to support. The result of this interaction? Cheryl did not seek connection with the Jewish community again for many years, and Sam never had a Jewish education or a bar mitzvah. Sadly, Cheryl's story is not unique. More than 30 percent of American Jewish children do not receive any sort of Jewish education at all.[1]

THE CURRENT STATE OF JEWISH EDUCATION

In the early 2000s, there was a huge push for Jewish education focused on continuity, the idea that kids who are raised actively Jewish go on to live a Jewish life as adults and marry other Jewish people. Using research from the National Jewish Population Study published in 2001, the researchers and educators who approached Jewish education from this angle concluded that individuals with two Jewish parents were more likely to receive a Jewish education and, as a result, to go on to have their own Jewish practice as an adult. These findings were in comparison to individuals who had one Jewish parent and one non-Jewish parent, who were less likely to receive a Jewish education and less likely to have a Jewish practice as an adult.[2] If a child had a Jewish education, they were more likely to continue to participate in the Jewish community as an adult. As a result, Jewish education aimed to turn Jewish children into Jewish adults who fit the statistics of individuals who stayed involved in Judaism. Those adult Jews married other Jews and joined synagogues, enrolled their children in Jewish education, and sent them to Jewish summer camps. There are significant challenges to this model, though. If, according to the 2020 Pew study on American Jews, 72 percent of non-Orthodox Jewish adults who married in the last decade married someone who isn't Jewish, then our institutions are defining and building an educational system that is not designed for the children of those families.[3]

Jewish education as it exists right now best serves people who already feel they have a seat at the communal table. While that's true for both youth and adult Jewish education, this chapter will focus on just the youth education piece of this ecosystem. Regardless of age, not everyone is invited to the table. Those who are invited typically were raised Jewish, had a Jewish education, have two Jewish parents, and grew up in a part of the country with a significant Jewish population. When our friends who are Jews of Color report repeatedly being mistaken for security guards or maintenance staff when they visit a new synagogue, or when our working or single parents feel that Jewish community is not designed with their needs in mind, we are reiterating an old problem of exclusion. Our institutions are prioritizing the limited segment of Jews who marry other Jews and look the most "typical."

The argument that Jewish education is an antidote to assimilation cannot be the version of Jewish education put forward in progressive communities anymore. That only serves to further exclude people. It sends the message that the children of multifaith families are not from the "right" kind of Jewish family. The idea of "continuity" rings hollow to children who are themselves the product of diverse family structures. They are still inheritors of Jewish tradition and members of the Jewish community. But if we keep telling them they aren't, they won't be active participants or members for long. The demographics are clear: Jewish children of color and children from multifaith and multicultural households are central to the Jewish future.

A further challenge to the current model of Jewish education is that it's mainly interested in working to connect children and families to the educating institution or synagogue. That may be great for an institution's fundraising, revenue streams, and future recruitment, but is that what serves the child or family? Not always. If the parents of children in a synagogue's religious school build relationships with the clergy and other families in the synagogue school, then perhaps they will stick around and invest their time and resources into the community by volunteering or donating money. If parents love the synagogue or day school where they send their children, they'll tell their friends about it and encourage them to enroll their kids. But that model reflects a prioritization of the needs of the institution for its own sake and deals with enrollment numbers and budgets over the needs of the children or families themselves.

In the 2000s, we saw a push for Jewish literacy in congregational schools based on the National Jewish Population Study 2000–2001 results. Largely, that meant a focus on preparation for bar or bat mitzvah as an event and having the necessary skills for that experience. Joseph Reimer, professor of Jewish education at Brandeis University, in discussing what makes congregational schools work, says, "it is a mistake to separate 'learning' from 'performance.'"[4] While Jewish literacy could mean having the tools to ground ourselves in Jewish wisdom as we experience joy and grow into the people we want to be, it rarely does. Instead, many institutions focus on rote facts or pieces of data with the bar or bat mitzvah celebration held up as the culminating performance of this years-long effort, rather than as a launching point for a rich lifetime undergirded by Jewish wisdom.

What does the landscape of Jewish education look like in 2021? Jewish education occurs in many places, including synagogue schools, Jewish day schools, Jewish camp, and Jewish after-school programs. Each of these arenas for Jewish education has tremendously dedicated professionals, varying degrees of funding, different levels of reach into the Jewish population, and distinctive barriers to participation.

Synagogue Schools

Synagogue schools are working to reinvent themselves, and there are shining examples of engaged families and thriving children. There is deep beauty and power in being embedded in a multigenerational community. That said, on the whole, synagogue schools still prioritize definitional or performative learning rather than affective learning, or learning that's about feelings, emotions, and application. Why is it more of a priority to know how many walls a sukkah has than it is to reflect on the moment in the biblical narrative when Jews were wandering in the desert to understand how powerful it is to live with a sense of vulnerability by connecting to nature and residing in a sukkah? Prioritizing learning that could be easily Googled or watched on repeat from a YouTube video is not the best use of our time and efforts in education. In a synagogue world where we emphasize identifying a sukkah over relating to ourselves or connecting to something larger than ourselves, this model may make sense, but we are then reinforcing continuity of information over building a deep relationship to Jewish wisdom.

Jewish Day Schools

You might think that Jewish day schools serve as a significant foil here, offering a deeper educational experience, but it's not that straightforward. Day schools are varied, from ones that are progressive in their pedagogy to ones staffed by primary-language Hebrew speakers who might not be trained educators at all, to *yeshivot* (Orthodox Jewish elementary or secondary schools) with varying degrees of Zionism and a ranging priority on secular education. They are also often denominationally siloed. Day schools do have some significant advantages. In having children learning together daily, there are many more organic opportunities for applying learning to a living community and a spaciousness of time for content. Children are also surrounded by peers whose families share their own values and approach to Jewish life. On the flip side, Jewish day schools are very expensive, costing about $235,000 per child from kindergarten to grade 12, thereby requiring significant funding from local Federations and foundations, which doesn't make them a sustainable system or readily available to families without deep pockets.[5]

Jewish Summer Camp

Then, of course, there's Jewish summer camp. It's informal and immersive and, as many of those who've attended can attest, joyful. Many Jews reflect on their deepest and most lasting friendships coming from this space. Jewish camps clearly know how to build experiences for effective learning and deep relationships, which is what makes them so attractive to parents and children alike. Like Jewish day schools, summer camps range in their approach to Jewish content and Jewish life. While they are often denominationally siloed, there is no denying the significant impact on the small percentage of people who do get to attend Jewish summer camp. However, like day schools, camp can be an expensive proposition, costing $5,000 for a single session, even with financial aid coming from local Federations and from the camps themselves. Because of the cost of Jewish summer camp and other barriers, only a small percentage of American Jewish children attend overnight camp each year.[6]

Jewish After-School Programs: A New Model for Jewish Education

Jewish after-school programs are pioneering a different form of Jewish education in the United States, and their pedagogy varies from leaning more into Hebrew language immersion to being a schedule-flexible Hebrew school These Jewish after-school programs are typically untethered from denominations. What unites them is an understanding of working parents' logistics and a flexible schedule to support today's children and parents while relieving the financial challenge of trying to pay for a child's Jewish education.

Like Jewish day school, daily programming is an advantage in the process here. Thanks to the increased contact hours, there is a natural rhythm to communal celebrations and immersive experiences. These experiences build deeper and more meaningful engagement with teachers, peers, and content. Judaism and Jewish values are infused throughout the environment, curriculum, and relationships. These programs put a lot of staff focus on the whole child, including supporting learning needs in after-school hours. Some of these programs excel at engaging both parents and children. After-school programs may vary tremendously in price and are only available currently in urban areas in a limited number of locations. Jewish after-school programs also vary in who makes up the staff, how staff are supported, how (or whether) the learning engages with spirituality, and how they approach Hebrew and text study.

The schools are hyper-local, often only serving a small geographic area due to logistical constraints of providing both pickup and childcare with Jewish education. As I write this, there are fewer than a dozen Jewish after-school programs in the United States. These are distinct from aftercare programs that take place at JCCs around the country but are not providing Jewish education.

These Jewish after-school programs bring together after-school childcare and Jewish education.

At present, this is not a form of Jewish education that has wide reach in the U.S. population, but among the families it reaches, it often excels at building relationships and individualizing learning across various programs. Makom Community, the seven-year-old nonprofit program I founded, is among these programs. Let me share with you how we came to understand the need for this unique communal learning experience for children, parents, and families.

MAKOM COMMUNITY: A JEWISH ENRICHMENT CENTER

At Makom Community, a Jewish after-school program in Philadelphia, we focus on teaching perspective, empathy, and self-knowledge from Jewish text and practice. We tailor our logistics for urban, working-parent families— picking children up from their public, charter, and private schools, Monday through Friday, and bringing them back to our home base for the time between the end of the school day and the end of the parents' work day. While children are at Makom Community, they are trusted and nurtured into becoming kind, confident, resilient leaders. They learn to do this through deep engagement with Jewish wisdom and practice. Our schedule is flexible, supporting children who want to attend two, three, four, or five days a week. Each week concludes with a Family Shabbat Celebration that invites families into sacred Shabbat time together and holds parents up as interpreters of Jewish tradition for their own families, whatever their individual backgrounds are.

Jewish Placemaking

At Makom Community, the pedagogy that we are developing centers around *Jewish placemaking*. Placemaking is a recursive process where learners explore a text and immediately apply their learning to their shared physical (or online) learning space and to their interpersonal relationships. The children then evaluate how well that worked, generate new questions, and bring those questions back to the original text in search of more ideas to try. Our *makom* (place) is for us. As children and adults, we get to articulate our needs as we understand them from Jewish text and look to our community to meet them. Some of the needs we meet daily at Makom Community include being seen and heard, making meaning of our lives through Torah, thriving as we become who we want to be, bringing our full selves to Torah learning, and building the community we need. The impact of having those needs met at a young age in Jewish community is far reaching and long lasting.

Consider this example of placemaking: Two pairs of children are drafting pieces of a mural that will soon be painted. One pair has already gotten their group of learners to agree on their piece of the mural—a quote from Deuteronomy and a large shape to make space for the other pair's art interpreting the text. One teacher is circulating and asking learners open-ended questions to advance their process. Another teacher is helping a pair of students prepare to share their proposal with their group to get agreement to move their interpretations of text to the painted mural. These children are immersed in communal placemaking and are making their learning space into what they want and need it to be, based on the content of the learning itself. What makes this a moment of *Jewish* placemaking is that the wisdom they are drawing on to shape their relationships and physical space is Jewish text. These children have deep ownership of our shared inheritance, Torah. And they have a deep understanding of their own self-efficacy in the world, with that inheritance in hand. The mural they are painting together is a reflection of each child's individual learning and how the class has woven together their growing understanding.

When people are immersed in placemaking, the content-knowledge is critical. It has to be there, but not in a rote performance. Jewish placemaking is the work of living in community in an iterative and self-reflective way, grounded in Torah. This model for Jewish education views great Jewish education not simply as an exercise in collecting and sorting facts and symbols. Rather, it is a grand adventure where children create spaces they love in ways that are as wise, unique, and dynamic as they are. The driving intention is then building the skills our learners need to create and lead community and access Jewish wisdom throughout their lives. With that, we can be confident that learners will return to Torah and Jewish community in moments of seeking meaning and connection.

Every afternoon, the Makom day concludes with *tefilah* (prayer). When it comes to accessible *tefilah* experience for kids and families, we don't start from the *keva* (specific set text), though we do get there and emphasize its meaning a great deal. Rather, we start with cultivating wonder in children at the natural world, at all they can be thankful for, at all they can be happy about. We look at the ways the children can show and feel love, nurturing a love for singing and movement in this context. We examine all the ways our community and world is in need of peace and healing. Then we model the ways that *tefilah* gives us a path to channel those human experiences in good company and without judgment. *Tefilah* is a fully embodied experience. We don't talk about tents with kids who live in a city. We take out a parachute and experience a tent in a playful and embodied way. We sing in call and response, mirror each other's movements, dance, jump, bring in gestures to give meaning to Hebrew words, tell and retell stories, play with metaphor, and reflect on how it all worked (or didn't work) for each of us on a particular day.

With great intention, our educators set up the *tefilah* experience every day. When we sing "Mi Kamocha" ("Who Is Like You?"), we embody the commandment to remember leaving Egypt every day. We retell the story in an engaging and age-appropriate way where we are the ones leaving Egypt. Both the Hebrew slaves and the Egyptians eventually call out, "We have had ENOUGH!" and that is one of the keys to redemption. Young children deeply understand what it means to be a *shaliach tzibur* (Jewish prayer leader) and lead each other in prayer when they stand in a line, bowing in unison to lead *Barechu* (the call to prayer), reflecting afterward on the power of getting something started as a leader or as the echo chorus who lets the leaders know they are ready to be present and be together. With our older learners, the process is still reflective but looks quite different. They have a prayer experience that looks more like what happens in a synagogue (no parachutes, scarves, etc.). Their educators still share intention-setting questions and ideas as they engage together in *tefilah*, but before prayer begins, they have time to work toward mastery. A child who has mastered a *tefilah* can read all the words in Hebrew, give a short summary of what the prayer is about, translate key words from the text, and ask three juicy questions about the text. Those three questions come with the child to a mastery check, and that rich conversation with an educator is part of a learner owning that piece of *tefilah*. They can lead it in front of their peers. Incidentally, they are as prepared as any b'nai mitzvah child. But they did not get there from rote learning; they got there through self-directed exploration, at their own pace, in order to be proud of their own mastery of that piece of our collective tradition.

Children as Co-creators

Holding up children as co-creators of our learning space is built right into the foundation of the program. In many classrooms across the country, children are asked to create classroom rules on day one, based on their previous understanding of how learning environments work. The idea is that if children create the rules, we can maintain clear expectations for the remainder of the school year, and children have buy-in because they created the rules. Here's a typical list of classroom rules one might find in a more traditional classroom setting:

- Be respectful.
- Keep your body to yourself.
- Don't hit.
- Have fun!

And that's it. In contrast, when a newly enrolled learner first arrives at Makom Community, we offer children an approach to placemaking that goes beyond making a few rules. Over the first few days at Makom Community, learners come to understand that this is their space to create in and shape. They are invited to rearrange furniture. They are asked to assess and share whether things are working for them. If that means grabbing a cozy blanket or a costume, that's great. If that means making a plan with their classmates about how quiet space works, that's also a win. Then comes time for text study. After hearing a narrative or excerpt, the teachers invite the learners into sharing their perspectives about the text, while offering empathy with the text itself and each other. They bring that empathy into the learning space, noticing their own emotions as they learn. We then look back to the text again to check how we're doing, implementing what the text offered us. This iterative process tells the children that they are powerful, their ideas and perspectives are valuable, and they have the ability to effect change in their lives and spaces.

While there are a few nonnegotiable starter rules, such as (1) be kind, (2) be helpful, (3) be safe, and (4) believe each other, the rest of the rules at Makom Community are rewritten every year. The Torah we study and the Torah we offer to the world are always changing, so the community that we create must be dynamic, too. We welcome new learners into our space every fall. In light of that renewal, we create anew our *brit* (two-way promise or covenant) each year after the first 10 weeks of reflecting on Jewish wisdom, ourselves, and our physical space. We empathize with the characters in the texts we study and their respective journeys. We apply what we're learning to choices we already made today and see whether we measured up to our own standards. We apply what we're learning to choices we can see coming down the road to make

Figure 11.1. A second-grade student points out her contribution to Makom's classroom *brit* (two-way promise). *Source:* Rachel Utain-Evans.

them in the kindest and most intentional way possible. We ultimately rely on the Torah we study to better understand ourselves as we grow. Rewriting the *brit* with the children each new school year is a powerful statement of what it means to live in community. It says, "Once you are here, you have an equal stake in creating something that works for everyone. You are a fully capable leader here to shape our community."

Empowering Teachers and Parents

To make all this happen, our teaching staff spends nearly equal time between preparing to teach and teaching, all on paid time. That is nearly unheard of anywhere in the world of education. This lends itself to depth of learning, collaboration, teaching, and a deep investment in individualizing learning for a child. Our staff also prioritizes making time to support our students and their families with robust pastoral care as life unfolds before them. We gather weekly to study text together to nurture ourselves, to give space for our own questions and journeys, and to prepare to teach. We also prioritize co-teaching where teachers can explicitly support each other and create an even more robust learning environment that is engaging to our students and better set up to individualize the learning experience based on students' learning preferences and needs. By investing in our teachers, we're investing in our students and our developing pedagogy.

At Makom, our focus is on empowering our young learners, but we also offer their parents resources and tools that make us different from traditional Jewish educational options. What message do we offer to a parent like Cheryl who might not find what she and her family need in other Jewish educational spaces? We want her, and all parents, to know from her very first point of contact with us that her needs matter and that she and her family have a place at the table. That means listening first to what brings her to us and, second, sharing with authenticity why people join our community. That requires having clarity about what value we add to people's lives and why we build Jewish education the way that we do. In some cases, this might mean sharing with Cheryl honestly whether a neighboring community might serve her better. Welcoming Cheryl in a genuine way means focusing on getting her the connection she seeks instead of focusing on making a "sale" as if her son were nothing more than a financial transaction.

To facilitate this relationship building, at Makom Community we have a standardized intake process that we use with parents in order to get to know them as people first as a part of a process of inviting them into community building and relationship with us, rather than seeing what we offer as a service to be purchased. Intake is a process we focus on and train public-facing staff at any level to manage. Below are a few of the questions and processes we work from, utilizing a reflective-listening process. Though this is a healthy set of conversational prompts, it is important to approach every new conversation with genuine curiosity and openness to follow the lead of the person you're speaking with. Here are some of the questions we ask:

- Thanks so much for taking the time to sit down with me. Tell me a bit about you and your amazing family.
  - We then share briefly about our own family in response.
- What drew you to our organization?
  - We then reflect back some of our favorite parts of the community.
- Tell me something about the role that religion played in your family growing up.
  - Note: This question doesn't assume that the parent you're talking to grew up Jewish or is Jewish currently. It's just getting context on their lives and whether there is tension here to take into account as you understand their needs. This question also comes with the implicit message that a person's whole self and whole journey are invited into the community and the journey of Jewish education.
- What brings you great joy?
- What keeps you awake at night?
- How could our program/school/community/institution add to your life? What are you looking for from us?
  - This is our opportunity to reflect on whether what we have to offer is a good fit for this family or whether the genuinely welcoming thing to do would be to help them to get to a place that would be a better match.
- What else can I tell you about our community?

Our intake process is unique in the way it invites parents to reflect on their personal stories and see that as a value added for the community, not a liability. From the very first conversation, parents are initiated as community builders, not members, and certainly not consumers. There is something particularly inviting about being reminded of your own self-efficacy, even as a newcomer. These notes are then entered into our database so families are known by our whole staff team as they meet more educators and don't have to repeat this process over and over to be seen and known in our community.

WHERE CAN YOU START?

Maybe you can't reinvent your synagogue school or create a new venue for Jewish education as a start-up. Let me suggest a few ways, though, to incorporate some of what makes Makom Community special into whatever setting where you bring Jewish education to children.

Start at the beginning. Make a list of who the first professional or volunteer contacts are for someone who calls or e-mails with interest about your school, camp, or program. Are your staff treating those interactions as the opening of a relationship? Are they aware that they are responsible for building a foundation to last for years to come? Are they listening deeply and sharing back with the rest of the staff what they learn? Do you have a database to collect and keep confidential what is uncovered in these conversations? Develop your own intake process for initial calls and e-mails, first conversations, and follow-up. When someone calls for an initial conversation, make sure you have clear plans about what happens after that, too. Make sure everyone who needs to know any of these steps has expertise in their pieces of the process and understands how the whole arc from contact to engagement should flow.

Consider the *why*. Why do you work in Jewish education? What is the primary purpose of your Jewish learning space? Get clear about that, and then shout it from the rooftops. Share it with your committee of lay leaders. Compare it with the rest of your leadership team. Help each other see what pieces may be missing in your articulation or in between your vision and what is happening on the ground. If it is connecting Jewish children to the global Jewish community, then make sure you have a diverse set of Jewish communities to connect with. If it is to continue a particular kind of Jewish practice, ensure that there is space to experience that practice and reflect on it, rather than only learning about that practice. Having clarity about your community's "why" and checking for how and where that is present in your programming and experiences will necessarily move you beyond definitional learning and into the affective realm where community is deeply felt.

Know your context and empathize with your community members. What are the schools you pull from? What are the stresses, challenges, joys, and fears of your population? Are the parents in your community generally holders of advanced degrees? What kinds of professions do they work in? How financially secure are the families you are working with? How rooted are your families in your community? How many families have extended family or deep networks of friends in your area to support them? Once you dig with empathy into who your community is, you are in a position to begin designing experiences that see and work for people in their entirety. You could even apply this process to reimagining a single yearly program rather than a more dramatic overhaul. Gradual change is easier to maintain. Once you have begun that process of user-centered design, talk to the participants and keep their feedback in mind for the next iteration. And don't be afraid to share that you are experimenting, reflecting, and iterating to offer the best you can to your families.

Find ways to infuse more support for your educators. Whether it is bringing in an outside teacher a few times a year, asking your school's or congregation's rabbi to meet with teachers and add their own depth and flavor to the content the teachers are planning, or participating in the growing array of remote learning options, we need to make sure our Jewish educators are well equipped for the content they teach before they begin planning for the classroom experience. Similarly, make sure teachers have enough understanding of cognitive and moral development to design learning experiences that are developmentally appropriate. I hear often that teachers feel seen and appreciated when this kind of investment is shown in them and the holy work they do. Teachers love learning, and it benefits everyone when we support them in continuing that process in an ongoing way.

Think deeply about a single piece of your curriculum. Perhaps start with a single segment of one grade. What would happen if you imagined that piece of curriculum while educating for self-efficacy? Ask yourself, "After learning this, what do I want kids to know, feel, and be able to do for themselves *for the rest of their lives?*" This is not learning for a near-term ceremony, a presentation to the class, or a task to check off a list. You are educating people for their life-long benefit. In your new piece of curriculum, create goals that differentiate between lifelong learning and definitional pieces that kids need to build their learning but don't have to retain forever. While this new piece of curriculum is implemented, plan to hear regularly from the teacher, make observations, and leverage what you've learned in the next iteration of this curriculum. As this unfolds, build in moments to share and show parents about this exciting new process. When you've done that once, you'll want to repeat this in other areas of your school with your own growing sense of self-efficacy.

Rethink your space. What can you do with your space? Perhaps your classrooms are all shared with the preschool, and that's tricky. What shifts in your classroom dynamics if the teachers invite their students to collect thoughts, questions, and art onto an inexpensive white tablecloth in fabric marker for a few weeks, and then that tablecloth is always spread out or hung on the wall, awaiting the students when they arrive for each class? What shifts when the learners are invited to reflect on what they need out of the physical space of the classroom and are supported in making it happen? Refer back to your purpose for Jewish education. Does your space support that purpose? If not, what can you begin to change? It could be as simple as creating small groups of students instead of all the desks facing forward. It could be thinking about a circle of chairs without desks, a mural on the wall, more time outdoors, or refreshing furniture altogether. Do consider the space itself as if it, too, was a source of learning and education. The physical space sets the tone for the learning before you can even begin speaking or setting up an activity.

Jewish educators already feel stretched too thin and often wonder whether their students are getting enough. I'm here with you. This is profoundly challenging work. At times, I'm exhausted from carrying it all and rarely being able to set this work aside. But we can still do better. We can invest deeply in knowing, seeing, and caring for people. We can invite people into an iterative process of learning designed for them, and we can take incremental steps toward creating the Jewish education we long for. We have to be bold enough to start and admit that we won't get it all right, but we won't give up either.

RESOURCES

Greene, Ross. *The Explosive Child: A New Approach for Understanding and Parenting Easily Frustrated, Chronically Inflexible Children*. 5th ed. New York: Harper, 2014.
Wiggins, Grant, and Jay McTighe. *Understanding by Design*. 2nd ed. Alexandria, VA: Association for Supervision and Curriculum Development, 2005.

NOTES

1. Laurence Kotler-Berkowitz, *The Jewish Education of Jewish Children: Formal Schooling, Early Childhood Programs, and Informal Experiences*, United Jewish Communities Report Series on the National Jewish Population Survey 2000–01, May 2005, 13, https://www.jewishdatabank.org/content/upload/bjdb/307/NJPS2000_The_Jewish_Education_of_Jewish_Children.pdf.

2. Steven M. Cohen, *Jewish Educational Background: Trends and Variations among Today's Jewish Adults*, United Jewish Communities Report Series on the National Jewish Population Survey 2000–01, April 2004, 9, https://www.jewishdatabank.org/content/upload/bjdb/307/NJPS2000_Jewish_Educational_Background_Trends_and_Variations.pdf.

3. Pew Research Center, *Jewish Americans in 2020* (Washington, DC: Pew Research Center, May 11, 2021), 39, https://www.pewforum.org/2021/05/11/jewish-americans-in-2020/.

4. Joseph Reimer, *Succeeding at Jewish Education: How One Synagogue Made It Work* (Philadelphia: Jewish Publication Society, 1997), 26.

5. Sherwin Pomerantz, "US Jewish Day School Tuition—Simply Out of Control," *eJewishPhilanthropy*, June 16, 2020, https://ejewishphilanthropy.com/us-jewish-day-school-tuition-simply-out-of-control/.

6. The 2020 Pew study indicated there were 2.4 million Jewish children living with at least one Jewish parent in the United States. Pew Research Center, *Jewish Americans in 2020*, 51. The 2016 Foundation for Jewish Camp Census shows 80,622 children in overnight camp in 2016. *Jewish Overnight Camps in North America: 2016*, Foundation for Jewish Camp, December 2016, 3, https://jewishcamp.org/wp-content/uploads/2017/01/FJC-2016-Overnight-Camp-Census.pdf.

CHAPTER 12

Minyans

Warren Hoffman

A number of years ago, I found myself sitting in a large urban synagogue for Rosh Hashanah services. I wasn't a member of the synagogue, but I had bought a ticket just for the High Holidays and was happy to be with a community as I sang along with all the familiar tunes and responses to the prayers during the participatory sections of the service. I was having quite an enjoyable prayer experience until the person in front of me turned around and asked me to stop singing. To say I was mortified and upset would be an understatement. "Shiru l'Adonai shir hadash. Shiru l'Adonai kol ha'aretz" ("Sing to the Lord a new song, sing to the Lord all the earth"), says Psalm 96. How better to express my love of God and Judaism than through singing? I wasn't singing over the cantor, and having sung with some of the top choirs and orchestras in the country, I don't think I was offering up an off-key rendition of anything. Totally thrown, I looked around this sanctuary easily filled with 1,000 people, and the thing was, almost *no one* was singing, even when a response was solicited by the prayers and the prayer leaders. At one point, the rabbi even asked the congregation to be more vocal. I left my seat and went to the back of the sanctuary, where I decided to finish the service unbothered but devastated and definitely less spiritually engaged than when I had begun.

In truth, I was an interloper at these services, only attending because my main place of worship and affiliation, an independent *minyan* (prayer group) called Heymish, did not offer High Holiday services. I helped co-found Heymish in Philadelphia back in 2006, and the group's main function was to meet for monthly Kabbalat Shabbat services and Shabbat dinners. But what Heymish lacked in terms of being a comprehensive one-stop shop for services, we made up for in heartfelt lay-led communal services, where the failure or success of services rested on no one but the *minyan*'s attendees. With no rabbi or cantor to call upon for help or guidance, the power and deep sense of Jewish community came from the collective power of the group itself. In fact, it was often through group communal singing that the *minyan* most fully came into its own.

There are, of course, many synagogues around the country that are not like the synagogue I just described. There are places full of robust participation, singing, clapping, and even, at times, dancing. I've been lucky to belong to synagogues like that, too. But many synagogues, many Jewish institutions, religious or not, continue to operate on the model of a "them versus us" system. There is leadership (clergy, staff, boards)—"them"—and then there are attendees/members—"us." Sometimes this structure is a chosen and desirable model, as the members themselves might feel that they lack the knowledge needed to be more fully integrated into the leadership and overall experience or because, even if they possess certain types of knowledge, they're happy letting someone else take the reins.

There is nothing inherently wrong with such a system, and for many people, it's what they're used to. But for others, such a structure can create a sense of separation. It limits the sense of investment that people might feel in the institution, and while the institution can welcome people in, if the organization doesn't create a culture that prioritizes or (better yet) empowers its members, its success at creating lasting community may be compromised.

This chapter is all about independent *minyans*, small prayer groups that meet on a regular basis for prayer, meals, learning, and other activities. Even if you have never participated in an independent *minyan*, the independent *minyan* movement and the related but distinct *havurah* (Jewish fellowship) movement have a lot that they can teach us about building warm and welcoming micro-communities, smaller groups that can offer individuals the sort of deep empowered connections that they might be lacking in larger institutional structures.[1] And while the attraction of micro-communities comes from just that—their size—there are aspects of such communities that can be adopted by larger organizations to make even large environments more friendly, welcoming, approachable, and inclusive. While this chapter will draw primarily from my involvement with Heymish, I've experienced similar services and mentalities through other independent *minyans*, including Shir HaMaalot in Brooklyn and Minyan Tikvah in Philadelphia, and the lessons learned from Heymish are valuable both for comparable independent groups and for more established institutions looking to incorporate some of the *ruach* (spirit) of these independent groups into their own offerings.

MINYANS AND HAVURAHS

According to the National Havurah Committee, as of 2020, there were more than 85 known independent *minyans* around the United States.[2] The independent nature of these groups, though, means that many fly under the radar and may only be known to certain individuals in a local community via a Facebook group, listserv, or word of mouth. Other *minyans*, like Kehilat Hadar in New York, have a much more established infrastructure with robust programming and a significant budget, even as they aim to operate much differently than a synagogue. The majority of *minyans* are quite small, and many may attract only 25–50 people, although, on occasion, some might attract several hundred attendees. But no one should dismiss these groups because of their size. Larger attendance doesn't necessarily make for "better Judaism." More sometimes is just . . . more. In fact, what many of these *minyans* lack in numbers, they make up for through in-depth personal connections and a richness of communal experiences.

Despite the rise in recent years of *minyans* that are attracting primarily Jews in their 20s–40s, the independent *minyan* movement is not particularly new. In the late 1960s, as counterculture pushed back against various sexual, racial, and organizational norms of the period (including the establishment of large suburban synagogues), a number of Jews in North America began creating small prayer groups as part of the *havurah* movement. Havurat Shalom is considered the first significant group to launch the *havurah* (from the Hebrew for "friends") movement and was founded in 1968 in Somerville, Massachusetts. It was a place, according to American Jewish historian Jonathan Sarna, "devoted to fellowship, peace, community and a 'new model of serious Jewish study.'"[3] Following the Havurat Shalom model, *havurahs* began to spring up all over the country both in independent formats and as part of synagogues. Writes Sarna, "In place of the large formal synagogue service, these havurot adopted sixties-era ideals, including egalitarianism, informality, cohesive community, active participatory prayer, group discussion, and unconventional forms of government."[4] In short, these *havurahs* exemplified many elements of what made a community warm and welcoming, eschewing structure and formality for multivocal community.

Though similar to *minyans*, the goal of these *havurahs* was to create not just prayer opportunities but also communal living environments where more "radical" or "hippie" Jews could come together and build their own collective versions of Judaism. These communities aimed to be different from the institutions of large synagogues and Federations that had been growing in size and number in the 1950s as Jews, for the first time, truly began to feel a part of American society. The *havurah* model was an interesting experiment in American Jewish life, capitalizing on the spirit of communes, *kibbutzim*, and other group living opportunities that young people were seeking out in the years of political revolution, antiwar protests, and free love.

Contemporary *minyans* are inheritors of this legacy, but as Elie Kaunfer, the founder of Kehilat Hadar, writes in his book *Empowering Judaism*, unlike *havurahs*, which often explicitly aimed to take on organizational Judaism and offer up a more communally driven model, the aim of the independent *min-yan* movement of the early 21st century is not to tear down established Jewish institutions like synagogues. Instead, contemporary *minyans* aim to create alternative spaces that many younger people felt were missing in the current Jewish landscape.[5] In fact, the creation of *minyans* goes exactly in the face of the common notion that Gen Z or millennial Jews aren't interested in religion, Judaism, or spirituality. If anything, Jews in this demographic want them even more so, *but on their own terms* in which they can have a say in both how the community is run and what it looks like. It's very different, in other words, to be invited into a "welcoming" space that someone else has created versus creating one's own space with peers, often preferring egalitarianism (both in terms of gender roles and in terms of leadership) over hierarchies. While many synagogues bemoan the fact that Jews in their 20s or 30s aren't joining or even attending their services, it's not simply because such individuals aren't interested in Judaism; rather, many are not interested in the *type* of Judaism that most established organizations have to offer.

The smallness and intimacy of most *minyans* enables them to make fairly democratic decisions about a number of things that they would not have the option to weigh in on at a more established synagogue.

Take, for example, the issue of *siddurim* (prayer books). In a traditional synagogue, congregants may be limited by the prayer book of the denomination to which the synagogue belongs or limited by the fact that the synagogue might not be able to buy new prayer books because of budgetary restrictions. A smaller *minyan*, though, has a number of options at its disposal, all of which can be utilized to create a more inclusive space. At Heymish, in the beginning, we encouraged participants to bring a siddur that they preferred while providing photocopies to participants who did not own a siddur. This was great except for the fact that following along during services could prove challenging with everyone using a slightly different text with different page numbers. If we wanted to create a sense of community, we needed a shared text to make sure that everyone was literally on the same page. As Heymish grew, we moved to buying the rights to bind and reproduce the text of a Kabbalat Shabbat service from the *siddur Chaverim Kol Yisrael*. The *siddur* met the community's need to have a complete Kabbalat Shabbat service in Hebrew (as prayers were led completely in Hebrew). The text was also entirely transliterated and had full English translations plus commentary, ensuring that wherever people were on their Jewish journeys, including attendees who were not Jewish, they could follow along and therefore participate meaningfully in services. Years later, when these bound photocopies wore out, the community came together to buy actual prayer books and could do so because the community was happy to invest in something that they saw as valuable and worthy. Without dues or building fees to pay, asking regular attendees to contribute $18 to a prayer book campaign that would benefit the entire community was an easy ask. The smallness and nimbleness of the *minyan*—not needing to buy, say, 700 new prayer books for High Holiday services—makes it possible to build consensus and cultivate community around something as seemingly mundane as a prayer book.

VOLUNTEERS AND LEADERSHIP

Another area in which *minyans* succeed and exemplify inclusivity is in their leadership models. While established organizations like synagogues may have rather fixed structures that involve boards, elections, terms, and giving requirements, *minyans*, while they frequently do have some sort of organizing committee, thrive on the ability to bring in more people who can serve the community in a variety of leadership roles. The demographics of most *minyans* require this flexible and inclusionary model. Many *minyans* are located in urban locations, and participants are squarely in the age range of their 20s and 30s, individuals who are no longer in college but who are not yet married or who might not have any desire to join a congregation. As such, the *minyan* might serve as their Jewish home in their current city as they build their careers and explore budding personal relationships. The constant turnover of participants who enter and leave the community requires a model of engagement that takes advantage of the transient nature of participants. As most *minyans* have opted out of dues or membership models of involvement, it becomes even more imperative for the *minyan* to create a sense of community that is predicated on involvement, participation, and volunteerism. That said, the very things that make a *minyan* nimble can also be their downfall. A *minyan* might not be encumbered by the financial burden of things like mortgage payments or salaries to clergy that can keep many synagogue executive directors up at night, but simple disinterest or apathy can easily cause a *minyan* or other lay-led group to fall apart and disappear overnight.

Because of the constant need for volunteers—people to send e-mails, people to coordinate food and meals, people to be prayer leaders, and people to set up chairs—*minyans* often exemplify best practices in cultivating volunteers, an area in which many organizations could improve. It's not uncommon, for example, to hear this request in a variety of organizational settings: "So, if you're interested in joining our leadership team or leading services next week, come speak with us." The not infrequent response to this solicitation? Silence. Yet the key to getting volunteers is precisely the action that all of us should be using all the time to foster inclusion: making a personal, direct ask. It's not enough to say that anyone is "welcome" or to issue an open invitation to volunteer. Best practices dictate that current leaders should explicitly invite individuals in on a one-on-one basis, based on that person's specific skills, interests, and strengths.

About eight years into running Heymish, I was ready to "retire" from leadership, but every time I made a broad announcement, asking whether anyone would be interested in joining the leadership team, all I got were blank stares. That's when I began to pick up the phone, not texting or e-mailing people, but making actual calls! "Hey, Sarah," I began, "you've been coming to Heymish for a number of years and are one of our regulars. I can tell you're passionate about the group, and I wanted to see if you would consider stepping up into a leadership role." I would then lay out the specific tasks that she would need to do and the time commitment involved. Sarah said yes. I did this with three other people, and in about a week, I had handed over the entire leadership of the organization to a new team.

With the exception of sitting in on a transition meeting where I functioned mainly as an observer to answer any questions, I empowered the new leadership team from the outset to make their own independent decisions, including making changes to aspects of the community that I might not have touched. It was important to me to make sure that the new team knew that the leadership was now in their hands. I was especially keen to avoid a case of "founder's syndrome" with Heymish, a "disease" in which the founder of an organization often unilaterally controls all aspects of the organization and refuses to share leadership with others, an illness that sadly befalls and often kills many organizations both small and large. In my experience, organizations that are plagued by "founder's syndrome" are often inherently unwelcoming, less diverse spaces as the group becomes more about the founder and what they want, as compared to the community that the group is ostensibly aiming to serve and engage. Only when multiple voices are truly heard and allowed to participate in the governance of an organization does that group have the chance to both thrive and become a long-lasting, durable organization that can withstand multiple changes in leadership. In fact, I was prouder of the fact that Heymish was able to continue *without me* than of the fact that I had helped to co-found the group in the first place; that was a true indication of the group's success.

Focusing on individuals, making the ask personal, making people feel special, and empowering the group to make decisions were the things required to make everyone want to say yes to joining Heymish's new leadership team. This strategy of targeted involvement is also particularly good for engaging people who are regulars to your group, but who might be shy or less vocal, and yet would still make great leaders. This one-to-one outreach helps cultivate new leaders and build investment in the future of the group. Like many of the strategies described in this book, this personal engagement takes work—whether that be a coffee date, a phone call, or some extra guidance and reassurance behind the scenes—but these are exactly the sort of steps needed to make people truly feel welcomed and, more important, invested in community.

ALTERNATIVE SPACES

One of the major problems that synagogues have in attracting individuals to religious services is not the services themselves but, often, the physical synagogue building, or at least what it represents. For individuals who grew up with negative Jewish experiences, whether lackluster services or years and years of uninspiring Hebrew school, the synagogue space itself can unfortunately be a trigger for years-old trauma. While a number of *minyans* and *havurahs* do meet in the basements, multipurpose rooms, and other secondary spaces in synagogues, a decision that itself can be quite fraught for a number of reasons, many independent groups meet in private homes, in non-Jewish communal spaces like community centers or libraries, and sometimes even outdoors in public spaces. This nimbleness allowed some *minyans* to continue meeting through much of the COVID-19 pandemic, particularly when prayer communities with buildings had to keep their doors shut.

Heymish took its name from the idea that not only did we want the community we were building to be warm and *heymish* (Yiddish for "homey"), but we were also physically meeting in people's homes, a defining characteristic of our group. While this did limit the number of people we could accommodate, and while not at all aiming to be exclusionary, we also were intentionally not advertising ourselves to dozens and dozens of people, so the smaller spaces worked for our purposes. A neutral non-synagogue space meant that people weren't coming in with any presuppositions of what services would be like, denominationally or otherwise. Rather, people simply felt like they were being invited into someone's home.

For a period of roughly three years, Heymish built a partnership with the local Moishe House in Philadelphia and essentially became the "in-house" *minyan* of Moishe House. It truly was a win-win situation. We were in a home with a built-in audience that we could count on month after month, and we didn't have to continually search for new hosts, which was a frequent challenge we faced. It opened the Moishe House community up to our group and introduced our audience to their programming as well. Only when our core audience began to age out of Moishe House's 20-something demographic did we decide as

Figure 12.1. Heymish aspired to be a "warm, comfy, and homey" group that met in people's homes and featured a door knocker as its logo. *Source:* Artwork by Fred Kogan.

a group to return to the roving house model. Not wed to a single space, the flexibility and coziness of our group meant that we could go almost anywhere within the geographical confines of Center City, Philadelphia. Our group was not about the physicality of one specific permanent location, such as often defines a synagogue; rather, the focus was on the community itself and the people in that community.

What does neutral or alternative space have to do with non-*minyan* groups? As Rabbi Mike Uram describes in his book, *Next Generation Judaism*, spaces like synagogues or Federations function in what Uram calls the "Club Model." He writes, "Institutions that operate as clubs do have certain norms that prevent newcomers from feeling welcome. These are also the same norms that help people on the inside feel like they are a part of something special."[6] Uram goes on to show how meeting people where they are—in terms of physical location as well as their stage in life—can go a long way toward getting people involved. In other words, rather than feeling like you need to bring everyone into the "club" or synagogue to feel welcome, you can curate experiences in a variety of spaces, thereby working to eliminate the "us/them" dichotomy. For many legacy organizations, this model can feel foreign and even threatening. Success is often measured by how many people physically attend events inside their buildings. When one has to pay a mortgage or rely on membership dues, then yes, bringing people "in" to the space seems like a goal in and of itself. Even in non-membership scenarios like arts organizations and some social service groups, success is measured, not only for the institution but also for some funders, through the number of attendees in a given fiscal year. But if the *real* goal of Jewish organizations is to make Judaism flourish in a variety of forms and circumstances, why should programming be tied to a single physical location? By focusing on one's mission statement, which might be something like "Our synagogue strives to create meaningful Jewish experiences for people of all ages and backgrounds," and not "Our synagogue aims to bring as many people into our synagogue building as possible," thinking about alternative spaces might get the organization that much further in achieving its *true* mission and goals.

SHARED DECISION MAKING

As much as we want to believe that the United States is a democracy, it's not, at least not in the purest sense. We're a representational democracy where citizens vote for leaders who will ostensibly represent and stand up for their constituents' issues and concerns. The United States is too large to be a true democracy, and the same is true for most Jewish organizations. But what is saved in efficiency through boards and leaders can at times cancel out the multivocal opinions of a group's members. Smaller *minyans* and *havurahs,* while also perhaps not true democracies, are able to better cultivate a sense of communal buy-in and participation around issues.

In 2017, Heymish, like other Jewish institutions, was confronted with a moral dilemma: Should the melodies and tunes of contemporary Jewish spiritual leader Shlomo Carlebach continue to be used in services in light of multiple allegations that Carlebach sexually assaulted and harassed a number of women and girls in his lifetime?[7] Carlebach's tunes had become so synonymous with Kabbalat Shabbat services that while some people wanted to completely do away with his music, to others, it would feel unsettling to face a service that suddenly had all new music. Unsure how to proceed, the leaders of Heymish posted the following on Heymish's closed Facebook group wall:

> Hey there, lovely community members! Last month we started talking about what impact, if any, renewed knowledge of Carlebach's history of sexual abuse should have on our services. This conversation will be continued with those who wish to participate over the dinners of the next 6 months, after which point we will determine what next steps are indicated by the community. . . . We are a community based in personal connections, and in welcoming one another into our homes. As such, we will have all conversations about this (or any other difficult topic) in person. I look forward to seeing you and talking with you at Heymish sometime soon![8]

This thoughtful campaign exemplifies a number of strategies rarely seen nowadays with most organizations: A delimited period of six months was set aside for discussions; discussions would only happen in person to prevent misunderstandings and potential flame wars online, and the decision would be informed by conversation and discussion, not a simple vote. This was not only a terrific model for how one *minyan* decided to address a specific challenge it was facing but also an opportunity for Heymish to invest in its core values of inclusion and building welcoming community by using this difficult issue to make Heymish itself stronger as a whole.

After months of discussion, here is what Heymish decided to do about the issue of Carlebach's music:

> Heymish has now had 6 months of conversation surrounding what to do with the legacy of Carlebach's tunes in light of his abuses. In keeping with the trend of those conversations . . . Heymish as a community will make an effort to learn new tunes, with the eventual goal of not using any of Carlebach's music. Toward this goal, each month the tune we are learning will be posted to the month's event on Facebook, in the form of a YouTube video, so everyone who wants to can learn it beforehand. . . . If you feel that your input was not fully taken into account in this decision, please pm me. It is my goal that everyone's voice be heard.[9]

Heymish reaffirmed its commitment to listening to different people's voices in the community and transparently articulated its resolution to the issue, concluding with an invitation for further discussion lest anyone felt their opinions were not heard. Heymish made resources available to assist in the process of learning new music to make sure that the entire community could come together as part of the next step in this process.

What would it mean for larger organizations to utilize such an approach? Unwieldy? Maybe. Challenging? Perhaps. But not impossible. When Kol Tzedek, the 12-year-old Reconstructionist synagogue in West Philadelphia, faced the departure of its founding rabbi, Lauren Grabelle Herrmann, in 2015, in addition to establishing a committee to lead the search for a new rabbi, the synagogue initiated a series of small, facilitated household meetings for synagogue members to talk about their hopes, goals, and concerns for Kol Tzedek. The search committee (on which I served) used the information from these meetings to help guide the selection process and make sure that the selected rabbi would truly be a reflection of as much of the congregation as possible and not the seven or so people who sat on the committee. Complemented by larger congregational meetings at the beginning and end of the search process, the leadership of Kol Tzedek recognized that, at this emotional and fraught junction for the congregation, making sure that as many people as possible had a voice at the table was key. The payoff was tremendous. When the new rabbi was selected, congregants felt that they had been not just informed of the process but also active participants. Eliminating the line between leadership and community—while it may feel scary at times, and challenging if not well managed, to allow the community to play such a large and vocal role in decision making—is more of an opportunity than a threat for the organization. Only with the buy-in of the community can an organization truly thrive and accomplish its mission. Otherwise, who is the organization serving?

The smallness of *minyans* might cause some readers to dismiss them as irrelevant examples in the larger landscape of communal Judaism. Can a bunch of people meeting in someone's home for services really matter all that much? If we only measure success by numbers, then the answer is no. But those numbers, as we all know, in all but a handful of synagogues, are steadily decreasing year after year. Fewer congregants. Fewer donors. Fewer members. By focusing exclusively on bottom lines and numbers instead of personal one-on-one relationships, depth of connections, transparency of policies, and decision making, numbers are irrelevant in what is already an environment of attrition and attenuation. Instead, by learning from smaller micro-communities whose size allows them to innovate and build community in genuine, meaningful, and lasting ways, larger organizations might learn new skills and tips to focus on what the real goals of their missions are: to build meaningful Jewish community, not to simply count the number of attendees. And for those larger institutions that *are* concerned about numbers, whether dollars or people, learning to listen and respond to diverse voices in the community, rather than lead from a top-down model, will ultimately draw in more participants in ways that are honest, authentic, and organic.

RESOURCES

Websites

Hadar (hadar.org/independent-minyanim) provides information on the history of *minyans* and resources for *minyans*.

National Havurah Committee (www.havurah.org) is a network of diverse individuals and communities dedicated to Jewish living and learning, community building, and *tikkun olam* (repairing the world) and has provided the tools to help people create empowered Jewish lives and communities.

Books

Kaunfer, Elie. *Empowered Judaism: What Independent Minyanim Can Teach Us about Building Vibrant Jewish Communities.* Woodstock, VT: Jewish Lights, 2010.

Prell, Riv-Ellen. *Prayer & Community: The Havurah in American Judaism.* Detroit, MI: Wayne State University Press, 1989.

NOTES

1. While the Hebrew plural of the words *minyan* and *havurah* are *minyanim* and *havurot*, in this chapter, as we describe American prayer groups and communities, we are using the Englishized plurals: *minyans* and *havurahs*. Even this word choice came with its own set of decisions about inclusion for our readers.

2. National Havurah Committee, "International Havurot Resources," accessed February 15, 2021, https://havurah.org/the-nhc/national-havurot-resources/.

3. Jonathan Sarna, *American Judaism: A History*, 2nd ed. (New Haven, CT: Yale University Press, 2019), 319.

4. Sarna, *American Judaism*, 321.

5. Elie Kaunfer, *Empowered Judaism: What Independent Minyanim Can Teach Us about Building Vibrant Jewish Communities* (Woodstock, VT: Jewish Lights, 2010), 75.

6. Michael Uram, *Next Generation Judaism: How College Students and Hillel Can Help Reinvent Jewish Organizations* (Woodstock, VT: Jewish Lights, 2016), 70.

7. Melanie Lidman, "After #MeToo, Some Congregations Weigh Changing Their Tune on Shlomo Carlebach," *Times of Israel*, December 20, 2017, https://www.times ofisrael.com/after-metoo-some-congregations-weigh-changing-their-tune-on-shlomo -carlebach/.

8. Naomi Socher-Lerner, "Hey there, lovely community members!" Facebook, March 4, 2018, https://www.facebook.com/groups/heymish/permalink/10160165222630341.

9. Naomi Socher-Lerner, "Heymish has now had 6 months of conversation," Facebook, October 15, 2018, https://www.facebook.com/groups/heymish/permalink/ 10161076676215341.

CHAPTER 13

Dues and Fundraising

Rabbi Kerry M. Olitzky

Nathan was a secular Israeli Jew. Kirsten grew up as a Roman Catholic in a small midwestern American city. As avowed secularists, Nathan's family eschewed synagogues and were ardently opposed to any religious interference in civil life. By contrast, Kirsten was raised in the bosom of the church. Her childhood memories were inextricably tied to religion and family.

Nathan and Kirsten met in graduate school on the West Coast and quickly fell in love. As their relationship grew more serious, Kirsten pushed Nathan to take her to synagogue, especially if they were to consider creating a Jewish family together, a decision that they were contemplating. It was the High Holiday season, and while Kirsten had limited previous interactions with Jews or Judaism, she knew that the High Holidays were of utmost importance to those who engaged with Jewish religious life. They found the closest synagogue to where they were living, looked up the times for services, and made plans to attend.

When they approached the crowded entry doors of the synagogue on the evening of Rosh Hashanah, they were first confronted by a table blocking their entrance. Behind the table, sitting next to a security guard standing at the ready, a synagogue representative asked for their tickets. Neither Nathan nor Kirsten had any cultural cues that would tell them to expect to need tickets for admission for a religious service. After they explained that they had no tickets and were only coming to worship and then inquired as to how to acquire tickets, they were ushered into an office where another synagogue representative was prepared to sell them tickets on the spot. When Nathan and Kirsten were told what they considered an exorbitant cost for tickets and they explained that they were graduate students, they were told that tickets were free for members if they wanted to join the congregation, a concept that was also unfamiliar to them. In any case, the price for membership was also quite high and beyond what they could afford. So this young couple was invited to sit in an auditorium where the service would be broadcast on a large viewing screen. Politely, they said, "No, thank you," and left the synagogue. Needless to say, they failed in their attempt to attend these holiday worship services.

Subsequent to this unfortunate and unwelcoming experience, Nathan and Kirsten stumbled onto the website for the organization that I was leading at the time, Big Tent Judaism, and reached out to me. They had no experience with the "pay to pray" culture that permeates North American Jewish religious life and were dumbfounded by it. I felt lucky that they were committed enough to continue their search and ended up in my office. More often, people encounter such barriers to entry and give up. All too frequently, finances, tickets, membership dues, and fundraising are obstacles that have to be circumnavigated by those who want to enter Jewish communal gates. They are all barriers to entry, and the vast majority of the unaffiliated and unengaged simply prefer to sit it out rather than knock on closed doors, especially after these doors have been slammed in their faces.

A BRIEF HISTORY OF COMMUNAL INSTITUTIONAL FINANCES

The biblical model of taxing individuals for the support of the community, first established in Exodus, followed the Jewish people throughout their historical wanderings: "The rich shall not give more, and the poor shall not give less, than the half shekel, when they give an offering to God, to make atonement for your souls" (Exodus 30:15). The membership model of the contemporary synagogue emerged in part from this biblical notion that all people who belong to a community are obligated to support it. There are some communities around the world, such as in Hungary and Germany, where variations on the Exodus approach still exist. People are taxed to support the entirety of the community and its institutions.

When synagogue dues were introduced about 100 years ago in the United States in response to a lack of any defined system for financial resource development in the American synagogue, they were considered an innovation over the church collection plate, such as Christians like Kirsten probably experienced. Previous common techniques for raising funds at the time included the auctioning of synagogue honors (such as an *aliyah*, or Torah honor, when one is called to offer a blessing before and after the public reading of the Torah); the fining of members for coming late to synagogue annual meetings or missing them entirely, or inappropriate behaviors, such as the use of a spittoon during synagogue meetings or talking during the reading of the Torah during worship services; and the renting/selling of synagogue sanctuary seats, particularly for the High Holidays. While the Reform movement objected on principle to some of these practices and discontinued them, practices that we now realize were also inherently unwelcoming, there are some Orthodox synagogues that still auction off Torah honors and the like.[1] Moreover, a large number of synagogues, regardless of religious orientation, sell tickets for the High Holidays and rent/sell sanctuary seats that are thereby permanently reserved. Other synagogues have introduced other fees, especially for religious/Hebrew school, life cycle events, building funds, and, more recently, for security. As other Jewish communal institutions such as Jewish Community Centers (JCCs) or Young Men's Hebrew Associations (YMHAs) emerged on the scene, they followed what had become the established dues model for synagogues. These other institutions also established fundraising methods that synagogues, in turn, followed such as gala events and fees for specific program services. And while there are numerous institutions that dot the landscape of the organized North American Jewish community, synagogues are the most numerous and usually lead the way in the area of dues and financial resource development.

VALUES PROPOSITION MORE THAN MISSION STATEMENT

Irrespective of what approach to dues that a membership institution undertakes—and this includes all Jewish communal institutions and is not limited to synagogues—it is important to note the changes in the North American Jewish community vis-à-vis supporting Jewish communal institutions. In the post–World War II period, which saw the Jewish community move into the suburbs amid a baby boom, a large percentage of these families felt an obligation to support Jewish communal institutions, even those in which they did not fully participate. Because of the explosion of these institutions in the suburbs in particular, leaders didn't have to consider the notion of being "welcoming." They were in an expansive economy, so to speak. Local Jews financially supported these institutions, feeling that the synagogues represented the American Jewish community's rightful place in American society. Synagogues, in particular, could now claim their place alongside churches and other religious institutions in the community. Many of these Jewish institutions were built on the backs of so-called three-day-a-year Jews who attended Rosh Hashanah and Yom Kippur services but nothing else. This support waned as new generations felt more comfortable being fully American, far away from any status as immigrants or quotas that limited or prevented their participation in the social, professional, and/or communal life of their community. Now, in the postmodern era, this sense of obligation has given way to the notion of *personal benefit*. In other words, institutions are now forced to answer this question: *How will participation in this community, generally, and in this institution, particularly, benefit my family and me?* Rather than considering the actual cost of membership or even its affordability, people are now probing its cost benefit, asking questions like *What am I getting out of my membership? Is the amount that I am spending worth it?*

This is why no matter what approach to finances is undertaken by an institution, it has to be built on the foundation of a persuasive *values proposition* and not simply a well-crafted, carefully word-smithed mission statement. Those institutions that have introduced new membership dues models that do not succeed most likely fail because they mistakenly assume that all that is needed is a tweaking of, or even a full replacement of, the traditional dues model. But then it's back to business as usual without any analysis of the institution itself or a needs assessment of the membership it seeks to serve.

Moreover, it is no longer possible, even if it ever was, to simply define an institution, particularly a religious institution, through its affiliation with a national movement and assume that is its defining mission. Nor is it adequate to define a mission in comparison to other institutions in the community. This may work for those who are actively seeking affiliation of a specific kind, but it will not work for the vast majority of North American Jews who may not be looking for Jewish community at all. A variety of major societal changes has made movement affiliation less relevant. Of note, political scientist Robert Putnam, in his classic book *Bowling Alone*, uses the example of bowling to demonstrate the challenge to membership-based organizations.[2] While more people are bowling, fewer people are bowling in leagues. They eschew membership commitments of most kinds. Similarly, in my own work, *Playlist Judaism: Making Choices for a Vital Future* (2013), I argue that the introduction of the music-sharing platform Napster was the beginning of the demise of membership-based models for Jewish communal institutions as well.[3] Just as the music industry had previously required the consumer to purchase an entire album just to listen to one song (and also controlled the order it would be played), synagogues and other Jewish communal institutions required full membership just to use one of their services: b'nai mitzvah or High Holiday tickets in synagogues, gym access, or preschools in JCCs. This was not a very welcoming posture for communal institutions, and people started to "vote with their feet," discontinuing their membership or not joining in the first place.

THE NEED FOR A NEW MODEL

While nearly all synagogues and other membership institutions have a "dues forgiveness policy" of some kind for those who cannot afford the cost of membership, and imply that everyone is welcome irrespective of their ability to pay, many of these institutions require copious financial information—and force potential members to go through an extensive and often embarrassing vetting process—for any reduction in dues. Some institutions even require evidence of financial need in the form of income tax returns. Even for those institutions that don't require this level of financial backup, there can also be the internalized social stigma attached to those who request any kind of dues reduction, sometimes called dues abatement or dues forgiveness. As a result, there are large swaths of the Jewish communal population who do not request any reduction in dues and simply avoid participation in Jewish communal institutions altogether.

A new model is necessary for one simple reason: the old model is no longer working. The traditional dues model (or membership model) is failing in cultural and religious institutions throughout North America, both within and outside of the Jewish community. Diminution in membership is not the sole province of the North American Jewish community; cultural institutions have felt it as well. Even commercial enterprises, such as fitness centers, have changed their approach to membership in response to this trend away from the commitment of membership.

There are those who argue that we need only reinstate a sense of obligation in people to support Jewish communal institutions.[4] Once that is accomplished, nothing else about the institution would need to change since it is simply—and always—about money. Nothing could be further from the truth. Jews can fulfill their spiritual, cultural, and social needs elsewhere, outside of the synagogue and other Jewish communal institutions—especially as Jewish thought has entered the marketplace of ideas and Jewish culture has entered the marketplace itself. Thus, just as the model for dues needs to be changed, the model for the synagogue and other institutions will require change as well.

Alternative Dues Models

The voluntary dues model has become the most popular and prominent of alternative dues models. There are more than 60 synagogues that have undertaken this model since 2017.[5] Perhaps it is because there is empirical evidence that it is successful.[6] But more likely, this change seems most palatable in the risk-averse environment of the contemporary Jewish community and its leadership because, in the voluntary dues model, the membership model itself doesn't change. Voluntary dues require no financial oversight on the part of communal leadership. Instead, potential members simply determine the amount that they want to pay, and that amount is readily accepted by design. In order to assist individuals in their self-determination of dues, institutions often list the sustaining amount of membership to help guide decision making. This is determined simply by dividing the operating budget of the institution by the number of presumed members. This approach usually motivates those who can afford it and value their membership to pay more than the sustaining amount. Those who can't afford it pay what they can without having to deal with anyone scrutinizing their personal finances or decisions. When people find value in membership, they will be willing to pay for it. This approach places the onus of responsibility on the institution to demonstrate the value of membership to its members and potential members.

While the model itself seems more welcoming than the former traditional dues model to potential members, like other aspects of synagogue and Jewish communal institutional life, whether it is actually welcoming is dependent on how the model is implemented and communicated to current and potential members. Tiferet Beth Israel (TBI) in Blue Bell, Pennsylvania, is a synagogue that moved to a voluntary dues system in 2020. While the approach to voluntary dues goes by various names in synagogues, TBI calls its model *Heshbon Lev* (literally, accounting of the heart). This synagogue is operating under the assumption that if members see what the synagogue provides, they will increase their financial commitment. This will extend to potential members as well. In addition, TBI reorganized its staff to include a director of engagement to focus on member relations in order to make sure that its value proposition is being clearly articulated to people and that the synagogue is meeting the needs of its members.

Given the successful experience of synagogues that have introduced voluntary dues programs, one would expect other Jewish communal institutions that are membership based to introduce similar programs, but this has generally not been the case. Synagogues have an advantage of engaging their members especially during liminal times in their lives such as births, weddings, and funerals, making a clear case for value. Most other institutions are not positioned to engage members in this same way. This is changing, though, as more and more Jewish organizations are finding ways to provide value to individuals at key life moments. Some JCCs are starting to do life cycle events because they think that it might transform their relationships with members and nonmembers. Federations and other organizations attempt to create touchstones through their missions to various countries.

Some JCCs have lowered their membership fees to what might be called minimal dues. This membership entitles members to access the basic services of the institutions and provides discounts for premium programs offered. In some cases, one may not register for other programs and services, such as day camps or preschools, without having paid these minimal dues. The JCC of Manhattan calls its approach to minimal dues "community membership." However, whenever an institution provides discounts to programs and services as a benefit of membership, it unintentionally asks people to consider the value of membership in strictly financial terms. In addition, this approach leads to a transactional membership model, also called fee-for-service. Such an approach undermines the goal of creating a welcoming community, which is the desideratum of nearly all Jewish communal institutions.

It is important to note that there are some institutions that do not offer membership at all and even provide their services for free. Chabad is a successful example of such an approach. Chabad rabbis are social entrepreneurs who succeed or fail in the midst of a free market economy. As a result, they have no boards of directors to support, challenge, or direct their decisions. Chabad Houses are generally known to be welcoming regardless of one's background or religious practice. As an alternative to no membership, other institutions, such as Congregation Shir Shalom in Woodstock, Vermont, provide free membership to all who are interested in joining their community. Shir Shalom has been free to members—and financially stable—since its founding in 1988. Shir Shalom has never had an explicit fundraising campaign, although its leaders have quietly solicited those who can give financial support. Thus, it mostly exists on relationship fundraising.

FUNDRAISING

Among the most challenging aspects of finances for Jewish communal institutions is the disparity among them with regard to whether the operating budget is covered by dues. In most membership institutions, dues generally only cover a portion of the operating budget. The institution is therefore faced with raising the remainder of its necessary income through the assessment of fees, which can include building funds as well as various kinds of fundraising activities. This is important to note when considering the introduction of an alternative dues program. While an alternative dues program is more welcoming on the surface than the traditional model, when the alternative dues don't cover the majority of the institution's operating expenses, the institution is forced to assess additional fees, and the institution's welcoming quotient, as I call it, is undermined entirely. As a result, some institutions with alternative dues programs include a promise to members that no additional fees will be assessed and that they will not be solicited if there is a necessity to conduct any additional fundraising. In this case, any new financial program must be comprehensive and support the entirety of the institution's budget. If additional fundraising is necessary, the models that followed the historical arc of traditional dues will require changing as well. Just as a value proposition needs to be clarified for the purpose of collecting dues, potential members and supporters will want to see the personal and perhaps communal benefit of the institution that is requesting their financial support.

Since there are institutions in the Jewish community that are not membership based, they have no choice but to raise funds to support themselves. Some institutions, such as those that make up the Jewish Federation system, were originally established to raise funds and disburse those funds to the community to support other Jewish communal institutions. While this is less of the raison d'être for Jewish Federations and the like today, many are still raising community funds, as well as funds for their own operating expenses. Some techniques that these institutions undertook proved effective in the past but are no longer effective. These included "card calling," in which an individual publicly announces their gift at an event and peer pressure encourages others to do so, too, or "caucusing," in which leaders during a Federation mission trip unpack the emotional experience with participants in an effort to pull heartstrings and ask them to publicly announce an increased gift. Providing elite access to leaders based on a certain level of giving (another common approach) is not only not welcoming but also likely to actually push people away.

A case in point: Not long after I finished rabbinical school, I was invited to participate in a "rabbinic mission to Israel"—a model for fundraising for the United Jewish Appeal that was started by Herbert A. Friedman and then copied by many Jewish communal organizations. Natan Sharansky, a longtime Soviet Jewish refusenik, had just been released from the Soviet Union and immigrated to Israel. We newly minted rabbis were offered a chance to meet with him—or so I thought. It turned out that only donors of a certain level were given the privilege to meet with him at the time. As a recent graduate, I was certainly not in a position to make a large pledge or gift to the local Jewish Federation. I have never forgotten that incident. I share it because I did not feel welcome, and I carry that memory with me. Others have had similar experiences in the Jewish community, and they carry those memories with them as well. Institutional fundraisers have to bear in mind how certain techniques that may seem successful in the short term can be off-putting and unwelcoming to others by creating unpleasant memories and experiences that can linger for a lifetime and hurt their bottom line in the future.

All institutions require funds to operate. All are forced to find efficient and effective ways to raise those funds. As Rabbi Elazar ben Azaryah famously states in *Pirke Avot* (3:17), "Im ein kemach, ein Torah," which can be understood as "Without physical sustenance, there can be no spiritual nourishment." There is no debate here. However, how we raise those funds and what techniques are used can determine the future of the institution as much as the funds themselves. As an institution considers a fundraising project or approach, an important question has to be asked: Is it welcoming, especially to newcomers? Will it affirm those already engaged by the institution? A common fundraising maxim is this: "People give to people." Fundraising, beyond the notion of a values proposition, as discussed above, has to be built on the development of personal relationships. If I feel like I really belong and people care about me, I will support the institution.

The cost of participating in the Jewish community and affiliating with it can be quite high. At the same time, the baby boomer population, which remains the largest segment of the community, is steadily moving out of the workforce and thereby losing a fixed income. The millennial population will not have the financial resources of their parents; therefore, it will be imperative to develop new strategies that don't depend entirely on members to support the institution. If institutions can serve the entirety of the community, and not just their members, which means welcoming in disparate segments of the community, then institutions have a larger universe from which to raise funds. This will demand a rethinking of the very nature of Jewish communal institutions.

The various changes and shifts in organization that have impacted Jewish communal institutions over the course of the 20th century have been expedited by the recession of 2008 and further impacted by the pandemic of 2020. These crises will yield a vastly different landscape for the Jewish community when this era concludes. The financing of these institutions and the various approaches to dues and fundraising will significantly impact the shape of these institutions and the community they serve. The cadre of Jewish communal professionals will also change. Some will be phased out by economic necessity. New trends will require new professionals with new skills. It is unclear when this current era of Jewish communal life will fully conclude, but what is clear is that the Jewish community and its institutions will look nothing like it did when this era began—and neither will its foundation of financial support.

RESOURCES

Chernov, Beryl P., Debbie Joseph, and Daniel Judson. *Are Voluntary Dues Right for Your Synagogue? A Practical Guide.* Innovations and Strategies for Synagogues of Tomorrow 8. New York: UJA-Federation of New York, 2015.

Cousens, Beth. *Connected Congregations: From Dues and Membership to Sustaining Communities of Purpose.* Innovations and Strategies for Synagogues of Tomorrow 3. New York: UJA-Federation of New York, 2013.

Judson, Daniel. *Pennies for Heaven: The History of American Synagogues and Money.* Waltham, MA: Brandeis University Press, 2018.

Mersky, David A., and Abigail Harmon. *Successful Synagogue Fundraising Today: Overcoming the Fear of Asking for Money.* Woodstock, VT: Jewish Lights, 2016.

Olitzky, Kerry, and Avi Olitzky. *New Membership and Financial Alternatives for the American Synagogue: From Traditional Dues to Fair Share to Gifts from the Heart.* Woodstock, VT: Jewish Lights, 2015.

Reisner, Lianna Levine, and Daniel Judson. *Connection, Cultivation and Commitment: New Insights on Voluntary Dues.* Innovations and Strategies for Synagogues of Tomorrow 14. New York: UJA-Federation of New York, 2017.

Union for Reform Judaism. *Strengthening Congregations: Reimagining Financial Support for Your 21st-Century Congregation: A Report from the 2013–2015 Community of Practice.* New York: Union for Reform Judaism, n.d. https://urj.org/sites/default/files/ReimaginingFinancialSupport.pdf.

Zevit, Shawn. *Offerings of the Heart: Money and Values in Faith Communities.* Bethesda, MD: Alban Institute, 2005.

NOTES

1. For a full discussion of seating in the American synagogue, see Jonathan D. Sarna, "Seating in the American Synagogue," in *Belief and Behavior: Essays in the New Religious History*, ed. Philip R. Vandemeer and Robert P. Swierenga (New Brunswick, NJ: Rutgers University Press, 1991), 189–206.

2. Robert D. Putnam, *Bowling Alone: The Collapse and Revival of American Community* (New York: Simon & Schuster, 2000).

3. Kerry M. Olitzky, *Playlist Judaism: Making Choices for a Vital Future* (Herndon, VA: Alban Institute, 2013).

4. See, for example, Mark Greenspan, "What the Shekel Teaches: Ten Commandments for Synagogue Fundraising," *eJewish Philanthropy*, March 7, 2011, https://ejewishphilanthropy.com/what-the-shekel-teaches-ten-commandments-for-synagogue-fundraising/.

5. Daniel Judson and Lianna Levine Reisner, "Connection, Cultivation, and Commitment: New Insights on Voluntary Dues," *SYNERGY Innovations and Strategies for Synagogues of Tomorrow* 14 (2017): 3, https://www.ujafedny.org/api/v2/assets/788990/.

6. See Beryl Chernov, Debbie Joseph, and Daniel Judson, "Are Voluntary Dues Right for Your Synagogue? A Practical Guide," *SYNERGY Innovations and Strategies for Synagogues of Tomorrow* 8 (2015), https://www.ujafedny.org/api/v2/assets/787643.

CHAPTER 14

Marketing and Communications

Miriam Brosseau and Lisa Colton

A few summers back, Miriam moved to a new area with her husband and new baby. While they knew some people in the area, they were eager for community and assumed that a great way to find that was to get involved in a synagogue. Thanks to Google, Miriam found a congregation within walking distance of her family's apartment and fumbled around on the synagogue's outdated website in an attempt to dig up times for Friday night services. Several pages (and too many minutes) deep, she found the information. She decided to go alone (sans baby, just this first time) to check it out and report back. She got all dolled up for the first time in months and walked out the door that Friday night, excited at the prospect of becoming embraced by a community so close to home.

When she arrived, she tried the door, only to find it locked. Confused, she looked for another entrance. Nothing. A sign outside listed times for services and other upcoming events, but, to her dismay, it didn't match what was posted on the website; services wouldn't begin for another hour. She didn't want to leave her still-nursing baby that long. Dejected, she walked home. Once home, she tried calling, but no one picked up. She poked around on Facebook but found nothing matching the congregation's name and location. Her sense of belonging to this community ended before it had ever really begun.

There's a story in the Talmud of a rabbi who announces that no student may learn with one who is not *tocho k'varo* (one whose insides are not like their outsides). The values they embody need to be reflected in their actions, and vice versa. It's the definition of authenticity. Too often, as communications experts, we see Jewish organizations that claim to be "warm and welcoming," but such language feels like false advertising. The congregation in the story above missed the mark on a basic test of *tocho k'varo*. By not providing information that was consistent or easily accessible, potential visitors couldn't accurately get to know their insides or outsides. Internally, something like this could simply be chalked up to an administrative error. As a newcomer, though, Miriam never got the chance to see what this community had to offer. If this was how the synagogue (mis)communicated something as basic as Shabbat service times, it didn't bode well for how she and her family would *feel* even if she could walk through their doors or how the synagogue was positioned to function as an organization overall. In today's busy attention economy, organizations are competing for nanoseconds of attention in order to build trust, and that trust buys you more time and attention to deepen the relationship.

COMMUNICATIONS AS A NERVOUS SYSTEM

Communication is an essential element of relationships, whether with a spouse, boss, friend, or customer. It's the nervous system of your community that connects and animates all the other facets of communal life—creating relationships, setting priorities, conveying energy and emotion, building momentum, and sharing information (like the correct time of Friday night services). But communication is much more than just providing your audience with facts or the *who, why, where,* and *when.* It's also about the *how.* Research conducted with 18–40-year-olds over the summer of 2020 by the Charles and Lynn Schusterman Family Philanthropies and the Jim Joseph Foundation found that, in the context of virtual events in particular, how such an event makes a young adult *feel* is more important than what information you get them to *know.* In their research, the participants who *felt* positively about a virtual event were more than twice as likely to engage again, particularly when they felt a sense of connection, fulfillment, and/or fun.[1]

A NEW WAY OF THINKING, A NEW WAY OF WORKING

Thanks to the internet and social media, today's younger generations are different from previous generations in how they consume and interact with media. Millennials (those born between 1981 and 1996) and Gen Zers (those born from the mid-1990s to the early 2010s) have fundamentally different characteristics than baby boomers and Gen Xers and thus are forcing companies and nonprofits to design and communicate in new ways. As of April 2020, the number of millennials in the United States surpassed the number of baby boomers for the first time.[2] Millennials also represent $2.5 trillion in annual buying power and command a strong voice in social media.[3] For a group that has never known life without a smartphone, the one-directional "broadcast" relationship doesn't capture their imaginations or serve their needs. Millennials and those younger than them expect brands to build relationships with them, listen to them, and engage with them.[4] Ease, accessibility, and customized experiences are paramount. Evan Spiegel, a co-founder of Snapchat, sums up millennial attitudes: "We do have a sense of entitlement, a sense of ownership, because, after all, this is the world we were born into, and we are responsible for it."[5]

In order to resonate with younger generations, we need to shift from broadcast communications to styles of communication that serve as the nervous system and connective tissue that coordinates and animates all of our endeavors in a multifaceted and relational experience. We've identified five interconnected strategies that best model how to achieve this style of communication:

1. **Emphasize "show" over "tell."** Instead of using a bullhorn to tell people about your organization, demonstrate what makes your organization special by working to make sure the "inside matches the outside."
2. **Speak not just to the head but also to the hearts, hands, and "hooks" (or relationships) of the people you seek to engage.** While the specifics of the information provided is important, rather than communicating only to share information, think about using communications to impact how people *feel* and experience *belonging* to a community.
3. **Serve people rather than chase technology.** Instead of adding a layer of technology to your "broadcast era" communications, consider redesigning the function of your communications to better serve not just millennials and Gen Z but all your constituents.
4. **Communications *is* the work.** The story you tell both reflects and becomes the story your community lives. Communicate to create connection, live your values, and build your culture.
5. **Communications is your organization's nervous system and is infused into every function.** Instead of consolidating all the communications with one person, explore how to infuse communications throughout your team.

EMPHASIZE "SHOW" OVER "TELL"

For many of us who grew up in the age of broadcast communications where information is shared out in a one-way flow of direction, we have been diligently (and unwittingly) taught that if we could only get *more people to see how very awesome we are*, the masses would come. We've been led to believe that marketing is merely a question of reach—that is, our job is simply to tell more people about all the great things we're doing. Broadcast communications were built on the premise that the more people you can *inform*, the more people will know about you and therefore buy whatever it is you are selling. The broadcast approach of simply shouting your message louder and to a larger audience worked well for a hundred years, but in an "attention economy" that is grossly oversaturated with messages, this strategy is no longer effective. Think about the last time a piece of marketing actually moved you to change your behavior, take any kind of action, or influenced your beliefs. How would you characterize it? What made it so effective? When we shift our perspective and consider the kinds of marketing we find most engaging, inviting, and, yes, even informative, it is not often broadcast- or announcement-style messaging. Rather it is the messaging that helps us feel seen, known, and understood. It's about *showing* your audience what their experience or lives will be like if they come to your organization and how what you have to offer will make their lives better, easier, or more meaningful.

If you're reaching out to an entirely new audience, or reintroducing your organization with a new brand or project, you need to do a certain amount of informing—just letting your target audience know you exist. But in the field of Jewish communal work, we're not selling widgets (or, honestly, even memberships); we're inviting people into *community*. Potential participants need to know that what you're offering is actually for people like them, and that the organization running things is both authentic and trustworthy. A synagogue website with a picture of a brick building may have a caption that says, "We're a warm and welcoming community," but there is no proof that they actually *are* "warm and welcoming." In fact, there's no proof that there's even a community at all. You need to show the communal culture and demonstrate the feeling of belonging, not just say that it exists and hope your prospective audience believes you.

Take Chevre Ahavas Yisroel (CAY), described on its Facebook page as "a lovely little shul located in the heart of Crown Heights, New York—for good people looking for good davening." The congregation began because many young people weren't finding their fit in other synagogues in the neighborhood, which catered to older, more established adults and families. Young singles exploring diverse interests and paths needed a place of their own. As such, the synagogue caters to a wide range of personalities, from tech entrepreneurs to artists. Every aspect of their marketing becomes a window into the unique community they are—and a mirror to the one they seek to serve. Their Facebook header image, for example, is a funky, colorful painting of a service in progress, done by artist Annita Sobel—a member of the community (see figure 14.1).

Contrast this image with the typical synagogue Facebook header image of the outside of a building, or the "dramatic" shot of rows and rows of empty pews, and a viewer quickly discerns that the difference in imagery is a difference in values. Shots of a building emphasize the *what*, the *vehicle* for the community. The CAY painting emphasizes the *why*: the community itself.

Think about your audience—who are you trying to reach? Consider their demographics: age, geography, income, and the like. But perhaps more

Chevra Ahavas Yisroel
@chevraahavasyisroel · Local Business

⊘ Send Message

Figure 14.1. Chevra Ahavas Yisroel uses its creative Facebook header image to show who the congregation is, not where it meets.

important, consider their psychographics: what they think, feel, believe, and value. And beyond where that person is today, ask yourself what kind of person your ideal "customer" wants to be, and how your organization can help them become that person. These questions represent the alignment of mission and aspiration. Seeking out these distinctions will lead you to the powerful intersection you want to speak to. *Show* who you are to those you seek to serve.

SPEAK TO THE HEADS, HEARTS, HANDS, AND "HOOKS"

Mishkan Chicago is a spiritual community committed to "inspired, down-to-earth Judaism" headed up by the insightful and exuberant Rabbi Lizzi Heydemann and a youthful and grounded staff deeply devoted to the persistent act of welcoming. Contrast the opening anecdote of encountering a locked synagogue with the wording on the "Get Involved" page of Mishkan Chicago's website:

> It can feel intimidating to walk into services on a Friday night and face a room full of strangers. We've figured out a cure for that feeling: Shabbat dinner with Mishkanites in your neighborhood. Or celebrating Havdalah on a rooftop with people who share a piece of your story. Or greeting people as they walk through the door at a holiday or Shabbat. Whether you're looking to just show up, get involved as a leader, or provide some kind of service in community, we'll hook you up.[6]

There is nothing hidden about this language, no digging deep through pages to unearth the information that matters. Even from this small slice of messaging, prospective attendees understand that more than informational data, Mishkan Chicago wants to provide a sense of what this community values and what attendees might *feel* if they participate. A reader immediately perceives a level of care in the conversational tone of the wording. The blurb acknowledges the needs of the potential congregant, what they're looking for, that they might feel vulnerable at the start, and how the Mishkan community

Figure 14.2. Skokie Valley Agudath Israel invites congregants to ease the rabbi's loneliness by booking one-on-one conversations.

might meet those needs. (And it's pretty much guaranteed that the times for services are accurate and updated on the website.) This is the essence of powerful communications: a radical acknowledgment of the humanity of the people receiving it.

While adept at welcoming communications, Mishkan Chicago is hardly unique. Figure 14.2 shows a post from the Facebook page of a synagogue located just a bit north of Mishkan Chicago: Skokie Valley Agudath Jacob congregation in Skokie, Illinois. This was posted at a time when the coronavirus pandemic was peaking in that state.

A traditional "broadcast" message would approach this opportunity very differently. "Book your conversation with the rabbi today!" it might read. But that approach is all about informing; it's all about the head. This post, however, takes a very different approach. It speaks to the *head* and informs the community of a new offering, but it also goes far beyond that surface level of information:

- It speaks to the *heart* by acknowledging the somewhat paradoxical sense of shared loneliness of life in a pandemic. The rabbi feels lonely, too.
- It speaks to the *hands* by giving a concrete action step and examples of what the conversation with the rabbi might entail. No topic is too small or trivial.
- It speaks to *hooks*, in this case the relationship between the rabbi and the congregants, by framing the offering as a two-way opportunity to heal, to connect, and even to contribute.

This special post is empowering during a time when most of the congregation might feel disempowered. The wording doesn't suggest that congregants are lonely and crave the presence of their spiritual leader (true as that may be). Rather, the rabbi himself is in need of company and solace. By participating in this offering, you're contributing; you're helping *him* out. Jewish tradition speaks deeply and powerfully of the importance of communal contribution, of everyone—regardless of status—putting in their proverbial half-shekel, their contribution to the communal pot. By framing this as an opportunity to *help*, rather than *be helped*, any sense of shame in asking for help is stripped away and the instinct to give kicks in. The idea that I can support my community's leader by taking a walk with him and unloading my troubles is quietly profound.

When considering the content and messaging of your marketing, take all these elements into account: the *head*, the *heart*, the *hands*, and the *hooks* (relationships). At its best, marketing and communications are not about programs or institutions or simply providing the information one needs to show up (though, again, the importance of accurate information cannot be overstated). Effective communication is about speaking to the whole of a person, emotional and spiritual, and not just the intellectual.

SERVE PEOPLE RATHER THAN CHASE TECHNOLOGY

Like you, your audience is probably overwhelmed by messaging. Digital marketing experts estimate that every single one of us is bombarded with more than 5,000 messages a day—up from 500 a day in the 1970s and far more than the human brain is capable of engaging with in any meaningful way.[7] As the communications ecosystem becomes more and more crowded, our internal filters are on high alert for irrelevance. Your marketing, therefore, needs to find a way to cut through the clutter.

Here's the key, though: the point of communications is not to master the Facebook algorithm or edit the perfect Instagram image. The "com" in the word "communications"—just like in "company" and "community"—means "together." Communications is about connecting with people first, and while we need to be familiar with new technologies in order to understand the array of possibilities at our disposal, our primary job is to figure out to how connect people to our mission and to one another. Technology may be the means, but it is certainly not the end to our goal of building community.

Before diving into the particulars of a communications platform, we need to understand how your audience allocates its most scarce and precious resources: time and attention. In the last decade, the normalization of social media and our digital lifestyle has fundamentally changed the way we consume information and make decisions. Americans use multiple screens simultaneously, often accessing content while in motion. According to a recent study from *eMarketer*, "In 2020, U.S. adults spent 7 hours, 50 minutes (7:50) per day consuming digital media."[8] While one might assume that the answer to communications, given this statistic, is simply to communicate online, the overwhelming surge of information means that other factors drive our decisions, too. For example, with so much digital media competing for our attention, many of us now turn to our friends, in whom, by virtue of their authenticity, we place a greater level of trust in helping us decide what products to buy, what programs to attend, and what organizations to support.

Foregrounding the need to connect with your audience in an authentic and meaningful way, take a look at your marketing from your audience's perspective: receiving your e-mail on their commute, catching a glimpse of your post as they scroll through Instagram, perusing flyers on the bulletin board of the JCC or local coffee shop. Whether they think this consciously or not, your potential audience has one question running through their mind, acting as that initial filter: "What does *this* have to do with *me*?" If your target person cannot come up with a compelling answer, if their attention isn't caught within a few micro-seconds of encountering your piece, then they will not continue to engage. It doesn't matter what delivery system you're using; if the message isn't there, the platform is moot.

This is a difficult balance to strike, especially on social media where posts on the newsfeed are collated for users. Every platform has its own specialized algorithm, which is constantly taking in information and determining what content rises to the top, for whom, and for how long. You can, through the minutiae of constant optimization and well-targeted ad spends, increase your chances of staying at the top of your audience's feed. While that may, in the moment, capture the attention of more individuals, your place of prominence in their feeds does not guarantee that you will build trust or move those same people to action.

Rather, focus on the person over the algorithm. Speak to their heads, hands, hearts, and hooks, and speak *with* them, not *at* them. One school asked on social media "bagels or muffins?" the day before a parent meeting (and learned how many gluten-free people would be attending). Another synagogue asked, "What's your favorite place to buy challah around here?" on behalf of some newcomers to town and got not only a plethora of responses but also multiple Shabbat dinner invitations for the new family. One rabbi posts a regular funny photo in "a day in the life of the rabbi" as a caption contest that invites lighthearted (fictional) captions. Like a good host, your communications should invite someone to see themselves (literally or figuratively) as part of the communal story, and your communications should affirm the importance of their place in that story.

COMMUNICATIONS *IS* THE WORK: THE ROLE OF STORYTELLING

Storytelling has become a bit of a marketing buzzword, which is unfortunate because there is real wisdom in this human-centered approach to our marketing and communications. Humanity is wired for story. Author Tahir Shah calls stories "a communal currency of humanity."[9] Story is how we make sense of all the disparate pieces of our lives. Judaism itself is rife with story; our collective stories are how we build a sense of coherence, purpose, and worth, both individually and collectively. Our goal as communicators is to demonstrate that our organizations' missions can be a meaningful part of our audiences' stories and that the people we serve can in turn be a meaningful part of our organizations. Both sides of the equation must be equally true for the story to hold together and for the relationship to feel fulfilling.

There are a few ways we can think about what storytelling means and how we can incorporate it into our marketing and communications. First is the idea of the organizational narrative, which is the overarching sense of shared history, experiences, values, and beliefs that tie a congregation, its mission, and its participants together. "Storytelling" in this context is less about sharing any one particular story; rather, it is about consistently demonstrating that sense of a shared past, present, and future through the language, tone, colors, and imagery we use.

In practical terms, how you tell your story and what story you're telling is what makes your *brand*. A brand is more than your logo. A brand is who you are and the story you are telling. While it may be tolerable, and even charming, to post home-spun flyers of upcoming events for the sake of speed or lack of resources, the drawback is in quality, consistency, and sense of connection. Rather than create a sense of connection by feeling casual or grassroots, unprofessional publicity can be alienating to your potential audience, conveying a sense that the organization doesn't know what message they want to send and don't care enough to send that message in a polished way. Having a consistent look and feel to your marketing collateral provides a sense of stability and groundedness—a reference point for the ongoing narrative your community is weaving together. Adherence to brand standards takes on the quality of a type of *minhag* (a communal practice that works to connect people to one another). Consistent branding then has the added benefit of capturing attention when that mold is consciously broken.

The other side of storytelling is, quite simply, telling specific stories. The key to this type of storytelling is knowing what to share—and how to share it well. And when we share stories, we need to be intentional about the moral of the story we hope our listeners will take away.

A while back, Miriam worked with SHALVA, a Jewish domestic abuse prevention organization, on a series of videos aimed at empowering upstanders— those friends, colleagues, and relatives who notice something is wrong and who may suspect abuse is happening but just need the language and tools to speak up. This organization had done life-changing work with survivors and hoped to expand its impact by reaching those who were not necessarily in an abusive relationship themselves but may be in a position to help others. Through a short initial research period, we uncovered the emotional arc of these upstanders' experiences, nailing down four basic stages they would go through, from expressing concern to effectively supporting their friend. To educate and activate these upstanders, we leaned on the power of storytelling. We developed an animation that told the story of a different upstander at each of the four points in the journey. We specifically centered stories of upstanders themselves, not survivors of abuse, because we wanted our audience to see themselves in these narratives and to emulate what our characters were doing. In the course of telling these stories, we found organic ways to integrate statistics on domestic violence, counter stereotypes about abuse in the Jewish community, and show—rather than tell—how these individuals made a difference.

At its heart, a well-crafted story is an *invitation*, not a *presentation*. We do not tell our stories to show off. We tell stories to help others understand, connect, and step inside of the story themselves. We tell stories to create a culture of permission for others to share their stories, be vulnerable, find points of connection, and enter into new narratives that we build together. Through stories comes understanding, relationship, and thus community.

THE COMMUNICATIONS NERVOUS SYSTEM IN ACTION: BRINGING IT ALL TOGETHER

Today, communications must function like a nervous system (not a bullhorn), which is a fundamentally different way of organizing your communications than you may have now. Organizations must invest time and effort to transition to different types of communication, but the benefits are worthwhile for the organizations and the community as a whole. A nervous system has feedback loops that send messages out and listen to the messages coming back in return. To run, your brain, muscles, and inner ear all work in close coordination to keep you balanced and moving forward. So, too, your communications infrastructure engages many people and systems across your organization in close coordination to have an elegant and effective impact on your community.

To work in the ways we've described in this chapter, communications professionals and their colleagues need to capture the "DNA" of your community— the values, personality, and essence of who you are. Honing in on this essence will empower the different levels of stakeholders within your institution to build a culture of engagement, listening, and responsiveness while maintaining sufficient consistency and cohesiveness. Just like each cell of your body has the same DNA, each cell also expresses it differently, from your eye color and your bone marrow to your likelihood to develop certain diseases. Your community's DNA and the culture you build from it will be the starting point for how all staff members and volunteers think about, understand, and talk about your community and organization. That DNA is expressed everywhere—from the photo on your website (brick building or multigenerational celebration?) to the tone of your social media posts (serious or snarky?) to how your staff answers the phone in the office. When everyone is expressing the same DNA, your organization's insides will start to match your outsides, allowing participants a more authentic experience. Furthermore, you'll find your community members relate this DNA through their networks, too, and that word of mouth is the best marketing you can ask for. As communications specialists, we are here to tell you that the best digital strategies are almost useless without the entire team aligned about what constitutes the DNA of the community.

Once you have a good shared sense of that DNA, the next step to make your communications hum is to clarify your goals. That may sound simple, but we encourage you to check your assumptions. What really is your goal, and how does that goal relate to your mission? Often, organizations are aiming (explicitly or implicitly) to get "more tushes in seats." But this goal is organization centric rather than community centric, and it's probably not actually the essence of your mission. Your communications will default to broadcast, and you'll slip right back into the status quo. When you align your mission, goals, and DNA, your communication strategy and tactics will become clearer.

From 2013 to 2015, Lisa collaborated with UJA-Federation of New York on a project called "Connected Congregations" to help a cohort of synagogues that wanted to work more as *communities* rather than as *institutions*. A Connected Congregation was defined as a congregation that "deeply understands the meaning of community, and works explicitly to build a strong, meaningful and engaged Jewish community. Connected Congregations prioritize relationships and shared values as the foundation of a successful synagogue, and *align all aspects of institutional management in service of this community*."[10] Because a Connected Congregation acknowledges that *connection precedes participation*, the goal of their marketing and communications is to offer multiple entry points for connection, not simply to blast out information about upcoming programs and expect people to appear in seats.

Communications designed as a nervous system measures progress by engagement, for example, the number and quality of comments on and shares of a post, or the dialogue that is organically generated online about issues related to your organization. How do you build a culture of engagement? Start by *asking questions* to invite replies. You might begin to see more replies to your e-mail newsletters and comments on your social media posts. Then you might start to see people talking *to each other* in the comments, not just talking back to you. Likes, followers, and views (sometimes called "vanity metrics") are only useful as leading indicators—a hint that you're doing something right to invite people in. While these indicators are easy to measure, on their own they do not indicate much about a healthy, warm, and connected community.

If this nervous system model sounds like more than you're prepared to do today, you may be right. This isn't a simple switch to flip; it's a transition that may take time. Evolving the culture of conversations with your audience takes consistency and patience. Moving from broadcast to nervous system likely means updating the job descriptions, skills, systems, and culture within your organization to match today's needs, rather than the needs of your organization 10 years ago. Together, the entire staff will function as a coordinated communications team "quarterbacked" by the person who is accountable for the communications strategy and calendar, who will also be tasked with coordinating and developing organizational culture. Communications should be increasingly embedded into many roles throughout your organization, and thus more people need strategic communications skills. Consider these as critical skills in every hire you make from here forward.

As you get your nervous system whirring, you will start to see opportunities for new roles that are emerging in organizations that are particularly savvy. Such positions might be a "network weaver," who intentionally and strategically connects people to each other and nurtures a community that "hums" together. A membership director might morph into a director of community engagement, a title that speaks more directly to the results and goals that marketing and communications can and should play for any organization. But simply changing the title does not change the operating system. The description, skills, activities, responsibilities, and measurements of success must change, too. Moving to a nervous system model of communications takes intentionality, patience, and culture change, but we promise that, when done well, reaching your audience will feel less like constantly swimming upstream, and more like surfing a wave.

Our society is in the midst of a communications revolution. Not since the advent of the printing press has there been so much change in society driven by changes in the way we communicate. While the printing press may have catalyzed social, political, economic, and religious revolution hundreds of years ago, the real lesson of the printing press is about literacy. When more people were able to share their ideas and get their hands on printed material, the general public had a motivation to learn to read. So while our current communications revolution may be dizzying, when used well, these strategies are powerful tools for a more connected, engaged, and literate Jewish community.

While you may want to seek out easy answers by becoming fixated on the latest technologies, remember that communications is about people, together on a journey to create meaning and support each other. In a world so dominated by technology, those who design for the human experience will be most effective at truly cultivating a warm and welcoming community that's *tocho k'varo*, where the insides match the outside.

RESOURCES

Brafman, Ori, and Rod Beckstrom. *The Starfish and the Spider: The Power of Leaderless Organizations.* New York: Portfolio, 2006.

Campbell, Julia. *Storytelling in the Digital Age: A Guide for Nonprofits.* Nashville, TN: CharityChannel Press, 2017.

Godin, Seth. *This Is Marketing: You Can't Be Seen until You Learn to See.* New York: Portfolio, 2018.

Kanter, Beth, and Allison Fine. *The Networked Nonprofit: Connecting with Social Media to Drive Change.* New York: Jossey-Bass, 2010.

Miller, Kivi Leroux. *CALM not BUSY: How to Manage Your Nonprofit's Communications for Great Results.* Lexington, NC: Bold & Bright Media, 2017.

Shirky, Clay. *Here Comes Everybody: The Power of Organizing without Organizations.* New York: Penguin, 2008.

NOTES

1. Benenson Strategy Group, *Virtual Engagement Research* (n.p.: Benenson Strategy Group, August 2020), 3–5, https://www.schusterman.org/sites/default/files/Virtual EngagementResearchFindings2020.pdf.

2. Richard Fry, "Millennials Overtake Baby Boomers as America's Largest Generation," Pew Research Center, April 28, 2020, https://www.pewresearch.org/fact-tank/ 2020/04/28/millennials-overtake-baby-boomers-as-americas-largest-generation/.

3. "Millennials & Gen Z Teens' Combined Spending Power Is Nearly $3 Trillion in 2020," *YPulse*, January 9, 2020, https://www.ypulse.com/article/2020/01/09/ millennials-gen-z-teens-combined-spending-power-is-nearly-3-trillion-in-2020/.

4. Lauren Freedman, "Here's What Millennials Really Want from Brands," *Total Retail*, September 28, 2017, https://www.mytotalretail.com/article/heres-millennials-really-want-brands/.

5. Evan Spiegel, "Snapchat CEO Evan Spiegel to Grads: 'This Is the World We Were Born Into, and We Are Responsible for It,'" *Time*, May 16, 2015, https://time.com/ collection-post/3881609/snapchat-evan-spiegel-graduation-speech/.

6. Mishkan Chicago, "Get Involved," accessed July 15, 2021, https://web.archive .org/web/20200928061126/https://www.mishkanchicago.org/get-involved/.

7. Sam Carr, "How Many Ads Do We See a Day in 2021?" *PPCProtect*, February 15, 2021, https://ppcprotect.com/how-many-ads-do-we-see-a-day/.

8. "US Adults Added 1 Hour of Digital Time in 2020," *eMarketer*, January 26, 2021, https://www.emarketer.com/content/us-adults-added-1-hour-of-digital-time-2020.

9. Tahir Shah, *In Arabian Nights: A Caravan of Moroccan Dreams* (New York: Bantam, 2008), 138.

10. "Theory," Connected Congregations, accessed July 21, 2021, http://connectedcon gregations.org/theory/ (emphasis added).

CHAPTER 15

(Almost) Everything Else

Miriam Steinberg-Egeth

I grew up in a small town with an even smaller Jewish community. In my professional capacities now, I see many times the number of Jewish people on a daily basis than I even knew existed when I was young. Part of my naïveté about Jewish communities as a child was that I perceived that everyone Jewish had to stick together; there were so few of us that we couldn't afford to be exclusionary, territorial, or anything other than genuinely welcoming to each other.

One of the greatest disappointments of my adult life was realizing just how wrong that perception was. Much of my motivation for my work in the Jewish community and my involvement in this book is to make good on what I believed to be true in my childhood: all Jewish communities must, by necessity, be open and accessible to anyone and everyone who wants to participate.

As my family's phone number was on the answering machine for the only local synagogue, from a young age, I learned that if I answered the phone and someone had a question about Judaism, I was to answer it to the best of my ability or to make sure that the person on the other end of the line knew that my parents would get back to them soon. To some extent, I have been striving to be the best person on the other end of the phone for anyone trying to connect to the Jewish community for my entire professional life, determined to treat each newcomer with care and concern and never taking anyone for granted.

I'm glad to be part of your journey as you, too, aim to create a genuinely welcoming, truly inclusive Jewish experience for the people around you. Reading this book, reflecting on the issues raised in each chapter, considering what tangible improvements you can make in your organizations—these have all been steps on that journey. And now you've reached the end—of the book anyway. You've made it. Sort of.

While you're at the conclusion of the book, there's no end in sight to the process of making our Jewish communities more warm and welcoming. Inclusionary work is never ending and always changing, and the commitment to examining our organizations is sometimes as important as the changes we choose to implement. In some cases, the act of *solving* an issue can even create a new issue. What if you decide to use amplification in your sanctuary on Shabbat to make services accessible to people with hearing disabilities, but that causes Shabbat-observant Jews to feel alienated by the use of electricity on Shabbat? Or what if you arrange a meet-up for families with young children to help create a safe space for noisy kids and, in the process, childless young adults feel excluded from their peers? These aren't theoretical examples; they are real-life ways that organizations are grappling with what inclusion means.

Making your institution a welcoming place means negotiating boundaries, thinking about how changes will impact people from a wide variety of backgrounds, and ultimately coming to terms with the fact that your space, organization, or project won't be able to be all things to all people. Rather, you need to determine what being "warm and welcoming" looks like in the context of your audience and the unique circumstances of your organization. By examining your institution's values and goals, you can determine which aspects of this book speak to you and your constituents and which won't.

Another challenge of inclusion work is that there are always more areas in which to make progress. The process of choosing what areas to focus on automatically means at least temporarily deprioritizing another group of people deeply deserving of attention and community resources. This final chapter gives voice to a few more topics, recognizing that "everything else" will always inherently be incomplete and unfinished.

TRANSLATION AND TRANSLITERATION

Warren shares the following story:

> A few years ago, my [then] boyfriend and I attended services at a synagogue that was new to us. The synagogue is known for its progressive politics and their truly impressive efforts at inclusivity. Before the service began, leaders touted their gender-inclusive and physically accessible restrooms. They had hired a sign language interpreter for the deaf and hard of hearing. They were proud to stand in solidarity with the Black Lives Matter movement and advocated for progressive causes like preserving the environment and fair immigration. Truly, it was a lot to be proud of.
>
> But as the service began, my boyfriend leaned over to me and whispered, "Uh, I think we're in trouble." As I opened the High Holiday *machzor* (prayer book), I realized that the synagogue had decided to haul out old Reform prayer books with only a bare smattering of transliteration tucked away at the back of the book. My boyfriend is not Jewish, and yet, since dating me, has been not only supportive of

my Jewish practice but has taken an interest himself in Judaism and likes coming to services, especially when there's music. But he doesn't read or speak Hebrew. Not a drop. And when confronted with a prayer book where he couldn't follow along or even sing the chorus, this was a major failing at inclusivity. How can he (or us as a couple) feel welcome here when the basic ability to verbally participate was essentially made impossible?[1]

It's not just most non-Jews who can't read Hebrew. Many Jews themselves lack this skill. According to the 2013 Pew study on American Jews, "Fully half of U.S. Jews (52%) say they know the Hebrew alphabet, though far fewer (13%) say they can understand most or all of the words when they read Hebrew."[2] Not surprisingly, the statistics on Hebrew knowledge also correlate to a person's level of religious observance. Orthodox Jews and individuals who have attended day school possess a higher level of Hebrew proficiency. Meanwhile, only 24 percent of "Jews of no religion" can read the Hebrew alphabet, a category of Jews who might attend High Holiday services once a year but no other time.[3]

But making services accessible to non-Hebrew readers isn't out of reach. Buying new, more inclusive prayer books may not be financially possible for every synagogue, but creating a few dozen photocopied supplements with transliteration should be a manageable undertaking. Making sure everyone stays on the same page between different books can be challenging, but having someone hold up page number cue cards is a reasonable volunteer job to add to your roster. Prayer books that include full transliteration can be cumbersome to hold onto, but prayer leaders can mark points in the service where the books can be set down. Even with the prayers written out in English, it's not always clear how to pronounce the words, where the syllable breaks are, and how the phonetic spellings correspond to the translations, but inviting congregants to sing along on wordless melodies can help relieve the burden to pronounce every word. Synagogues owe it to their attendees, Jews and non-Jews alike, both to make these changes and to acknowledge the limitations of how much inclusion transliteration can provide.

Transliteration and translation also goes beyond prayers and prayer books. Anytime someone speaks publicly for a Jewish organization or at a Jewish event, any Hebrew or Yiddish words used in sermons or announcements should be translated on the spot or not used. Sometimes it's true that certain words can create an inclusive feeling for people who are in the know. But at least as often, those same phrases end up excluding others, and those who are left out, without translations, are more likely to be those who are otherwise unsure whether Jewish spaces are really for them. It's not worth the cute pun in your marketing language or the laugh during announcements at the expense of those in your congregations who may not understand.

One way of explicitly including people is through an invitation to participate. But asking someone to read something in Hebrew can be terrifying for some, so even those invitations should be offered carefully. When inviting the congregation to sing along, prayer leaders can teach the refrain and offer opportunities to practice as a community. This can happen either in the service itself or through prerecorded videos in advance of services. Prayer leaders can also offer translations and pronunciation help in real time during a prayer service, and while, yes, this can add to the length of services, the cost/benefit of including the whole community as full participants is a worthwhile consideration. Some communities are set up to project transliteration and translation during services, but even if that is outside the scope of what is possible in your space, looking at serving people who don't read Hebrew as an inclusion issue to address creatively helps create a culture that speaks to the reality of the people in your seats. One notable advantage of virtual services during the pandemic was the ease with which prayer leaders could screen share transliterations much more nimbly than using photocopies or new prayer books. As organizations think about lessons learned from 2020, I hope this is one area that continues to receive attention.

FOOD

You may be nodding along at the idea that reading or singing in another language has a high potential to leave people out, but perhaps the idea of eating together seems universally inclusive. Food, though, while a crucially important aspect of Jewish events and gatherings, is also a potentially polarizing element that can divide people based on religious practice, health issues, and ethically held preferences. When organizations consider what to serve at a *kiddush* luncheon, happy hour, or Hanukkah party, they are setting the tone for how and whether a variety of dietary needs are taken into account. If a person shows up to a Passover seder and finds that there is nothing she can eat, she's unlikely to seek out that organization again in the future.

The laws of keeping kosher dictate many of the decisions around food for a certain set of Jewish organizations. There may be a preferred caterer list for Conservative and Orthodox synagogues to make sure catered events adhere to that community's standards of keeping kosher. Not everyone in a community always "holds by," or accepts the same *hashgacha* (kosher certification), so even when an event is catered, there may be questions around who eats what. Further complicating matters, I remember the first time I heard someone say she prefers eating food that *isn't* certified kosher, citing the often exclusionary beliefs of the usually male rabbis who oversee kosher establishments. You are likely to encounter new food needs and opinions at every turn, but being prepared for and sensitive to people's reactions will help you provide for them appropriately.

Potlucks are popular in many communities and have led to terminology like "kosher-style," "ingredient kosher," and the "two-table system."[4] If you know what these things mean, you know where to put your food when you arrive at Shabbat dinner. If you're a newcomer, you're likely to be left standing around holding a tray of baked ziti with no idea where to put it and how you'll be judged based on where your food ends up. Even these designations aren't standardized, and the rules may vary from community to community. In an attempt to be inclusive (everyone brings a dish to share!), potlucks can sometimes lead to exclusion (your food doesn't meet our standards) or confusion (where do I put this? what can I eat?). Minyan Tikvah, an independent *minyan* I helped found in Philadelphia, came up with a "sticker system," in which everyone's potluck contribution had an attached notecard that answered a variety of questions ranging from "Does this include peanuts?" to "Was this made in a kosher kitchen?" In this way, everyone's contributions were subject to the same scrutiny, and everyone could see for themselves how the food matched their personal needs.

Even though we're talking about food, Shabbat observance also factors in. Another item on the potluck sticker sheet was "Was this transported in a car on Shabbat?" While this is a non-issue to some, for others, it might render the contribution inedible because of the prohibition of using electricity on Shabbat. The host of an event may go out of their way to get food from a kosher caterer, only to realize they've made it impossible for their Shabbat-observant guests to eat by heating the food up on Shabbat. Food, the very thing we often depend on to unite us, can unwittingly cause problems because of these subtle and hard-to-navigate differences in observance. Knowing your intended audience and communicating with participants in advance can help mitigate some of the more divisive aspects of food in Jewish institutions.

Many organizations, in an attempt to reach people outside the boundaries of their walls, may host events in bars or restaurants. The relaxed atmosphere of a familiar bar may make some individuals feel at ease and may break down the barriers that could make it challenging for someone to step into a new, distinctly religious space. The other side of this issue, though, is that some people may feel out of place because their kosher observance means that they won't eat or possibly drink anything in a non-kosher establishment. While these questions appear to be strictly about observance, they're really about Jewish identity and how individuals and organizations relate to the secular world.

Beyond the inclusion issues inherent in laws of keeping kosher, many Jews, just like many people in the general population, have restrictive food allergies or sensitivities. From 2014 to 2019, I planned a large-scale, community-wide Shavuot event in Philadelphia. It's traditional to eat dairy on Shavuot, and alongside our midnight cheesecake and 2:00 a.m. ice cream sundae bar (which does include dairy-free options), we put out a bowl of Lactaid pills for the many among us who are lactose intolerant. Though this addition always got a laugh, it also allowed participants to partake of special foods without risking their comfort and well-being. I also worked with the caterer to be sure that different dietary needs were met and that we provided ingredient lists for everything we served. Our registration form asked about dietary restrictions so that people knew even before they arrived that we were sensitive to their needs. At the event itself, we invited people with allergies to go up to the buffet first before any of the platters might be cross-contaminated. A community member with celiac disease served on the planning committee to advocate and educate the rest of the community. She was introduced at dinner as the point person for food allergies so that she could help all attendees eat safely at the event. Providing multiple options may feel overwhelming, but when someone feels taken care of by the food provided, they're more likely to think their other needs will be met by the organization as well.

Considering the needs of vegetarians and vegans is also important. When organizations are thinking about serving kosher meat, a complicated and expensive prospect, opting for vegetarian meals is often an easier default than considering some of the other intricacies of kosher laws. But when meat is the primary meal, ensuring that the vegetarian option feels substantial is respectful of the needs of your vegetarian guests. Even when there is a vegetarian sandwich or salad, if there's no protein, and vegetarians go home hungry, they may conclude that the organization is not taking their needs seriously and isn't equipped to welcome them fully into the community.

One extremely inclusive way to address diverse food needs is that rather than provide alternative options—such as gluten free or vegetarian—at a meal, provide a meal that can inherently play to the most common denominator. For example, a 20s/30s group hosted a Shabbat dinner and, rather than serving a traditional meat meal, offered up vegetarian Thai food that was rice based, thereby circumventing gluten issues. This not only simplifies the central meal that all are eating by not having to keep count of who needs a "special meal" but also helps individuals with food restrictions feel more included. And remember that small steps are still valuable: Maybe the main meal can't be adjusted to suit everyone's needs, but all the desserts could be gluten free and dairy free. Maybe the exact meals served still need to be different, but the plates and utensils they're served on can be the same for everyone.

Finally, as we move into the next section on ashkenormativity, the typical fare of Shabbat chicken and kugel on Friday nights, herring on Shabbat afternoon, bagels on Sundays, and latkes on Hanukkah show a cultural prioritization of certain types of foods over others. When you examine what elements of your organization or event speak to particular segments of the population, what people eat, the cultural cues around what you serve, and how the food is presented and prepared set the tone for how your organization considers the full range of what it means to nourish relationships.

ASHKENORMATIVITY

"Ashkenorma-what?" you may be asking yourself. Derived from the term "heteronormativity" (which is the belief in heterosexuality as the only "normal" expression of sexuality), "ashkenormativity" is the belief that Ashkenazi Jewish culture—that is, the cultural traditions of Jews from Central and Eastern Europe—are the default and "normative" ways that Jewish culture is and should be defined in the United States. As we saw in the earlier sections, decisions as routine as the languages we speak and the food we eat may have deep cultural contexts that indicate how open an organization may be to those from different backgrounds. For many Jewish organizations, ashkenormativity is so much a part of our institutional lives and expectations that the entire concept that this may be exclusionary is a new and deeply challenging one.

It's true that the large majority of Jews in the United States are of Ashkenazi descent. Most of those individuals can trace their family roots to the great waves of migration in the late 19th and early 20th centuries from Russia, Poland, Hungary, Romania, Lithuania, and other places. Other individuals can trace their lineage back even further to the German Jewish immigration wave of the mid 19th century. The traditions that these Jews brought with them, from the language that many of them spoke (Yiddish) to the foods they ate (bagels, gefilte fish), to the tunes and melodies that they would chant in synagogues, came from these diasporic homelands where Jews had lived for hundreds of years. Even as the majority of modern American Jews have assimilated into American culture, many of these Jewish traditions carry on today. What many think of as a "traditional" Shabbat dinner—roast chicken and potato kugel, with babka for dessert—has direct ties to Eastern Europe. Traditions are wonderful and have kept Judaism alive, but when Ashkenazi Jewish culture is conflated with or becomes a stand-in for Jewish culture, that's a problem. That's ashkenormativity.

While the majority of American Jews are of Ashkenazi descent, it's not the whole picture. There are Sephardic Jews of Spanish descent, and Mizrahi Jews from North African backgrounds. Beyond these categorical differences that sometimes impact Jewish practice and customs, there are also South African Jews, Israeli Jews, Venezuelan Jews, Karaite Jews, Turkish Jews, Iraqi Jews, and Jews from the former Soviet Union, just to name a few, each with their own fantastically unique and special culture and traditions. Emphasizing Ashkenazi culture likely means that Jews by choice feel left out as well. When we default to Eastern European Jewish culture, we minimize the importance of the cultural backgrounds of the rest of the Jewish community, we risk erasing these identities from our understanding of what it means to be Jewish, and we prevent people in our communities from participating as their full selves.

If the only time we talk about Sephardi Jews is to emphasize differences in culinary traditions on Passover, we're reducing an entire culture to one way that it exists in contrast to the dominant culture. One woman of Sephardic descent told me that many congregations make "assumptions that using Yiddish makes the community seem more warm, friendly, accessible and welcoming," but in reality, she experiences the use of Yiddish in communal spaces as "alienating and uncomfortable." She also highlighted that clergy, who are often from Ashkenazi backgrounds themselves, are unable to support Sephardic "children in their preparation for bar or bat mitzvah in the family's cantillation tradition."[5] Even if we sometimes offer a Ladino (traditional Sephardic language) version of a prayer or a recipe during Passover for Moroccan *charoset* (a mixture of fruit and nuts served at the seder), how often are Ashkenazi-dominated synagogues acknowledging Torah cantillation from other cultures or asking our Sephardic members what will make them feel at home? We need to make sure that being aware of and sensitive to these differences is at the forefront of our planning, not only when we want to flaunt multiculturalism but also each and every time we aim to make our constituents feel welcome and represented.

Ignoring these other traditions and experiences of what it means to be a Jew not only damages the experience of non-Ashkenazi Jews but also robs Ashkenazi Jews of the multitude of experiences, music, languages, and foods that can be part of Jewish tradition. Does this mean that we need to repudiate Ashkenazi Jewish culture? Not at all. But it does mean that we should try to name it for what it is: one of many ways of being Jewish, but not the only way. Broadening how you conceive of Jewish culture not only will make your space more inviting to Jews of all cultural backgrounds and heritages but also will provide novel ways to engage Ashkenazi Jews who will be excited to learn how their Jewish siblings from around the world celebrate their Jewishness. Of course, in doing so, community leaders should be in consultation with people who hold these traditions personally so as to be sensitive and authentic and to avoid appropriation in the name of diversity.

PARENTS OF YOUNG CHILDREN

I used to help run a small, independent *minyan*, which my husband and I and a few friends started in order to meet our Jewish needs that weren't being met by the local established synagogues (and, as described earlier, to have creative potluck solutions!). We rented space from a variety of community centers that required, at various turns, carrying strollers up two flights of stairs, using an elevator that notoriously let strollers in but not out, and renting an additional room where young children could play during services while adults took turns missing services to babysit. Despite my time spent coordinating in advance, arriving early to set up, and thinking carefully about the logistics, even in the *minyan* that I founded, I couldn't figure out how to integrate children into the experience such that all the members of my family could participate at once.

Synagogues offer Tot Shabbats, Mini Minyans, and pajama *havdalah* (ritual ceremony to mark the end of Shabbat) services to help provide spaces that are child centered. Many synagogues have in-house preschools, which both provide important childcare resources to families and can help create a direct channel from preschool to Hebrew school and, they hope, family memberships. With the emphasis in many Jewish organizations on continuity and the next generation, on the surface, it may seem as though institutions are already prioritizing the needs of families with young children. But what of the parents who want a traditional prayer experience for themselves with their children alongside them? Or the parents who want to pray uninterrupted on their own? Or the parents who want to participate in adult education classes?

Many synagogues advertise themselves as family friendly, but this often means they offer an early childhood program, rather than that children themselves are welcome in services. One father of a very enthusiastic three-year-old wrote to me looking for advice about his son: "He loves attending services at our synagogue. He sings along and is very happy to be there, but he doesn't always sit still. I'm sure to take him out when he's making too much noise, but when he's generally quiet, I let him be. On a recent Shabbat, he was walking up and down the aisles walking—not talking, and an older person turned to me and said, 'That's very distracting. Can you keep the noise down?'"[6] No one wants to be the center of attention for the wrong reasons, and attracting the attention of an entire congregation unintentionally and without receiving even silent support is enough to keep parents away until their kids are older and can attend Junior Congregation or participate more quietly in the main service.

Different synagogues have different norms around children in services, but it's impossible to know what experience you'll have when you show up somewhere new. A mom of an elementary-school-aged child shared this experience: "My daughter was singing along and actively participating in the adult service. She and I were both told separately that her participation was inappropriate because she was singing too loudly."[7] Some synagogues have a soundproof room where parents can listen to services but the congregation can't hear their child. This option serves an important purpose if parents choose to go there, but if the expectation is that that is where crying or even talking children *must* go, then parents are reduced to less than full participants in the goings-on in the main service.

Along those lines, once an adult is identified as being a parent of small children, it's hard to cross the boundaries back into being an adult member of a congregation. Social events are typically geared toward young professionals or retirees. Adult education programs are scheduled at times that are difficult for parents to attend (though event organizers can hardly be blamed for this because any time you choose is going to be *some child's* naptime or bedtime).

Parents likely long for the company of other adults, but within the structures that currently exist, finding those opportunities can be extremely challenging.

Our organizations can help, though. I have heard rabbis say in front of the whole congregation that a cooing or crying baby is praying along, which creates an environment where children are acknowledged without being shunned. Synagogues can consciously enact a culture shift to help congregants take kids' noises in stride. Having a designated area in the sanctuary where there are toys and books also sends a message to families that they are welcome there. Even more important, perhaps, having such an area sends a message to the rest of the congregation that children are welcome and included as members of the community.

Providing childcare during events and services is another simple solution. It comes at a cost, but it's a small one relative to losing parents' participation for up to a decade. Other easy opportunities to welcome parents include changing tables in all restrooms, clearly marked stroller parking, and special roles during services for children who are in attendance. Our changing ways of gathering during the COVID-19 pandemic have also shown institutions that livestreaming events increases accessibility to people who can't attend in person for all kinds of reasons, including parents of young children. To prioritize the Jewish future, organizations have to acknowledge and accommodate the needs of young children and their parents.

SINGLE PEOPLE AND CHILDLESS PEOPLE

At the same time, despite the messages that some Jewish institutions put out, the Jewish future doesn't rest solely on the shoulders of children and parents. All people who want to participate in Jewish institutional life ought to be valued and welcomed for being who they are. The final "everything else" issue I want to tackle is single people, who are often excluded, shut out, and made to feel invisible in ways that can echo the experiences of some of the other groups discussed so far, even while many synagogues claim to serve people in every stage of life. Single people exist across every age and demographic, and while they may feel excluded for different reasons at different points in time, many have felt consistently marginalized for decades of their lives.

As we saw in chapter 5, many organizations have emerged over the past 20 years specifically serving Jews in their 20s and 30s. Their events often are either implicitly or explicitly geared toward coupling—the dreaded "meet market" vibe, which supports the notion that being coupled is everyone's goal. These programs are also nearly always inherently (if tacitly) heteronormative, focusing on *straight* singles in the community and thereby alienating LGBTQ singles at the same time. And even if someone *wants* to be coupled, the assumption that these singles events will address the entirety of their Jewish needs is so often shortsighted.

These organizations also often default to happy hours or other purely social programs, furthering the lowest common denominator idea that millennials and Gen Zers are not interested in content. Certainly many people in their 20s are single, and many are interested in socializing, but these individuals also often have a wide range of interests in Jewish life, culture, and community building that extend beyond either drinking or meeting someone. Providing high-quality, content-driven programming can attract 20-somethings who want to engage with the topic and the community. If someone meets a significant other along the way, that's great for the individuals, provided that's what they're looking for, and nice for the community to be a place where people make those connections, but coupling can't be the only end goal of programming.

The ways in which single people are often made to feel "less than" in Jewish spaces is demoralizing and othering. Synagogues are not typically the organizations that people between the ages of 22 and 29 seek out, so many synagogues are ill equipped to welcome them. In cases when "young professionals' do attempt to integrate themselves into synagogue life, they often encounter numerous barriers. At the top of that list of barriers is the idea, once again, that if they're coming to an event, it means they must be there looking for a romantic match. This can be intensified even more in an intergenerational setting where older community members may not know what else to say to people several decades younger than they are. People in their 20s— when older members find out they're not part of a couple—have even been asked point-blank, "What's wrong with you?" While some attempts at setups are well intentioned (and may even be appreciated by a single person!), when that's the only topic that anyone is willing to discuss with a single person, these community members can feel reduced to a potential match for someone, rather than the whole person that they are.

If young professionals do manage to find a place for themselves in a synagogue, the structures often don't support them. Young adults have been priced out of holiday events and synagogue camping trips where the costs are calculated based on families. They've been excluded from "family-friendly" events, which is often just code for "don't come without kids," and may find themselves sitting all alone. And words matter. One woman told me, "I abhor the demographic titled 'post-college, pre-family,' which makes a lot of assumptions about a person's and couple's life journey. I stay away from organizations with that language."[8]

When synagogues don't have plans in place to accommodate single people, they are willfully ignoring many of their constituents or potential constituents. A man in his 30s describes being told by the membership director at a synagogue that there was one price for dues, whether you're a family or a single adult, and he could "take it or leave it."[9] A woman in her 30s showed up for Rosh Hashanah services and was asked by the usher, "just you?" before being directed to an overflow seat.

Synagogues need to be flexible with their membership rates and plans without penalizing single people or making them feel like an afterthought. Administrators should be sensitive as to whether their membership rates have fair-priced options for single people, and whether people without children are required to subsidize Hebrew schools and childcare through their fees. Staff and volunteers need to be trained in how to respond to requests from single people, how to greet single people when they arrive, and how to avoid making assumptions or insensitive comments. Lists of good *kiddush* conversation starters can help shift the culture toward more sensitivity, and leadership should model how to talk to and greet people at every stage of life without assumption or judgment.

Communal mazel tov announcements, often a given at the end of services or in synagogue e-mails, may seem like a benefit to the community, until you consider what's being celebrated. Esther Kustanowitz, a writer living in Los Angeles who has been consistently involved in Jewish communal institutions throughout her life, describes these announcements like this: "Honestly, congratulatory synagogue emails are just another nail in the coffin of how non-married, non-parents are treated in Jewish life. . . . Single all my life, not going to have children at this point, I've always known I'm seen as a second-class Jewish community member who will always feel a bite of bitterness when rabbis preach about what we should do for our children or how we behave in our marriages. No matter how else I contribute to the communal discourse, I know that until/unless I'm married with children, I'll be a disappointment, or worse, invisible."[10]

While more inclusive life cycle announcements alone won't fix that sting that Esther describes, instead of limiting announcements, either in person or through e-mails, to traditional, often exclusionary life cycle goalposts, consider expanding what is deemed worthy by the community of congratulations. Rabbanit Dasi Fruchter, of the South Philadelphia Shtiebel, says her community shares mazel tov announcements for any life cycle accomplishment. This includes "buying a new house, completing a graduate thesis, gallery openings, a lot of things. It is really important to me to feature as much as possible that the life cycle expands beyond birth, marriage, b'nai mitzvah, and death. But it's worth noting that people don't really submit these. As the spiritual leader, I have a sense of what's coming up in people's lives and just ask, and the response is usually 'I didn't know that counted.'"[11]

As people start to move beyond the 20s and 30s demographic, the feelings of isolation remain, but the specifics change. As one woman describes it, "BAM, you hit 40 and nothing caters to 'adults.' I have zero in common with the 20-something just out of college." As people get older still, whether they have been consistently single or are newly single due to divorce or the death of a spouse, different challenges emerge. Though lots of synagogues do have "boomer" programming, many of the attendees there are long-time couples themselves. A Jewish professional who describes herself as a "single female empty nester" has gone out of her way to create programming for people like herself because "rabbis all knew there was a demographic group they didn't have the bandwidth to address."

Though the barrage of quotes I've provided should give you pause, this is not a hopeless problem, and, to be clear, single people themselves are not the problem at all. Rather, the structures, priorities, and cultures of our organizations need to shift to ensure that no one is excluded because they show up solo. At whatever age someone is single, they should be included and welcomed as the whole person they are—not in search of a partner, not a potential match for your grandchild, and not someone who is less than a full participant in the life of the community.

Single parents face an additional combination of challenges, which combine some of the challenges of this section with some of the challenges of the prior section on families with young children. Acknowledging the vast array of circumstances of your constituents and considering how all these factors impact their Jewish lives will help you find new perspectives to consider how you're including or excluding people. To help implement these goals on a policy level, synagogues and other community organizations would do well to invite young professionals and single people of all ages to be on their committees and boards, not as a token representative, but in order to hear, understand, and incorporate their perspectives into the overall life of the organizations.

There is yet another category of people worthy of our attention in this mix: couples without children. Just as no one appreciates being asked why they're still single, couples will likely find it both intrusive and painful to be asked when they're having children. Both in Jewish institutional realms and in the rest of life, it's a question that should never be asked. Couples I spoke to recall being ignored at events after telling synagogue staff that they don't have children. One woman says, "I tried to join a *shul* (synagogue), and when I told them I was married, they only offered me events for parents and tried to sell their preschool/religious school. When I said that we didn't have kids, they basically dropped me. No more outreach after that." Another person says it's as if "people without children are not worthy of these events," and yet another says, "While they may say they're open to everyone, it never feels that way."[12] Indeed, that last statement ought to strike a chord regarding single people, people without children, and every other group discussed in this book. The goal isn't to say that everyone is welcome. The goal for all Jewish organizations must be that everyone actually is welcomed, completely, not despite who they are but because of who they are.

WHAT NEXT?

Whatever thoughts and feelings this book may have brought up for you—frustration, anger, confusion, hopefulness—we hope you'll sit with those feelings for a bit and reflect on where your organization has been and where you hope it's going to go. Perhaps you hear the phrase "warm and welcoming" differently now, compared to how you felt at the beginning of the book. We hope you'll see it as a phrase to aspire to, rather than a stamp you can put on your flyers and website to prove you've already accomplished some ultimate goal. We hope these chapters will be a resource you can return to again and again to check in on your progress and to examine your organization's goals, priorities, and accomplishments.

Along the way, you may have felt challenged by some of the suggestions, defensive about why certain topics don't apply to your organization, or at a loss for how you can possibly implement everything that's been suggested. Maybe you feel righteously justified by how many of these things you're already doing well, and you think your work is done. Experiencing that range of emotions is what will allow your community, and the Jewish community as a whole, to grow and change. All Jewish institutions won't evolve at the same rate or with the same goals or results, but our hope in sharing these chapters with you is that, wherever you are, you'll be able to push yourselves to go a little further.

Just as situations in which people have been made to feel unwelcome were not created overnight, so, too, many of them cannot be corrected quickly. Many of these issues require new funding sources to support new initiatives, and very few organizations can or should be expected to tackle everything in this book right away. Rather, we suggest forming a committee that can begin by doing an "audit" of the areas discussed in these chapters. Where are you succeeding and where are you falling short? Are there some easy wins you can achieve now? What will take more time and planning? Some issues might seem obvious and may have already been brought up multiple times by your organization, while other areas might not be relevant to your group at all.

Create a plan (you don't need to hire an expensive outside firm to do this!) with specific goals and action steps, metrics, and deadlines to keep your organization accountable. Share your plan with your constituents and invite feedback and involvement, especially from the people you are most trying to engage, and share your progress along the way so that your constituents know that you're invested in this continuing, ever-changing work.

Don't be afraid to listen and have open, honest, and even difficult conversations with people who are not like you. If you are lucky enough to have someone come to you and say that they had a negative experience with your organization, embrace that opportunity to make amends and do better next time, maybe even under the guidance of the person who approached you. We can often only see the world through our own experiences, unable to see the blind spots that are pain points for others. While each of us still needs to do the work in learning about diversity and inclusion and should not expect any one person to serve as the encyclopedia for a certain group of disenfranchised people, learning from others who are not like us is a blessing and is one of the most tangible ways to make progress.

Again and again, our contributors referenced the concept of *"b'tzelem Elohim,"* that we are all made in the image of God. Interacting with, learning from, and including those who are not like us is a holy act. The commitment to making your institution "warm and welcoming" will be lifelong and never ending, and this process will likely be the difference between institutions that continue to be relevant in the coming years and institutions that fade from the Jewish landscape. Committing to being inclusive is a journey that we must all be on and that has no single end point. Rather, aspiring always to be more inclusive, more self-reflective, and more committed to living up to our "warm and welcoming" goals will carry all of us into the future. We wish you strength, patience, and fortitude on this journey you are about to undertake. May it bring you and the communities you serve new insights, joy, happiness, and fulfillment to make the Jewish community as a whole a more diverse, inclusive, and truly welcoming space.

RESOURCES

Websites

Alma (heyalma.com) is a blog that covers everything from Jewish pop culture to what's happening in the news to personal pieces about identity and feminism. The name comes from the Hebrew word meaning a woman of child-bearing age who has not had kids.

Be'chol Lashon (globaljews.org) aims to strengthen Jewish identity by raising awareness about the ethnic, racial, and cultural diversity of Jewish identity and experience.

Jewish Veg (jewishveg.org) aims to inspire and assist Jews to embrace plant-based diets as an expression of Jewish values.

Jimena (jimena.org) is the only organization in North America exclusively focused on educating and advocating on behalf of Jewish refugees and Mizrahi Jews from Arab countries.

Kveller (kveller.com) is a blog geared toward Jewish parents, featuring frequent, timely posts from a variety of perspectives with the attitude that there's no one way to parent Jewish kids.

My Jewish Learning (myjewishlearning.com) has thousands of articles, videos, and other resources to help people navigate all aspects of Judaism and Jewish life. Many of the sections on prayers and rituals include translations and transliterations.

PJ Library (pjlibrary.org) sends free Jewish children's books to families across the world every month with the goal of helping families talk together about values and traditions.

The Open Siddur Project (opensiddur.org) is an open-source, community-contributed archive for sharing prayers, geared toward crafting one's own prayer books. It features many transliterated sources and resources for creating transliterated sources.

Shmayim: Jewish Animal Advocacy (www.shamayim.us) offers programs, campaigns, and educational opportunities to teach the Jewish community about animal advocacy and veganism.

Books

Khazzoom, Loolwa. *The Flying Camel: Essays on Identity by Women of North African and Middle Eastern Jewish Heritage.* New York: Seal Press, 2003.

Miller, Sloane. *Allergic Girl: Adventures in Living Well with Food Allergies.* Hoboken, NJ: Wiley, 2011.

Ruttenberg, Danya. *Nurture the Wow: Finding Spirituality in the Frustration, Boredom, Tears, Poop, Desperation, Wonder, and Radical Amazement of Parenting.* New York: Flatiron, 2016.

NOTES

1. Warren Hoffman, "Want Your Synagogue to Be Truly Inclusive? Embrace Transliteration," *Forward*, September 17, 2018, https://forward.com/scribe/410291/want-your-synagogue-to-be-truly-inclusive-embrace-transliteration.

2. Pew Research Center, *A Portrait of Jewish Americans* (Washington, DC: Pew Research Center, October 1, 2013), 63, https://www.pewresearch.org/wp-content/uploads/sites/7/2013/10/jewish-american-full-report-for-web.pdf.

3. Pew Research Center, *A Portrait of Jewish Americans*, 63.

4. "Hilchot Pluralism, Part 1: The Two-Table System," *Mah Rabu*, February 23, 2006, http://mahrabu.blogspot.com/2006/02/hilchot-pluralism-part-i-two-table.html.

5. Personal communication with the author, January 15, 2021.

6. Miriam Steinberg-Egeth, "Ask Miriam: Young Children in Prayer Spaces," *Jewish Exponent*, December 16, 2019, https://www.jewishexponent.com/2019/12/16/ask-miriam-young-children-in-prayer-spaces.

7. Personal communication with the author, October 1, 2019.

8. On October 20, 2020, I posted the following on Facebook: "If you are a single person, I would love to hear the top 1–2 things that synagogues and other Jewish institutions have done that have made you feel excluded, and/or the top 1–2 things they could do better for single people. Feel free to pm me. Thank you!" These are some of the more than 60 comments I received, with the promise that I would quote them anonymously.

9. Personal communication with the author, October 21, 2020.

10. Facebook correspondence with the author, June 9, 2021.

11. Facebook correspondence with the author, June 9, 2021.

12. Facebook post, October 20, 2020; Facebook Messenger communications with the author, October 20, 2020.

Index

217

About the Contributors

Rebecca Bar is executive director of Challah for Hunger, inspiring communities of leaders to take action against hunger at the 85 college campuses and 10 community sites nationwide. Rebecca has been part of the Schusterman ROI community since attending Summit in 2009. She was one of the founding residents of Moishe House Philadelphia when it opened in May 2007. Rebecca has worked in the Jewish community for more than 20 years. Prior to Challah for Hunger, she was a strategic consultant for the Mayberg Foundation through MyZuzah, as well as the vice president of community partnerships for Honeymoon Israel, the director of operations for Bible Raps, and the senior regional director for Moishe House. Bar is an active individual who enjoys working out (at home). She also loves to cook and is incredibly close to her family and friends. Rebecca lives outside Philadelphia with her husband, Matt Bar, and their two boys.

Jodi Bromberg has been a part of 18Doors (previously InterfaithFamily) since October 1, 2013—the day that the Pew study on Jewish Americans came out—and became the 18Doors CEO in 2015. She has written for numerous publications and spoken at conferences, synagogues, and Jewish institutions around the country about the importance of creating comfortable, inclusive spaces for interfaith families in Jewish life. Jodi lives outside of Boston with her wife and twin boys, where she remains a diehard New York Yankees fan. Prior to joining 18Doors, Jodi was a corporate attorney in the Philadelphia area and is a proud graduate of the University of Pennsylvania and the Temple University Beasley School of Law.

Miriam Brosseau is principal of Tiny Windows Consulting, a digital communications consultancy built to help awesome Jewish leaders get creative and build community online. Before launching Tiny Windows in 2018, Miriam held various positions inside the Jewish nonprofit world, including running the Jewish TED-style platform ELI Talks, and consulted with organizations like Make-A-Wish America on storytelling skills and strategy. In addition to her current consulting work, Miriam is an adjunct marketing instructor at the University of Chicago's Graham School. She and her husband, Alan Jay Sufrin, are frequent creative co-conspirators, having five years touring as the "biblegum pop" duo Stereo Sinai and later co-hosting the podcast *Throwing Sheyd: Better Living through Jewish Demonology*. Miriam is a graduate of University of Wisconsin–Madison and holds a master's degree in Jewish professional studies from Spertus Institute. She is a member of the ROI network of young Jewish entrepreneurs and was named to the *Jewish Week's* "36 under 36" in 2013 and Chicago's "Double Chai in the Chi" in 2019. In real life, Miriam is mom to two gorgeous humans and spends her free time reading, drinking too much coffee, and roller skating.

Lisa Colton is the founder and president of Darim Online, which helps Jewish leaders and organizations align their business models, strategy, culture, and communications for today's connected, digital age. For 20 years, she's helped synagogues, schools, federations, foundations, and many others understand the profound shifts in our society and economy so they can most effectively lead their communities confidently into the future. In addition to her consulting and coaching work, Lisa founded and executive produced the Great Big Jewish Food Fest and the Big Bold Jewish Climate Fest, which together engaged more than 25,000 individuals in online community and learning during the COVID-19 pandemic. She is a graduate of Stanford University and the Pardes Institute for Jewish Studies and is a Wexner Heritage Fellow. She lives in Seattle.

Marilyn Levitch Hassid is a retired Jewish communal professional in Houston, Texas. Her career included 10 years as a formal Jewish educator and 35 years with the Evelyn Rubenstein JCC (the J), where she produced visual, literary, film, and performing arts programs, as well as numerous special events. Within the J, she built collaborations with fellow colleagues, particularly working in tandem with the Bobbi and Vic Samuels Center for Jewish Living & Learning pairing Jewish learning and arts and culture experiences. A significant focus of her work was developing meaningful lay committee engagement opportunities. Marilyn has served on national planning projects with the Jewish Book Council (JBC), the Jewish Community Centers Association (JCCA), and the Foundation for Jewish Culture. Currently, she is a consultant with the Jewish Book Council, onboarding and mentoring new staff and participating sites. Marilyn lives in Houston with her life partner, Marc A. Gessner. She has two sons: one in Houston and one married and living in Maryland with their three grandchildren.

Rabbi Lauren Grabelle Herrmann (she/her) serves as rabbi of SAJ-Judaism that Stands for All (historically Society for the Advancement of Judaism), the birthplace of Reconstructionism. Lauren's rabbinate has been driven by a desire to create inclusive Jewish communities of meaning and a passion for justice. Rabbi Lauren is a member of T'ruah (The Rabbinic Call for Human Rights), JFREJ (Jews for Racial and Economic Justice), and the Global Justice Fellowship with AJWS (American Jewish World Service). Rabbi Lauren has been an active champion of LGBTQ rights within and beyond the Jewish community, from her time as an intern at CBST (the world's largest synagogue for LGBTQ folks) until today. She has been arrested in protest of the Muslim ban and the profiling of undocumented immigrants. Before coming to SAJ, Rabbi Lauren was the founder of Kol Tzedek in West Philadelphia, a congregation rooted in justice and equality. There, she was a founding clergy member of POWER (Philadelphians Organized to Witness, Empower and Rebuild). She graduated from the Reconstructionist Rabbinical College in 2006 and is a proud alumni of JOIN (Jewish Organizing Initiative and Network). Rabbi Lauren lives in New York City with her husband Jon and her children Niko and Nadiv.

Warren Hoffman currently serves as the executive director for the Association for Jewish Studies in New York, where he leads the largest membership organization of Jewish studies scholars, teachers, and students in the world. Warren brings more than 15 years of experience in the Jewish, arts, academic, and nonprofit sectors. In Philadelphia, he was the associate director of community programming for the Jewish Federation of Greater Philadelphia and was also the senior director of programming for the Gershman Y in Philadelphia, where the *Jewish Exponent* named him the "next wave" of arts and culture in the city. Warren also served as the literary manager and dramaturg for Philadelphia Theatre Company and was the associate artistic director of Jewish Repertory Theatre, where he produced and dramaturged a season of Jewish musicals in concert. Warren holds a PhD in American literature from the University of California–Santa Cruz and has taught at multiple universities. He earned rave reviews for his book *The Passing Game: Queering Jewish American Culture*. The second edition of his critically acclaimed book *The Great White Way: Race and the Broadway Musical* hit bookstores February 2020. For more information, visit warrenhoffman.com.

Gabrielle Kaplan-Mayer is an experienced Jewish educator, having worked in various capacities in the field for more than 20 years. At Jewish Learning Venture (JLV), she works as the chief program officer and directs JLV's Whole Community Inclusion initiative. Her most recent book, *The Little Gate Crasher*, is a memoir of her great-uncle, who overcame society's prejudices about dwarfism to lead a remarkable life. She's also written a journal created for fellow parents raising children with disabilities. Gabby holds a BFA in theater and creative writing from Emerson College and an MA in Jewish studies from the Reconstructionist Rabbinical College. When not working at JLV, she can be found having fun with her family, walking with her Saluki, cooking, practicing yoga, reading, writing, and teaching online workshops about writing for spiritual growth.

Idit Klein is a national leader for social justice with more than 25 years of experience in the nonprofit sector. Since 2001, she has served as the leader of Keshet, which she has built from a local organization with an annual budget of $42,000 to a national organization with a $4 million budget. Under her leadership, Keshet has supported tens of thousands of rabbis, educators, and other Jewish community leaders to make LGBTQ equality a communal value and imperative. She served as executive producer of Keshet's documentary film, *Hineini: Coming Out in a Jewish High School*. A magna cum laude graduate of Yale University, Idit earned her master's in education with a focus on social justice and anti-oppression education from the University of Massachusetts–Amherst. She serves on the Leadership Team of the Jewish Social Justice Roundtable and the Advisory Board of the Safety Respect Equity Network. Idit was honored by the Jewish Women's Archive with a Women Who Dared award, by Jewish Women International with a Women to Watch award, and by the *Forward* as one of the *Forward 50*, a list of American Jews who have made enduring contributions to public life. She lives in Boston with her family.

Rabbi Kerry M. Olitzky is the former executive director of Big Tent Judaism (previously the Jewish Outreach Institute). He served as visiting professor at the Abraham Geiger Kolleg in Germany and was a Fellow at the City University Graduate Center (New York). He has been named as one of the 50 Leading Rabbis in North America by *Newsweek*. Formerly, he served as vice president of the Wexner Heritage Foundation and was national dean of Adult Jewish Learning and Living of Hebrew Union College–Jewish Institute of Religion, where he served on the faculty and administration for 15 years following his tenure as rabbi at Congregation Beth Israel in West Hartford, Connecticut. A leader in the development of innovative Jewish education, he has shaped training programs for clergy of all faiths, especially in the area of pastoral care and counseling. He has done pioneering work in the area of Jewish 12-step spirituality, as well as Jewish gerontology. He is the author of more than 75 books and hundreds of articles in a variety of fields, including four books on addiction and recovery. His opinion pieces are published in leading publications throughout North America and in Israel.

Gamal Palmer is the senior vice president of diversity, equity, and inclusion at the Los Angeles Federation and a diversity and inclusion specialist and keynote speaker. He is the principal and founder of Conscious Builders.

A graduate of Yale and a student of Oxford University with a strong background in organizational leadership and inclusion, Palmer has worked with hundreds of leaders, executives, and CEOs to help them diversify their teams and increase effectiveness and collaboration. He's worked with large-scale businesses and nonprofits including Sempra Energy, Live Nation, Intuit, Yale, UCLA, USC Business School, ITVS, Cultivate Advisors, and Wexner Heritage Fund. Through the Diversity Gym, he's worked with thousands of individuals to help them find acceptance and foster inclusion. He has worked with social impact entrepreneurs in more than 15 African countries, the Middle East, and the United States, and he is an International Career Advancement Program (ICAP) Aspen Institute Fellow, Schusterman Foundation Global Leader Fellow, Los Angeles Global Justice Fellow, and Durfee Foundation Spring Board Fellow. Palmer sits on three national boards: UpStart Lab, Jews of Color Initiative, and American Jewish World Service.

Rabbi Sid Schwarz is a senior fellow at Hazon, where he directs the Clergy Leadership Incubator (CLI), a program that trains rabbis to be visionary spiritual leaders. He also created and directs Kenissa: Communities of Meaning Network, which is identifying, convening, and building the capacity of emerging spiritual communities across the country. Rabbi Sid is the founding rabbi of Adat Shalom Reconstructionist Congregation in Bethesda, Maryland, where he continues to teach and lead services. He holds a PhD in Jewish history and is the author of two groundbreaking books—*Finding a Spiritual Home: How a New Generation of Jews Can Transform the American Synagogue* (2000) and *Judaism and Justice: The Jewish Passion to Repair the World* (2006). Rabbi Sid was awarded the prestigious Covenant Award for his pioneering work in the field of Jewish education and was named by *Newsweek* as one of the 50 most influential rabbis in North America. Sid's most recent book is *Jewish Megatrends: Charting the Course of the American Jewish Future* (2013).

Beverly Socher-Lerner is an innovative and passionate Jewish educational leader who believes that inviting learners to explore Jewish wisdom with emphasis on their own agency builds joyful and deep experiences in Jewish community. She is the founding director at Makom Community, which is built around creating learning experiences for whole families and children that are both joyous and meaningful. Beverly received a BA in Jewish studies from the University of Maryland (UMD). While she was at UMD, she researched Israeli education and the history of Jewish education. She was also a fellow at Yeshivat Hadar, an egalitarian yeshiva in New York City. Beverly received her MSEd from the University of Pennsylvania in Jewish education. She spent 12 years teaching in and directing synagogue schools and then opened Makom Community in 2014. She has developed more than 100 new curricula for students and families of all ages. Beverly is a 2019 recipient of the Covenant Foundation

Pomegranate Prize and a Shalom Hartman Created Equal Fellow in 2020. She lives with her spouse Naomi and their two children in Philadelphia.

Rabbi Toba Spitzer has served Congregation Dorshei Tzedek in West Newton, Massachusetts, since she was ordained in 1997 at the Reconstructionist Rabbinical College. She served as the president of the Reconstructionist Rabbinical Association from 2007 to 2009, becoming the first LGBTQ+ person to head a national rabbinic organization. She also served as president of the Massachusetts Board of Rabbis from 2017 to 2019. Rabbi Spitzer has been involved for many years in American Jewish efforts to help foster a peaceful resolution to the Israeli-Palestinian conflict as well as work in the United States for economic and social justice. She has served on the board of T'ruah: The Rabbinic Call for Human Rights and was a founding member of the Advisory Board of J Street. Rabbi Spitzer's writings on process theology, Judaism and social justice, and explorations of biblical texts have been published in *the Reconstructionist Journal* and *CCAR Journal: The Reform Jewish Quarterly*, on MyJewishLearning .com, and in the anthology *Torah Queeries: Weekly Commentaries on the Hebrew Bible*. Her book *God Is Here: Reimagining the Divine* will be published in 2022.

Miriam Steinberg-Egeth has been a leader in the Philadelphia Jewish community since 2006, providing interdenominational and intergenerational opportunities for Jews of all backgrounds to connect with communal experiences that work for them. During that time, she has served as the sole staff person for multiple Jewish organizations: the Center City Kehillah, the Board of Rabbis of Greater Philadelphia, and Hillel of Greater Philadelphia's Jewish Graduate Student Network. In all of these roles, she has focused on the importance of relationship building, resource sharing, and creating meaningful connections. She is the creator of "Miriam's Advice Well," the *Jewish Exponent*'s advice column, which she has been writing since 2011, fielding questions on parenting, dating, Jewish rituals, and the little issues of daily life. Miriam's writing has also been featured by 18Doors, Kveller, and the Horn Book. Miriam holds degrees from Goucher College and Lesley University. She lives in Center City, Philadelphia, with her spouse, Marc, and their children, Aliza and Solomon.

Rabbi Mike Uram is the chief vision and education officer for Pardes North America. Before that, he served as the executive director and campus rabbi at Penn Hillel for more than 16 years. He is the author of the best-selling book *Next Generation Judaism: How College Students and Hillel Can Help Reinvent Jewish Organizations*, which won a National Jewish Book Award in 2016. He is a sought-after speaker and consultant on the changing nature of the American Jewish community, Jewish innovation, cutting-edge engagement, and how legacy organizations can reinvent themselves in the age of millennials. Mike has worked with dozens of Jewish organizations including Jewish Federations of North America, the Wexner Foundation, United Synagogue, the Rabbinical Assembly, Central Conference of American Rabbis, Hillel International, and many local federations, synagogues, and JCCs. He also served as lead faculty and Jewish coach for the Schusterman Fellowship. Mike was part of a small working group that developed a new educational framework for Birthright Israel. Mike holds a BA in history and religious studies from Washington University and rabbinic ordination from the Jewish Theological Seminary. He lives outside Philadelphia with his wife Leora and their three children.

Rabbi Josh Warshawsky is a nationally touring Jewish musician, song leader, and composer. Josh seeks to build intentional praying communities, and he travels to synagogues, camps, and schools across the country sharing his music and teachings on prayer. He is originally from Chicago and has released three albums of Jewish music, with a fourth on the way in 2021. Josh composes melodies to open up new possibilities for understanding the deep meaning of the words of our tradition. Josh was ordained by the Ziegler School of Rabbinic Studies in Los Angeles. For more information, check out www.joshwarshawsky .com.